FIGHTING *for* PUBLIC JUSTICE

Cases and Trial Lawyers
That Made a Difference

FIGHTING
for PUBLIC
JUSTICE

Cases and
Trial Lawyers
That Made a
Difference

**Trial Lawyer of the Year Award
Finalists and Winners**

By Wesley J. Smith
Foreword by Erin Brockovich

For information about permission to reproduce
selections from this book, write to Permissions,
The TLPJ Foundation, 1717 Massachusetts Avenue,
NW, Suite 800, Washington, DC 20036-2001.

Library of Congress Control Number: 2001089979

ISBN 0-9710949-0-X

First edition, June 2001
Printed in the United States of America

Book design by Whitney Edwards Design, LLC
Printed by Fontana Lithograph, Inc.

To Trial Lawyers for Public Justice

and attorneys everywhere

who strive to realize the ideal of

equal justice under the law.

Author's Note and Acknowledgements

This book would not have been possible without the assistance of the many lawyers who took time out of their busy lives to provide me with case material and submit to my incessant questioning. Thanks so much to one and all. I hope I did you justice, as you did your clients.

The approach I took throughout this book was extremely straightforward. In each chapter, the stories of the cases handled by the Trial Lawyer of the Year Award finalists for that year are told first. Then a longer account of the winning case is provided. While I purposefully gave more details on the winning cases, any other differences in my treatment of cases or lawyers stem solely from differences in the resource materials and pictures we were able to gather. In my view, every case and lawyer mentioned in this book is important and worthy of praise.

I also wish to honor the good folk at Trial Lawyers for Public Justice and The TLPJ Foundation who conceived of this book and made sure it became a reality. Special appreciation to Peter Perlman, President of The TLPJ Foundation, who had the vision for this book, and to the staff members at Trial Lawyers for Public Justice and The TLPJ Foundation staff who ensured that vision was achieved — Arthur Bryant, Jonathan Hutson, Adele Kimmel, Michael Quirk, Carol Phillips, Renita Stevenson, Jill Morris, Clarisia Lovelace, and Tonya Farmer.

Finally, as always, my deepest appreciation to my wife and total sweetheart, Debra J. Saunders.

Contents

Foreword *by Erin Brockovich*

I USED TO HATE LAWYERS.

I thought all they cared about was power and money.

I thought they didn't give a damn about ordinary people.

Now I know better. Now I know that there are lawyers throughout America – trial lawyers throughout America — who spend their whole lives fighting for ordinary people. Trial lawyers who spend their time, their energy, and their money working to hold huge corporations, oppressive governments, and other wrongdoers accountable. Trial lawyers committed to ensuring that justice prevails.

Most people don't understand that — and neither did I. That's why this book is so important. Because there are companies in this country that would sacrifice lives for profits in a minute — like Pacific Gas & Electric did in Hinkley, California. And the one thing they're desperate to hide is the truth.

This book tells the truth. It doesn't add false details for dramatic effect. It is not a novelization or a made-for-TV script. It simply reports the facts of some key cases brought over the past 20 years.

Just by telling the facts, however, this book shows that what I uncovered in Hinkley — as big as it was — is just one small part of a much larger story. The story is simple. Every day, people with greed, hate, or something missing in their hearts are inflicting outrageous injustices on others — usually the poor and the powerless. Every day, government officials are doing little or nothing to stop them (or worse). And, every day, trial lawyers are fighting like hell to expose the wrongdoers and make them pay.

This is, of course, a story that the wrongdoers know well. But they're doing their best to make sure the rest of us don't. That's why, day after day, Corporate America and its public relations mouthpieces are spewing out propaganda designed to demonize trial lawyers and destroy public respect for our system of justice. They know that, if trial lawyers weren't able to take them on and juries couldn't hold them accountable, they'd usually get off scot-free. And they'd sure like that profit-maximizing result.

The problem with propaganda, however, is that it can't stand up to the truth. That's why the facts of these cases are so devastating. They show the kind of outrages taking place in this country. And they demonstrate that, without trial lawyers and our civil justice system, most plain decent folks wouldn't stand a chance. As you read these case reports, just ask yourself this question: what would have happened if cases like these couldn't be brought?

Now, don't get me wrong. I know there are problems with our justice system and I sure know that trial lawyers aren't perfect (despite what some of them may think). But what most people don't appreciate, as I didn't appreciate, is how willing the greedy and powerful are to hurt the rest of us — and how hard trial lawyers are fighting to stop them.

Let me give you an example. If you saw the movie bearing my name, you know about the case I worked on and what we had to overcome. The odds against us were enormous. The case is discussed in the chapter on the 1997 Trial Lawyer of the Year Award finalists and winners. As you'll see, however, that same year, there were several other cases that had even greater hurdles to overcome. In the winning case, an Oregon woman was horribly burned and disfigured when, through no fault of her own, her car collided with a 1976 General Motors pickup truck with side-saddle gas tanks that burst into flames on impact. But she couldn't sue GM, because Oregon law included a statute of repose — a special law passed at the manufacturers' urging that barred any lawsuit against a manufacturer for a product more than eight years old. So, her lawyer first had to persuade the Oregon state legislature to amend the law over GM's (and its lobbyists') opposition. Then he had to take on and beat GM in court. (Now, product manufacturers are pushing Congress and most state legislatures to enact similar statutes of repose.)

In another case, the plaintiff's lawyer fought the federal government for 15 years to try to win justice for his client, a woman whose scalp was pulled off when her hair was caught in a machine that lacked proper safety guards. He finally won a $1 million verdict. In the 16th year, after he was honored, the federal appeals court held in the fourth appeal of the case that the government was immune from suit — and threw out the verdict and the case. In the 17th year, the U.S. Supreme Court denied review.

As this case reflects, justice isn't always won. That, too, is a fact repeatedly documented in the pages that follow. But we don't have to like it. And like the lawyers in this book, we sure don't have to accept it.

At the start of this note, I told you that I used to hate lawyers. That's true. And there are still some lawyers I hate — those who spend their lives working for power against people.

The trial lawyers featured in this book — and thousands of other trial lawyers throughout America and the world — spend their lives fighting for people against power. For them, I have nothing but appreciation and love.

Introduction

Twenty years ago, 200 of the nation's outstanding trial lawyers decided to create a new type of organization: a national public interest trial lawyers' firm. They believed that trial lawyers — working together — could be a powerful force for the public good. In January 1982, with their support, Trial Lawyers for Public Justice ("TLPJ") opened its doors.

In its first year, TLPJ and its supporters gathered a great deal of information on how trial lawyers could advance the public interest. They also learned the exceptional extent to which individual trial lawyers were already pursuing high-impact public interest cases. In response, The TLPJ Foundation, the non-profit membership organization that supports TLPJ's work, established the *"Trial Lawyer of the Year Award."* The purposes of the award are:

1. To educate the public,
2. To inspire others to take on cases in the public interest, and
3. To honor the individual lawyers.

Now, to mark TLPJ's 20th anniversary, The TLPJ Foundation is sharing the stories of the cases brought by the Trial Lawyer of the Year Award finalists and winners — cases that have had a tremendous public interest impact. These are stories that need to be recorded and told.

Before we turn to these stories, however, we want to tell you a bit more about Trial Lawyers for Public Justice, The TLPJ Foundation, the Trial Lawyer of the Year Award, and this book.

Trial Lawyers for Public Justice has a special place in the American legal system, bringing together the trial lawyer and public interest communities. TLPJ's mission statement describes its role well:

> Trial Lawyers for Public Justice is a national public interest law firm that
> marshals the skills and resources of trial lawyers to create a more just
> society. Through creative litigation, public education, and innovative
> work with the broader public interest community, we:
> ■ protect people and the environment;
> ■ hold accountable those who abuse power;

- challenge governmental, corporate, and individual wrongdoing;
- increase access to the courts;
- combat threats to our judicial system; and
- inspire lawyers and others to serve the public interest.

Because TLPJ is dedicated to using trial lawyers' approaches to advance the public good, its litigation is not limited to any one area. It has a wide-ranging docket of cases designed to advance consumer rights, preserve the environment, uphold civil rights and liberties, prevent toxic injuries, defend workers' rights, and safeguard the civil justice system. It also has special projects devoted to fighting unnecessary court secrecy, federal preemption of injury victims' claims, mandatory arbitration abuse, and class action abuse. TLPJ prosecutes its cases by forming litigation teams that include its public interest staff attorneys and appropriate trial lawyers from across the country.

The TLPJ Foundation is a charitable and educational membership organization that supports TLPJ's public interest litigation and educates the public about the critical social issues addressed by TLPJ's work. It currently has over 2,500 members throughout the world, including many of the nation's most accomplished attorneys. Membership is open to everyone interested in supporting TLPJ's activities.

The TLPJ Foundation issues publications, sponsors speakers and educational programs, recruits and serves members, raises funds, networks with others in the public interest and legal communities, plans and coordinates meetings and other membership activities, and otherwise seeks to increase awareness of and involvement in TLPJ's activities. More information on TLPJ and/or The TLPJ Foundation can be obtained from our national headquarters in Washington, D.C.; our West Coast office in Oakland, California; or our web site — www.tlpj.org.

The Trial Lawyer of the Year Award is presented annually to the trial attorney or attorneys who have made the greatest contribution to the public interest within the past year by trying or settling a precedent-setting case. It is the single most prestigious award given to trial lawyers.

The finalists for and winners of the Trial Lawyer of the Year Award are chosen by a special committee of TLPJ Foundation Board members. Nominations are solicited nationwide. Then the committee evaluates the nominated cases, considering the dedication, tenacity, and skill of the trial lawyer(s) involved; the public interest significance of the case; the harmfulness of the defendant's conduct; the result obtained; and the extent to which the case advances any of the goals set forth in TLPJ's mission statement.

This book summarizes the facts of the cases brought by the Trial Lawyer of the Year Award finalists and winners. Those facts are important. They show the kinds of injustices that have occurred in the past and, regrettably, still take place today. They demonstrate the incalculable value of our civil justice system. And they prove, as TLPJ's founders believed, that trial lawyers — working individually and together — can be an enormously powerful force for the public good.

Arthur H. Bryant

Executive Director
Trial Lawyers for Public Justice

Peter Perlman

President
The TLPJ Foundation

CHAPTER ONE

1983: The Case That Made Justice State-of-the-Art

Product Safety *Airco, Inc. v. Simmons First Nat'l Bank*

Civil Rights *Bell v. City of Milwaukee*

Auto Safety *Dorsey v. Honda Motor Co.*

Medical Safety *Harbeson v. Parke Davis, Inc.*

Insurer Accountability *Sarchett v. Blue Shield of California*

Access to Justice *Von Stetina v. Florida Medical Center*

Winner
Beshada v. Johns-Manville Products Corp.
The Case That Made Justice State-of-the-Art

The finalists for the 1983 Trial Lawyer of the Year Award obtained justice for victims of unsafe products, hate crimes, medical malpractice, and insurance company abuse. The winner achieved an important legal victory in the Supreme Court of New Jersey, ensuring that the burden of harm caused by asbestos-related products would be placed on manufacturers of the unsafe products, rather than their innocent victims. The case honored with the first annual Trial Lawyer of the Year Award would also lay the groundwork for future suits against Big Tobacco.

Product Safety
Airco, Inc. v. Simmons First Nat'l Bank
Bernard Whetstone

The TLPJ Foundation named Bernard Whetstone of Little Rock, Arkansas, as a finalist for Trial Lawyer of the Year honors for demonstrating the vital role that tort litigation plays in maintaining a safe and humane society. Whetstone not only obtained redress for a woman killed by a defective medical product, but forced needed safety improvements that benefited surgery patients in the years to come.

On May 14, 1980, Georgia Hutchinson underwent surgery to remove a benign brain tumor. The operation should have saved her life. Instead, due to a faulty artificial breathing machine, Hutchinson's brain was denied vital oxygen, leading first to her profound disability and eventually to her death.

The machine in question regulated the flow of air to her lungs by providing alternate positive and negative pressure, so that Hutchinson's lungs would expand and contract normally. The alternate pressure was provided, part of the time, by a flexible bag that an anesthesiologist squeezed and released by hand and, at other times, by a ventilator that also created alternate pressure. During the surgery, the means of providing alternate pressure had to be switched back and forth between these two methods.

There were two ways for the anesthesiologist to change from mechanical to manual ventilation in the ventilator: (1) manually, or (2) by using a selector valve on the ventilator, which performed the switch mechanically. It was the defective design of this selector switch that cost Georgia Hutchinson her life.

The hook-up for this optional valve was comprised of three identical black hoses and three smaller ports, all situated very close together. There were no warnings or labels on the machine's surface. Due to human error — facilitated by the faulty design and lack of warning on the selector valve of the ventilator — the hoses that were to regulate Hutchinson's breathing were attached improperly to the machine. As a result, the machine pumped anesthetic gases into her lungs and there was no way for the gases to escape. This interfered with the flow of oxygen to her brain and left Hutchinson in a coma. Twenty months later she died.

Before Hutchinson died, her guardian retained attorney Whetstone to sue Airco, the manufacturer of the defective selector valve. Just prior to trial, the company and the medical partnership that provided the anesthesiologist for the surgery admitted liability. The case proceeded to trial on the issue of damages only.

Whetstone solicited testimony that devastated the defense. For example, the staff engineer who designed the ventilator admitted that, from the beginning, Airco had been aware of the hazard that caused the Hutchinson tragedy. Indeed, he acknowledged that the company had received reports from hospitals and physicians around the country concerning the danger and likelihood of the kind of deadly mistake that ended Hutchinson's life. At least one such incident had previously occurred in 1977 — three years before the date of Hutchinson's fateful surgery.

The jury awarded $1.07 million in compensatory damages and an additional $3 million in punitive damages to hold the company accountable for its failure to fix the defective ventilator despite the known dangers.

The good news, if it can be called that, is that Airco heard the jury's message loudly and clearly. The company issued a bulletin to anesthesiologists, anesthesiology publications, and other medical venues instructing that the selector valves be removed from all ventilator machines. Thus, the admirable legal work performed by attorney Whetstone in *Airco* demonstrated the dual purposes of the civil justice system. First, it compensated the victims of a deadly wrong with significant monetary damages. Second, it induced a corporation to improve the safety of its product so that others would not be hurt.

The reported decision in this case can be found at *Airco, Inc. v. Simmons First Nat'l Bank*, 638 S.W.2d 660 (Ark. 1982).

Civil Rights
Bell v. City of Milwaukee
Walter F. Kelley and Curry First

Racism is a blight on our nation that thwarts dreams, perpetuates injustice, and can even lead to physical injury or death. Racism takes an even uglier turn when its perpetrator is a police officer who is sworn to enforce laws even-handedly and protect the lives of all citizens. That is what happened in *Bell v. City of Milwaukee.*

David Bell, a 24-year-old African American, lost his life in a hate crime perpetrated by two law enforcement officers, Thomas Grady and Louis Krause, who, one otherwise uneventful night, decided to fill their arrest quota by bringing in "some niggers." Toward that end, the two policemen stopped the car in which Bell was riding for one reason — Bell was black. As Officer Grady approached the automobile to make the arrest, Bell jumped out of the car and fled down the street. Officers Grady and Krause pursued. Grady caught Bell and shot him in the back. To cover his tracks, the policeman then took a pocketknife out of his own pocket and put it in the dead man's hand to make it appear as if the shooting had been in self-defense.

Justice too often grinds slowly. In this case, 21 years passed before Milwaukee trial lawyer Walter F. Kelley, assisted by Curry First, successfully exposed the cover-up and the criminal activity that ended David Bell's life.

The official version, based on the police officers' lies, was that Bell's death resulted from a justified shooting. Bell's family never believed that to be true because the evidence pointed the other way. For example, David Bell was left-handed, and the knife was found in his right hand. Family members also knew that Bell never carried a knife. Moreover, they shared a popular perception that Milwaukee police officers carried "throw away" knives to plant on the bodies of victims of bogus shootings. In this case, there was also a common belief that the Milwaukee Police Department chose to take care of its own, rather than seek the truth in the killing of a black man. Officer Grady was quickly exonerated from any wrongdoing.

Bell's father filed a wrongful death action in 1959 — an act of remarkable courage considering the tenor of the times. The case ended in a mistrial. The City then offered the plaintiff an insulting $1,800 to settle the matter. He refused. Nothing further happened for almost 20 years. But a guilty conscience stalked one of the officers.

New life was breathed into the case when Officer Krause's conscience finally caught up with him. In August 1979, he came forward to confess the true story. Attorneys Kelley and First tried the case and obtained a jury verdict of $1.5 million. It took 21 years, but the Bell family finally obtained a modicum of justice, and a message was sent to law enforcement agencies that institutional racism is unacceptable and that cover-ups of official misconduct would be punished severely.

The reported decision in this case and the subsequent case history can be found at *Bell v. City of Milwaukee,* 498 F. Supp. 1339 (E.D. Wis. 1980), 536 F. Supp. 462 (E.D. Wis. 1982) (entering judgment for plaintiffs), *aff'd in relevant part,* 746 F.2d 1205 (7th Cir. 1984).

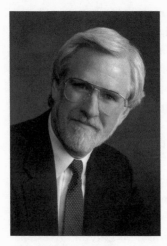

Walter F. Kelley

Auto Safety
Dorsey v. Honda Motor Co.
Larry Stewart

Larry Stewart of Miami, Florida, earned his nomination as Trial Lawyer of the Year by proving that the Honda car company ignored its own safety tests when it released its AN 600 compact car. Stewart's client, Glen Dorsey, suffered injury when his Honda, traveling at about 30 miles per hour, collided with a Ford. The left front of the Honda's passenger compartment collapsed approximately 10 inches. Dorsey's seat came off its back, ramming him forward and to the left. His seat belt failed to restrain him and his legs were jammed against the front of the passenger compartment, causing multiple fractures. Dorsey also suffered a severe concussion that left him with permanent double vision, a speech impairment, and partial paralysis.

The most appalling aspect of the story is that, if Honda had followed the recommendations of an employee in its own research and development department, much of this tragedy would have been avoided.

Dorsey and his wife, also injured in the crash, retained attorney Stewart. During discovery, the trial lawyer learned that Honda knew about the safety defect in its car from crash tests and that injuries of the type suffered by Dorsey were likely to occur in a 30 mile per hour collision. Despite this knowledge, Honda executives had refused to redesign the car to make it safer.

Stewart wanted punitive and compensatory damages from Honda. The problem was that, under Florida's law at the time, it was not at all clear that *failing to act* would give rise to punitive damages in the same way that acting wrongly could. Yet Stewart convinced a jury to award Dorsey $5 million in punitive damages. Honda appealed, arguing that because the company had complied with the federal safety regulations for some parts of the car that were affected by the crash, it should be automatically protected from punitive damages. The U.S. Court of Appeals in New Orleans disagreed, affirming the punitive damages award.

By protecting his client and clarifying the law on punitive damages, Larry Stewart promoted public justice through the civil justice system. As a result, product safety took a great stride forward.

The reported decision in this case and the subsequent case history can be found at *Dorsey v. Honda Motor Co.*, 655 F.2d 650 (5th Cir. 1981), *opinion modified*, 670 F.2d 21 (5th Cir. 1982), *cert. denied*, 459 U.S. 880 (1982).

Larry Stewart

Medical Safety
Harbeson v. Parke Davis, Inc.
Samuel Pemberton

When Jean Harbeson gave birth to a son in 1971, she had a grand mal epileptic seizure. Her doctor prescribed the drug Dilantin to control her epilepsy. All was well until the next year when the Harbesons decided that they wanted to have another child. Before attempting to add to their family, the Harbesons consulted with three U.S. Army physicians to learn whether there were any risks associated with taking the drug during pregnancy. Each of the physicians informed them that Dilantin could cause cleft palate and temporary hirsutism, both minor and correctable problems. In actuality, the drug is associated with far more serious birth defects.

Based on the information given by the Army physicians, Mrs. Harbeson continued to take Dilantin during her two subsequent pregnancies. Unfortunately, both children, Elizabeth and Christine, were born with "fetal hydrantain syndrome." The syndrome manifests itself in mild to moderate growth deficiencies, mild to moderate mental retardation, wide-set eyes, drooping eyelids, low-set hairline and other developmental defects — all caused by Dilantin. If the Harbesons had been properly informed about the risks, they would have chosen not to have more children.

Faced with many years of expensive special treatment and education costs associated with the proper care of their daughters, the Harbesons retained attorney Samuel Pemberton of Tacoma, Washington. Pemberton sued the federal government for medical malpractice. The trial court found that the Army doctors had failed in their duties to inform their patient of the risks of taking Dilantin during pregnancy. What made the case novel was that the plaintiffs also requested damages to pay for the care of the girls after they reached adulthood. The court agreed, awarding $338,000. This case helped to open the door to "wrongful life" suits by disabled children seeking compensation for the harm caused by being born with severe disabilities — even though, absent the malpractice, it is unlikely that they would have been born at all.

The reported decision in this case can be found at *Harbeson v. Parke Davis, Inc.*, 656 P.2d 483 (Wash. 1983).

Insurer Accountability
Sarchett v. Blue Shield of California
William Shernoff

Legal problems associated with health care of a different sort faced Claremont, California, attorney William Shernoff in a case involving the financing of medical treatment. John E. Sarchett visited his family physician after experiencing disturbing symptoms, including abdominal discomfort and severe weakness. Sarchett's long-time family physician, Dr. Bruce Van Vracken, feared that his patient might have internal bleeding, so he ordered Sarchett into the hospital for tests. The tests all proved negative and Sarchett was discharged after a three-day hospital stay.

That's when the problems began — not with Mr. Sarchett's health, but with his insurance company. When he submitted his $1,100 bill to his health insurer, Blue Shield, the company denied the claim, relying on a clause that excluded from coverage hospital stays for primarily diagnostic purposes.

Sarchett brought the insurance coverage issue to his doctor's attention. Dr. Van Vracken immediately wrote Blue Shield to inform the company that he hospitalized his patient based on Sarchett's symptoms, not primarily for testing. To do otherwise, he told Blue Shield, would have endangered his patient.

Blue Shield reviewed the case and considered the doctor's letter. Instead of granting the claim, however, it continued to deny it. Sarchett's claim was then supported by the Foothill Presbyterian Hospital utilization review committee. The committee reviewed Sarchett's records and backed the doctor's claim that the hospitalization had been necessary to protect Sarchett's health. The review concluded that Dr. Van Vracken's decision to hospitalize his patient was based on sound medical advice. Still, Blue Shield stubbornly refused to pay the claim.

Frustrated at being denied coverage to which he felt clearly entitled, Sarchett retained attorney Shernoff. Shernoff tried to settle the claim, but when Blue Shield *still* refused, he filed suit. It would be a decision that would cost the insurance company $100,000, both to compensate Sarchett and to punish Blue Shield for refusing to honor the claim. Considering the attorneys' fees Blue Shield had to foot, the decision to deny Sarchett's claim was an expensive one indeed.

In 1987, after Shernoff was honored, the verdict was reversed by the California Supreme Court and remanded to the trial court for a new trial. At retrial, the jury found that the "defendant breached its duty of good faith and fair dealing by failing to advise plaintiff of his right to peer review and arbitration" and again awarded significant damages. This case promoted public justice, in

Bill Shernoff's words, by ensuring that the "treating physician's judgment should be given great weight in determining whether a treatment is medically necessary rather than the insurance company deciding for itself."

A reported decision in this case and the subsequent case history can be found at *Sarchett v. Blue Shield of California*, 204 Cal. Rptr. 534 (Cal. App. 1984), *rev'd*, 729 P.2d 267 (Cal. 1987) (vacating award for plaintiff and remanding for damages determination).

William Shernoff

Access to Justice
Von Stetina v. Florida Medical Center
Sheldon Schlesinger

Tort reform is the bane of a just and equitable civil justice system. One tried and true attempt to stack the deck against individuals and in favor of the financially powerful is the "loser pays rule," a scheme that requires the loser of a lawsuit to pay the winner's attorney's fees. The rule works in favor of wealthy corporations and against injured individuals because a large company can well afford to pay for a lost case, but an individual who loses a large, complex case against a corporation could easily be bankrupted by a seven-figure judgment for attorneys' fees. Obviously, such a law could deter an individual from suing when she believes a large, well-heeled corporation has wronged her.

The Florida legislature had enacted such a "loser pays rule" for medical malpractice claims. The point of the law, clearly, was to deter patients injured by their health care provider's negligence from filing suit. However, attorney Sheldon Schlesinger successfully hoisted the malpractice insurance industry on its own petard.

The case involved Susan Ann Von Stetina, who was badly injured in an auto accident in November 26, 1981. An ambulance rushed her to the Florida Medical Center, where a team of surgeons removed her pancreas, put her fractured legs in traction, and attended to her other injuries. Thereafter, she was placed on a respirator.

Von Stetina was making steady progress until December 3, when the ventilator failed and left her brain deprived of oxygen for nearly half an hour. This resulted in a profound cognitive disability that would require Von Stetina to be hospitalized for the rest of her life. Von Stetina's parents retained attorney Schlesinger to help them recover a monetary award to pay for their daughter's lifelong care and for their pain and suffering.

During the two-week trial, the defense contended that the injuries sustained in the auto accident left Von Stetina's lungs unable to properly assimilate oxygen. Schlesinger countered that the overworked nurses in the unit simply did not have time to adequately monitor their patients. As a result, he argued, the nurses did not detect the ventilator failure until Von Stetina's brain had suffered profound damage.

The jury returned a verdict of $12.4 million after just three hours of deliberation. In an ironic twist, Schlesinger then relied on the "loser pays" statute — designed to hurt malpractice claimants — to seek reasonable attorney's fees from the hospital's insurance company. Stating that the lawyer's trial work was the finest he had ever seen and relying heavily on expert testimony presented in a separate hearing, the judge granted attorney's fees in the amount of $4.4 million over and above the $12.4 million awarded to the plaintiffs.

A later reported decision in this case and the subsequent case history can be found at *Florida Medical Center, Inc. v. Von Stetina*, 436 So. 2d 1022 (Fla. Dist. Ct. App. 1983) (affirming in relevant part), *rev'd sub nom., Florida Patient's Compensation Fund v. Von Stetina*, 474 So. 2d 783 (Fla.1985) (vacating judgment and remanding for new trial).

1983 Trial Lawyer of the Year Award Winner
Alan M. Darnell
The Case That Made Justice State-of-the-Art

The first case to win the Trial Lawyer of the Year Award was not only significant in its own right, but would echo through the years. Alan M. Darnell of Woodbridge, New Jersey, the only attorney to win the Trial Lawyer of the Year Award twice, filed suit on behalf of workers injured by one of the great health hazards of the 20th century — asbestos. He won the award for obtaining a landmark decision in the New Jersey Supreme Court that prevented asbestos manufacturers from mounting a "state of the art" defense which, if successful, would have shifted the burden of harm caused by asbestos from corporate defendants to innocent victims.

The case served public justice in a most significant and vital way. *Beshada v. Johns-Manville Products Corp.* not only helped open the door to justice for victims of asbestos poisoning, but also expanded the law of products liability in New Jersey to ensure that the party ultimately responsible for bearing the financial burden caused by unsafe products would be the manufacturer.

Asbestos is a group of naturally occurring fibrous minerals used extensively in construction during much of the 20th century because of its insulating and fireproofing properties. Asbestos was usually found in ceiling tiles, pipe and vessel insulation, floor tiles, linoleum, and mastic, and it was also commonly blown onto structural beams and ceilings. Though it was useful as building material, asbestos ultimately proved too dangerous to use. The problem is that asbestos is composed of microscopic fibers that can be swallowed or inhaled unknowingly. Once inside the body, the fibers slowly cause great harm to bodily tissues. Because the harm is often proportional to the amount of asbestos that finds its way into the body, the longer and greater the exposure, the more significant the risk of disease.

> *What is public justice? The manufacturers of dangerous products, not their injured victims, pay for the harm caused by the products.*

Asbestos poisoning causes a variety of deadly diseases. For example, asbestosis is a chronic lung disease caused by inhaling asbestos fibers that progressively penetrate and irritate the outer parts of the lung. At first, this merely causes inflammation, but it culminates in pulmonary fibrosis, a pronounced thickening and scarring of lung tissue. This leads to symptoms of breathlessness, which become increasingly severe, resulting in respiratory failure. Asbestosis also causes greater vulnerability to other lung diseases, such as tuberculosis and lung cancer — especially if the asbestos exposure is accompanied by smoking. There is no treatment for asbestosis, and it almost invariably leads to disability and/or death.

Another deadly disease caused by asbestos exposure is mesothelioma, a tumor on the outer part of the lung (the pleura). The disease is quite rare — unless the patient has been exposed to asbestos. One form of the disease can be treated with surgery, but the cancerous version generally leads to death.

Adding to the dangers of asbestos exposure is the pronounced latency period between exposure and the onset of disease. Indeed, many years usually pass before the exposed victim realizes that something is wrong — a crucial time in which many victims compounded their injury by continuing to expose themselves to asbestos. Thus, in years past, many victims, primarily workers in the building industry, continued to work with the dangerous fibers, unaware that they were sealing their own doom.

Tens of thousands of individuals were exposed to asbestos over the years, ultimately resulting in terrible personal tragedies and widespread litigation that remains ongoing to this day. One of the most important asbestos cases was *Beshada*, spearheaded by attorney Darnell. *Beshada* involved six consolidated personal injury and wrongful death cases brought against manufacturers and distributors of asbestos products by workers and their families. The complaints alleged that, due to asbestos exposure from as far back as the 1930s, the plaintiffs contracted asbestosis or mesothelioma.

The suits were not filed until the 1970s — in some cases nearly 40 years from the onset of exposure — due to the extended time lapse between exposure and recognition of symptoms. The key question facing the plaintiffs in the litigation was the applicability of the "state-of-the-art" defense mounted by the asbestos defendants. The asbestos companies argued that they should not be held liable for the plaintiffs' illnesses or deaths because they did not know about the dangerous propensities of their products during the time in which the plaintiffs were exposed and, thus, they could not have warned or protected the plaintiffs against the dangers. The plaintiffs disputed the defendants' claim of ignorance, but the issue promised to be a bruising factual dispute. Thanks to

Darnell's work, questions of what the asbestos companies knew and when they knew it became irrelevant to the litigation.

Darnell opened his legal gambit to strip the defendants of their "state-of-the-art" shield by filing a motion to strike the affirmative defense from the litigation. "The question as I saw it," Darnell recalls, "is who should bear the burden of the harm that was unquestionably caused to the plaintiffs by being exposed to asbestos? Should the injured individual have to pay for the burdens of asbestos-caused disease or should the manufacturer of the unsafe product? In my mind, this involved an analysis of which parties were in a better position to spread the risk and bear the costs associated with asbestos-related illnesses. It seemed to me that the answer was quite clear: a successful state-of-the-art defense would force those sickened by asbestos to bear the consequences of their illnesses rather than the parties who caused the problem. This would have worked a substantial injustice which I was determined to prevent if I possibly could."

The issue was a matter of first impression in New Jersey, so the trial judge was in no position to grant the motion. This was not entirely unexpected. Yet the matter was of such extreme importance to the plaintiffs and their families that Darnell immediately took the necessary steps to have the matter heard by the New Jersey Supreme Court. This was a crucial turning point in the case. Much was at stake. If New Jersey's highest court were to reverse the trial court, then much of the grinding fact-finding work needed to prevail in the litigation could be avoided and the case would become strictly a matter of determining damages. If the Court were to rule against the plaintiffs, then the victims might have to bear the financial brunt of treating their asbestos-related injuries.

On July 7, 1982, the Supreme Court of New Jersey issued its unanimous decision. The news was good. The Court reversed, striking the state-of-the-art defense. The Court's ruling was unequivocal, sweeping, and conclusive:

> Essentially, state-of-the-art is a negligence defense. It seeks to explain why defendants are not culpable for failing to provide a warning. They assert, in effect, that because they could not have known the product was dangerous, they acted reasonably in marketing it without a warning.

But, the Court noted, this litigation did not concern a failure to warn — it was about the production of dangerous products:

> In strict liability cases, culpability is irrelevant. The product was unsafe. That it was unsafe because of the state of technology does not change the fact that it was unsafe. Strict liability focuses on the product, not the fault of the manufacturer.

The Court then proceeded to dismantle the alleged justifications for permitting the state-of-the-art defense in *Beshada*:

When the defendants argue that it is unreasonable to impose a duty on them to warn of the unknowable, they misconstrue both the purpose and effect of strict liability. By imposing strict liability, we are not requiring defendants to have done something that is impossible. . . . [A] major concern of strict liability — ignored by defendants — is the conclusion that if a product was in fact defective, the distributor of the product should compensate its victims for the misfortune that it inflicted upon them.

In other words, "fault" was not the point. The purpose of the strict liability standard is to compensate the victim for injuries caused by a defective product. The key issue, as Darnell had hoped it would be, was the extent of harm caused by the asbestos, not when the companies knew of the dangers associated with the product. Therefore, the defendants' assertion of prior ignorance was beside the point.

The efforts of Darnell and the many lawyers and support staff who worked with him in obtaining this important legal ruling resulted in a substantial monetary settlement for the injured workers and their families. But the case served the public justice as well as the individual plaintiffs, making it easier for people injured by defective products to hold manufacturers liable, even if the companies claimed to be unaware of the harms they were causing. Although the reasoning of the New Jersey Supreme Court was not accepted in all jurisdictions, some other states followed New Jersey's lead, allowing many others whose health was severely impaired by asbestos exposure to obtain justice.

Unfortunately, what the Courts give they may also take away. "While there is no state-of-the-art defense in asbestos litigation," Darnell says, "the rule of law enunciated in *Beshada* was subsequently limited by the New Jersey Supreme Court to apply solely to asbestos cases."

Ironically, the issue of the asbestos defendants' knowledge soon became a matter of great import in asbestos litigation. "Lawyers for asbestos plaintiffs," Darnell points out, "have subsequently shown that many asbestos companies knew of the hazards of their products and took active steps to make sure nobody else knew what they knew. That led to many bankruptcies and many punitive damage awards over the last twenty-five years of asbestos litigation." These legal battles are still being fought across the nation, with Darnell in the thick of the action two decades after receiving first Trial Lawyer of the Year Award.

What neither The TLPJ Foundation nor Darnell could have known in 1983 was that history would only enhance the significance of *Beshada*. That important asbestos case subsequently led to Darnell and others suing tobacco companies in the famous *Cippolone v. Liggett Group* case, for which he and his co-counsel won the Trial Lawyer of the Year Award in 1988. In *Cippolone*, Darnell teamed up with an asbestos industry *defense* lawyer, Marc Edell, and his colleague Cynthia Walters, to bring an asbestos-type suit against some of the world's most powerful tobacco companies. *Cippolone* proved to be the turning point in the decades-long struggle by dedicated trial lawyers to force Big Tobacco to pay for its wrongful conduct. For the first time, a jury would award damages to a smoker for the harm caused by cigarettes. More important, in the larger picture of public justice, *Cippolone* generated a domino effect that would eventually break the back of the tobacco industry's long-standing grip over the American civil justice system. Thus, Darnell's work in asbestos litigation proved to be not only monumental, but path-breaking.

The reported decision in this case can be found at *Beshada v. Johns-Manville Products Corp.*, 447 A.2d 539 (N.J. 1982).

Alan M. Darnell

CHAPTER TWO

1984: The Case of the Atomic Downwinders

Drug Safety *Oxendine v. Merrell Dow Pharmaceuticals, Inc.*

Government Accountability *Meyers v. Philadelphia Housing Authority*

Auto Safety *Burgess v. Ford Motor Co.*

Product Safety *Butcher v. Robertshaw Controls Co.*

Drug Safety *Alboher v. Parke-Davis Div. of Warner Lambert Co.*

Auto Safety *Edwards v. General Motors Corp.*

Insurer Accountability *Keller v. Vermeer Mfg. Co.*

Medical Safety *Pedroza v. Bryant*

Winner
Allen v. United States
The Case of the Atomic Downwinders

The Trial Lawyer of the Year Award finalists for 1984 demonstrated how public justice can be obtained through tort law and the civil justice system. The finalists sought redress for harm caused by unsafe products, deaths caused by the failure of public housing officials to install smoke alarms, hospital-caused medical malpractice, violations of federal consumer protection laws, and insurance company neglect of duty. The winner took on the biggest defendant of all — the federal government — for harm caused to people living downwind of atomic bomb tests who become seriously ill and/or died from the resulting radioactive fallout.

Drug Safety

Oxendine v. Merrell Dow Pharmaceuticals, Inc.

Barry Nace

When Mary Virginia Oxendine, a registered nurse, suffered morning sickness during her pregnancy, she asked her doctor for treatment. He prescribed a drug known as Bendectin. Knowing that the health of the fetus was most vulnerable in the first trimester, Oxendine double-checked her doctor's recommendation by looking up the drug in the *Physician's Desk Reference* (PDR) to assure herself that her developing child would not be in any danger. The PDR report on the drug, manufactured by Merrell Dow Pharmaceuticals, contained no warning about possible birth defects. Assured that it was safe, Oxendine took the medication to combat her nausea.

Oxendine's daughter was born with a deformed hand. Oxendine's sadness turned to anger when she learned that birth defects in the babies of the millions of women who had taken Bendectin were widespread. She and her husband vowed to prevent other children from experiencing the same fate as their daughter. They hired trial lawyer Barry Nace of Washington, D.C. to sue Merrell Dow.

Nace, who holds a degree in chemistry, studied the research principles used by scientists when testing a drug for safety before marketing. The key issue in determining the risks to pregnant women, he learned, was whether the drug is a teratogen — that is, whether it will pass through the placenta and potentially impact the unborn child's development. At trial, Nace presented evidence of animal studies showing that some of the chemicals in Bendectin were indeed teratogens and that fetal deformities and deaths were dosage-related. He also introduced evidence that pregnant women who took the drug were in danger of having a baby with birth defects. Nace ultimately persuaded the jury that studies cited by the defense to rebut the case were seriously flawed.

The jury awarded the Oxendine family $750,000 in compensatory damages. Within two weeks, Merrell Dow took Bendectin off the market. But the Food and Drug Administration did not mandate a recall, and the product remains available in Canada under the name Diclectin. The jury verdict in *Oxendine* was subsequently overturned on appeal. (See the follow-up to this story in Chapter Four on the 1986 Trial Lawyer of the Year Award finalists and winner.)

A later decision in this case can be found at *Oxendine v. Merrell Dow Pharmaceuticals, Inc.*, 1996 WL 680992 (D.C. Super. Ct. Oct. 24, 1996) (vacating jury verdict and entering judgment for defendant).

Barry Nace

Government Accountability
Meyers v. Philadelphia Housing Authority
James Beasley

A house fire, six children dead, and a mother seriously burned — these were the tragic facts that led James Beasley of Philadelphia to sue the Philadelphia Housing Authority on behalf of the grief-stricken mother, Jean Meyers. When the housing agency rehabilitated Jean Meyers' home in 1975, it had failed to install smoke alarms, which soon thereafter became a required safety precaution under federal regulations.

With no law requiring that smoke alarms be placed in public housing, Beasley argued that simple foresight demanded the installation of the safety devices. Those who rely on public housing, Beasley believed, were least able to provide for smoke alarms themselves. In contrast, the agency could purchase smoke alarms cheaply due to economies of scale, so there was no excuse for the agency not to have installed smoke alarms to protect its tenants.

At trial, Beasley showed that even after 1976, when federal regulations required that smoke detectors be installed in newly refurbished houses, the Philadelphia Housing Authority refused to allocate funds for the required smoke detectors. Moreover, Beasley proved that more than 130 fires within the five-year period before the Meyers' tragedy had cost the agency over $1.3 million in property damages. Despite the relatively common experience of fires in public housing units, the agency never considered allocating a portion of the insurance proceeds it received to pay for smoke detectors. The jury agreed that such misfeasance was inexcusable and awarded Meyers more than $8 million in damages. While on appeal, the case settled for an undisclosed but reportedly "substantial sum." Beasley donated part of his attorney's fees toward the purchase of $10,000 worth of smoke detectors.

There is no reported decision on the merits in *Meyers*.

James Beasley

Auto Safety
Burgess v. Ford Motor Co.
William Smith and James R. Pratt, III

College student Rebecca Lynn Burgess was catastrophically injured while riding as a passenger in a Ford Pinto on her way home from dance class. She was rendered a spastic quadriplegic, unable to talk and requiring constant care. Because Ford had not equipped the Pinto with a simple and effective safety device — a passenger-side airbag — a question arose as to whether Rebecca's injuries could have been prevented if she had been riding in a more crash-worthy car.

Attorneys William Smith and James R. Pratt, III, of Birmingham, Alabama, were determined to find out. The premise of a crashworthiness case is that the manufacturer is duty-bound to design a product that is safe to operate in fore-seeable circumstances. This includes reasonably withstanding the forces of an auto accident. Smith and Pratt learned that when the Pinto's front end was crushed, the steel A-pillar (where the windshield and side window intersect) had crashed inward, causing Rebecca's injuries. They also discovered that Ford knew of the problem. But they did not restrict their case to the known defect. They sought to prove that by failing to install airbags in the vehicle — a common safety feature today — Ford had been doubly negligent.

Smith and Pratt researched the issue and learned that airbags were known to be effective since the 1960s. They also discovered that Ford had tested the Pinto with airbags and had determined that the interior safety of the automobile was enhanced when the bags deployed in front-end collisions. Indeed, the bags were designed to protect passengers in the very kind of accident that so catastrophically injured Burgess.

Bringing their two-pronged case, Smith and Pratt obtained a $1.8 million settlement after just four days of trial. More important, by pursuing the untried tactic of accusing Ford of wrongdoing for failing to install airbags, the lawyers not only improved their case, but also contributed to the ultimately successful cause of having auto manufacturers install airbags in all new automobiles.

There is no reported decision on the merits in *Burgess.*

James R. Pratt, III

Product Safety
Butcher v. Robertshaw Controls Co.
James McKenna

One morning, when Patrick Butcher bent down to check the control valve on his water heater, the heater exploded without warning, engulfing Butcher in a wall of flame. Butcher saved his life by having enough presence of mind to run outside and roll his body in tall grass to extinguish the flames. Following a frantic ride in an ambulance, and quick work by doctors, Butcher unexpectedly survived, despite suffering burns to 85 percent of his body.

Butcher retained attorney James McKenna of Rockville, Maryland, to seek justice for the agony and expense caused by this sudden explosion. McKenna relentlessly investigated the affairs of Robertshaw Controls Co., the manufacturer of the heater's gas intake control valve. He also made novel use of a largely ignored section of the federal 1972 Consumer Product Safety Act (CPSA) to obtain compensation for Butcher and safer water heaters for consumers.

Robertshaw had an infamous history, dating back to the mid-1950s, of being sued for injuries and property damage allegedly caused by its intake valves. McKenna was stunned to discover that, even though the company had been sued regularly for nearly 30 years, the consumer watchdog agency created by the CPSA to protect Americans against unsafe products had never investigated the company or called it to task for its safety violations. Much of the fault for this omission fell squarely on the shoulders of Robertshaw. Despite being legally required to report the maiming and killing of consumers by defective products, the company never informed the government of the problems with its valves. Instead, it falsely informed the government that it knew of a "potential defect" that had led to just one fatality and one injury.

McKenna used these egregious violations of the self-reporting rule to add new causes of action to Butcher's case. He found a provision in the CPSA that permitted victims of defective products violating a consumer product safety rule to sue the manufacturer in federal court for additional damages. Accordingly, McKenna sought punitive damages against Robertshaw for fraud and deceit in concealing the known dangers of its product from the government. Winning the right to pursue this approach earned McKenna his nomination as Trial Lawyer of the Year.

The reported decision in this case can be found at *Butcher v. Robertshaw Controls Co.*, 550 F. Supp. 692 (D. Md. 1981) (denying defendant's motion to dismiss).

Drug Safety
Alboher v. Parke-Davis Div. of Warner Lambert Co.
Alfred Julien

When Parke-Davis created the drug Dilantin, it was hailed as a medical miracle. Used to control epileptic seizures, the Food and Drug Administration (FDA) had warned that it be prescribed only to treat the symptoms of epilepsy. Unfortunately, when Ellen Alboher experienced only transient muscle twitches and spasms, Dilantin was prescribed. Worse still, when Alboher became pregnant, she continued to take the drug. This caused her daughter Elyse to be born with a severe physical deformity — the baby girl had no eyes or eye sockets.

An attorney named Fred Peters took the case. Five months before trial, Peters was killed in an airplane accident. The judge in the case granted one continuance while members of Peters' firm frantically sought a trial lawyer to replace him. Meanwhile, attorney Alfred Julien of New York had been retained to handle Peters' plane crash case. When the judge insisted that a jury be selected or the case be dismissed, Julien stepped in.

Julien was given responsibility for the case on a Thursday — with the trial beginning the next Monday. He and five of his staff worked around the clock all weekend to prepare the case. He then conducted a three-week trial. To counter the argument by Warner-Lambert Co., the parent of Parke-Davis, that the birth defect was inherited, Julien demonstrated that the condition almost never happened unless the parents were related. Elyse's parents were unrelated. Julien also proved that Parke-Davis researchers had never tested the drug itself, but relied instead on outside reports to assure the safety of their drug. Even so, the medical literature had reported that adverse effects were likely to occur if pregnant women took Dilantin. Thus, Parke-Davis should have warned against taking the drug during pregnancy and/or should have conducted greater safety tests to protect patients from the adverse effects of their drug.

The jury awarded Alboher $7 million after two weeks of deliberation. Attorney Julien not only acted in the best traditions of the legal profession by taking the case at the last minute, but for the first time, he forced Parke-Davis to pay for the severe birth defects caused by taking Dilantin in early pregnancy.

A later decision in this case can be found at *Alboher v. Parke-Davis Div. of Warner Lambert Co.*, 1984 WL 2739 (E.D.N.Y. Mar. 1, 1984) (upholding jury verdict).

Auto Safety
Edwards v. General Motors Corp.
R. Ben Hogan, III

Imagine the horror of being struck in a rear-end collision and having your car burst into flames. Worse yet, think about having to drag your wife out of the car with her clothes and hair aflame. Then contemplate the very worst: before you can rescue your two screaming boys from a back-seat inferno, you and your wife see them burn to death.

This is the tragedy that befell Bob Edwards and his family when a speeding car slammed into the back of their Chevrolet Chevette. Although the vehicle that struck them was speeding, the impact speed was only 20-25 miles per hour because both cars were traveling in the same direction. Normally, such a low-level impact would not be fatal and would cause only minor injuries. However, defects in the Chevette's fuel storage system made the car a death trap, transforming what should have been a survivable accident into a lethal catastrophe.

The Edwards retained Ben Hogan of Birmingham, Alabama, to hold General Motors (GM) accountable for their terrible loss. Hogan discovered an all-too-common story. GM executives knew from company crash tests that the rear doors were likely to jam shut upon rear impact and that the gas tank was in a position where it was likely to be crushed on impact. Indeed, the Chevette model in which the Edwards were riding failed one-third of all crash tests run between the beginning of its production and 1981. Despite their knowledge of these dangers, GM executives never directed that the safety problems be corrected.

The jury held GM liable for negligence and awarded the plaintiffs more than $4 million for their loss and personal injuries. The size of the award had the salutary effect of warning other consumers of the dangers of the Chevrolet Chevette. Moreover, the decision became the first crashworthiness case affirmed by the Alabama Supreme Court.

The later reported decision in this case and its subsequent case history can be found at *General Motors Corp. v. Edwards*, 482 So. 2d 1176 (Ala. 1985) (affirming judgment for plaintiff with remittitur), *overruling recognized by Brooks v. Colonial Chevrolet-Buick*, 579 So. 2d 1328 (Ala. 1991).

R. Ben Hogan, III

Insurer Accountability
Keller v. Vermeer Mfg. Co.
Francis Breidenbach

Gary Vermeer revolutionized the farm industry with his invention of a hay baler that permits one man to do the work of five. But the machine was potentially dangerous. The "wringer" can grab an object and pull it inward at a rate of seven feet per second. Because of this danger and because Vermeer did not have detailed knowledge of farm machinery safety, he relied on Liberty Mutual Insurance Company to provide him with advice and assurances that the design and engineering of the hay baler would be safe for farm workers.

Unfortunately, the kind of accident that Vermeer relied upon the insurance company to prevent in fact occurred. While the machine was running, its operator tried to dislodge a dirt clod in front of the wringer's rollers. The machine quickly grasped the operator's hand and yanked him into the baler up to his shoulder. The man's arm was eventually amputated.

The farm worker, Mr. Keller, retained Los Angeles trial attorney Francis Breidenbach to represent him, suing both Vermeer Manufacturing and Liberty Mutual. Breidenbach argued that when an insurance company undertakes responsibility for providing safety advice to a manufacturer, it should be responsible along with the manufacturer for a defectively designed product that causes injury. The jury agreed, finding Liberty Mutual liable for 13 percent of the $504,000 damage award.

This was the first time that an insurance company had been held liable in a products liability case for providing negligent safety advice to a manufacturer. There is no reported decision on the merits in *Keller*.

Francis Breidenbach

Medical Safety
Pedroza v. Bryant
Daniel Sullivan

Daniel Sullivan of Seattle, Washington, had the unique distinction of being honored as a finalist for the Trial Lawyer of the Year Award for a case he *lost*. Sullivan represented the family of Maria Pedroza, who died because of the gross incompetence of a doctor. The doctor had failed to heed her alarming symptoms in late pregnancy — symptoms that led to toxemia and death. Despite three different attempts by Pedroza to get help, all her doctor ever did was prescribe aspirin.

Late in her pregnancy, Pedroza lapsed into a coma and her family rushed her to the hospital. Doctors tried in vain to save Pedroza's life, though they were able to operate and save her child. Pedroza's doctor was not present to assist her because, as the Pedrozas later learned, his obstetrical and newborn privileges had been severely curtailed more than a year earlier.

Pedroza's husband, Rudolfo Pedroza, sued the doctor and the hospital, quickly settling with the former. The trial court then dismissed the case against the hospital because Washington State courts had never held a hospital liable to a patient for its decisions concerning the selection, supervision, and retention of the physicians on its staff. Sullivan handled the appeal from this dismissal.

Sullivan convinced the courts that hospitals have a duty to maintain the quality of their medical staffs. If a hospital permits a physician to use its facilities, it cannot avoid its responsibility to patients. Part of that responsibility is to assure patients that when a hospital grants doctors the privilege of associating with the hospital, those doctors will perform quality work. The potential for a hospital to be held financially responsible for failing to fulfill this obligation made life safer for all patients in the State of Washington.

Sullivan lost the case, despite making new law, because the malpractice that cost Pedroza her life occurred in the doctor's private office, not the hospital.

But the case established a critical principle: that hospitals should be held accountable for the quality of their doctors' professional conduct.

The reported decision in this case can be found at *Pedroza v. Bryant*, 677 P.2d 166 (Wash. 1984).

Daniel Sullivan

1984 Trial Lawyer of the Year Award Winner
Dale Haralson
The Case of the Atomic Downwinders

T he second annual Trial Lawyer of the Year Award was presented to Tucson, Arizona, attorney Dale Haralson for his short-lived victory against the federal government for injuring people living downwind of atomic bomb testing sites during the early 1950s. The government knew that the testing would expose Haralson's clients to dangerous levels of radiation, but actively hid the truth. As a consequence, the "downwind" citizens did not realize that the government had caused their deteriorating health. Outraged, Haralson took the difficult case, battling the power of the government to a trial court victory. Unfortunately, what one court allowed a higher court ultimately took away. In the end, Haralson's clients found that justice is sometimes an elusive concept when the wrongdoer is "Uncle Sam."

During the early 1950s, as the Korean War raged and the Soviet Union came into the atomic age, the U.S. entered the "arms race." President Harry Truman and his national security advisers decided to dramatically improve our atomic weapons capability. Part of this effort entailed the explosion of atomic bombs in the Nevada desert. However, detonated atomic weapons spread poisonous radiation known as "fallout," and detonating atomic bombs within the borders of the U.S. meant that fallout would spread to downwind communities. This atomic testing carried with it the potential of an immense public relations problem for the government. Instead of dealing with the safety hazards responsibly, the government adopted an ends-justifies-the-means mentality.

What is public justice? The government is held accountable when it lies about the public health risks of its conduct and innocent men, women, and children are injured and killed.

The federal government, then trusted by its citizenry, betrayed the people's confidence by lying about the dangers of atomic fallout. The government issued press releases before each test assuring the public that the test was being conducted safely. It also worked to obtain favorable press coverage of its false safety assurances. That was not difficult. In that era, the media were generally compliant — especially when it came to issues of national security. Press releases celebrated the advance of science and even invited local inhabitants to come watch history being made as the bombs blossomed into mushroom clouds.

The first atomic bomb was dropped over Frenchman Flat on January 17, 1951. The fallout cloud from this explosion and others that soon followed drifted east over sparsely populated areas of the Great Basin, located primarily in Nevada and Utah. On May 7, 1951, the fallout from a bomb blast passed over the little town of Tempiute, Nevada, contaminating more than 110 men, women, and children. Monitors showed that the fallout was the greatest ever recorded for a populated area, yet none of the citizens was warned or told what precautions to take to avoid harm. Other fallout clouds would pass over small towns such as Ely, Nevada, and larger cities such as Salt Lake City, Utah.

By early June, the poisonous effects of the fallout were beginning to appear in livestock. In the first incident, the fallout burned cattle grazing 25 miles from ground zero. Meanwhile, testing accelerated, subjecting increasing numbers of people to atomic fallout without their knowledge. Many years later, people exposed to this deadly fallout would find their lives destroyed and/or ended by radiation-caused sickness.

Fast forward to the summer of 1977. Haralson was attending a lawyers' convention in Maui where he was approached by a Holbrook, Arizona, lawyer who asked him to look over a couple of cases that he was thinking of referring. One of these cases involved a Justice of the Peace from Holbrook named Vonda McKinney whose husband Lenn had died of leukemia in 1964. Haralson's lawyer-friend suggested that Mr. McKinney died because he had been exposed to the fallout from atomic bomb explosions at a Nevada test site.

Haralson was initially dubious about accepting the case. "I explained to him that I thought it would be impossible to prove the connection," Haralson recalls. "I was also concerned that the statute of limitations would have run, not to mention the difficulties associated with government immunity. But I didn't feel I could take the good referrals and refuse to at least consider those that seemed more difficult. So, I agreed to talk with Mrs. McKinney and see where matters went from there."

Haralson had no familiarity with radiation-associated health issues when he first spoke with his future client by phone. After their initial conversation, Haralson remained unenthusiastic, but he felt duty-bound to meet with the determined Judge McKinney and they agreed upon a time. It was at that meeting that Haralson's legal antennae began to twitch.

"She brought an article with her about a veteran who successfully brought a claim against the Veterans Administration based on contracting leukemia after being exposed to radiation in the tests," Haralson recalls. "And she told me about seven people dying of the disease in another little town near where she lived. All had lived downwind of the bomb tests. I had grown up in a small town and I had never even heard of anyone contracting the disease during my entire upbringing."

McKinney asked Haralson if he would be more interested in accepting the case if other survivors would participate. He said that might make a difference. Soon he found himself in a small town interviewing widows and parents of leukemia victims. He learned from these people that the government had announced when tests were to be conducted, but that there had been no warnings of health dangers. Indeed, the townspeople had been told that there was no danger and they had no reason to believe otherwise. It would be years before a leukemia epidemic struck the small towns.

Haralson was now intrigued. He agreed to conduct some research to determine whether a medical connection could be made between the bomb tests and the leukemia hot spots. This would lead him to intense discussions with several radiation experts from around the country. He also delved deeply into the scientific literature concerning radiation and its effects. Haralson used the Freedom of Information Act to disgorge 90,000 pages of documents and 20 reels of microfilmed data — much of which had to be declassified before he could see it. Eventually he concluded that a direct connection could be made between the deaths of his clients' spouses and the atomic bomb tests. Moreover, he learned that the assurances of safety to the downwind regions' inhabitants were utterly disingenuous; government scientists *knew* that radiation fallout could cause cancer.

One of the biggest hurdles facing Haralson was the sovereign immunity defense. Citizens can only sue the federal government if permitted to do so under the Federal Tort Claims Act. Haralson believed he could overcome that obstacle and decided to take the case. Thus began a long odyssey that would lead first to triumph and then to heartbreak.

Haralson soon filed suit on behalf of five plaintiffs. The charges were very serious, claiming that the U.S. should be held to account. The lawsuit alleged:

■ that the government failed to adequately warn off-site residents of known or foreseeable long-range biological consequences to adults and children from exposure to fallout radiation from open air atomic testing;

- that the government failed to measure adequately and concurrently with open air atomic testing the actual fallout near the test site on a person-specific basis;

- that the government failed to adequately warn communities during the testing of ways to prevent long-range biological consequences of exposure to fallout;

- that such failures constituted negligence; and

- that the plaintiffs who incurred leukemia or cancer were made ill from the fallout radiation.

It is not hyperbole to describe the case as a potentially groundbreaking suit of major proportions.

Word of the lawsuit quickly spread throughout the downwind area of the country. It turned out that nearly everyone within a 300-mile radius east of the test site had family members or close friends who had died of cancer or leukemia in the late 1950s or early 1960s. The lawsuit soon mushroomed like the cloud from an atomic bomb test. Eventually, 1,192 people came forward to press their claims against the government. A sample group of eight cases went to trial in September of 1982. The record consisted of 6,825 pages of transcript containing the testimony of 98 witnesses. Nearly 1,700 documents were admitted into evidence, totaling more than 54,000 pages.

The court reached its decision in 1984, 17 months after the trial. United States District Court Judge Bruce S. Jenkins ruled in favor of the plaintiffs in a 489-page, book-length decision that carefully analyzed the science and the law. For the first time, in all eight of the sample cases that were tried, a federal court had ruled that the atomic tests had caused cancer. These were real people, including children, whose lives had been shortened due to the government's conduct. The court described four children who had most likely died due to exposure to radiation fallout:

- Karen Hafen was born on August 4, 1941. She spent her entire life in St. George, Utah. When atmospheric testing in Nevada began, she was nine years old. She was diagnosed as having acute myelogenous leukemia in February of 1956, at the age of 14. She died nine months later.

- Sybil Johnson was born on November 6, 1952, and spent her life in Cedar City, Utah. At the age of 11, in May of 1964, she was diagnosed as having acute lymphoblastic leukemia. She died a year later, on May 15, 1965. The probability of pre-natal in utero exposure to fallout radiation is apparent from the face of the record, particularly where exposure in the first trimester is concerned. At the time of the heavier fallout from the seven tower shots and four air bursts of UPSHOT/KNOTHOLE (1953), she was five-seven months old.

- Sheldon Nisson was born on June 17, 1946, and lived in Washington, a small community near St. George, Utah. In March of 1959, at the age of 12, he was diagnosed as having acute myelogenous leukemia. He died four months later. At the commencement of NTS atmospheric testing, Sheldon Nesson was four years old. The heavy fallout series UPSHOT/KNOTHOLE had concluded only two weeks before his seventh birthday. Six years later, his leukemia was diagnosed. His home community...lay directly in the path of heavy fallout...in 1953. Other tests likely contributed to additional exposures.

- Peggy Orton, born January 12, 1946, was five years old when testing began with Operation RANGER at NTS (Nevada Test Site) in 1951. She lived in Parowan, Utah. On November 11, 1959, at the age of 13, Peggy Orton was diagnosed as having acute lymphoblastic leukemia. She died six months later, on May 29, 1960....

As to these children, the court ruled that: "The factors of age, apparent latency period, type of leukemia, proximity to NTS fallout patterns, when added to the persuasive statistical evidence in the record justifies the rational inference that exposure to fallout radiation was a substantial factor contributing to the incidence of leukemia in each of the four cases listed above."

Adults, too, died premature deaths due to the fallout from the atomic tests. According to the court:

- Arthur Frederick Bruhn, a resident of St. George, Utah, from 1951 through 1962, was born on September 30, 1916. He was 34 years old when atmospheric testing began at NTS. He was diagnosed in December 1963 as having acute lymphoblastic leukemia. He died seven months later. Testimony indicates that he may have been exposed to significant fallout radiation from shot HARRY in 1953 following observation of the shot from a hillside west of St. George.

- Lavier C. Tait was born on April 5, 1928. He was 22 years old when atmospheric atomic testing began in Nevada. He resided in Orderville and Mt. Carmel, Utah, and Fredonia, Arizona, until his death on September 13, 1965, at the age of 37. He was diagnosed in August 1964 as having chronic myeloytic leukemia....Increased potential for direct exposure to fallout in the case of Arthur Bruhn adds a factor in addition to the statistical evidence available. The latency periods in each case are wholly consistent with radiation etiology if calculated from the 1953 fallout series....The evidence in the record reasonably justifies the inference that it is more likely than not that fallout radiation was a substantial factor contributing to the leukemia.

- Jacqueline Sanders was born on November 3, 1945. She was five years old when atomic testing began near her home in St. George, Utah. On March 20, 1967, at the age of 21, she was diagnosed as having adenocarcinoma of the thyroid. Like that pertaining to breast cancer or leukemia, the human data and scientific literature concerning radiation-induced thyroid cancer is extensive....The latency period for development of thyroid cancers on the average appears to be between nine and 20, or more depending on the study....The figures reported...indicate a statistically significant increase of thyroid cancer, particularly among women.

- A resident of Fredonia, Arizona, Lenn McKinney, was born on December 1, 1918. He was diagnosed as having leukemia in June of 1961, though the specific type was in dispute at trial. He died on May 14, 1962. Dr. Clark Heath identified a 'cluster' of leukemia in Fredonia, Arizona, that appeared between 1960 and 1964 with an observed incidence exceeding that expected for the community by a factor of twenty. Eight years prior to detection of Lenn McKinney's illness, Fredonia had been in the direct path of significant fallout from shot SIMON (April 25, 1953) as well as being in close proximity to that from other shots.

The court awarded damages to the survivors of these Americans who died because of their government's wrongdoing. The wife and two children of Arthur Bruhn were to receive $625,000. The wife and six children of John E. Crabtree were to receive $210,000. The mother of Karlene Hafen was awarded $250,000. The parents of Sybil D. Johnson were each awarded $125,000. The wife and three children of Lenn McKinney were awarded $300,000. The father of Sheldon Nisson was ordered to receive $250,000. Peggy Orton's mother was awarded $250,000. Lavier Tait's wife and four children were to receive $400,000.

Haralson's victory created a tremendous stir throughout the legal community, for it opened the courthouse doors to the thousands of Americans whose health had been destroyed by atomic testing. For this monumental victory, The TLPJ Foundation named Haralson the 1984 Trial Lawyer of the Year.

Three years later, however, the U.S. Court of Appeals for the Tenth Circuit slammed the courthouse doors shut with a loud bang. Overturning Judge Jenkins' near-500 page opinion with a mere 10 pages of analysis, it dismissed the entire case on the basis of governmental immunity. Specifically, the court held that the government's actions in testing atomic weapons constituted a "discretionary function" that could not be the subject of a suit under the Federal Tort Claims Act. "We must conclude," the court ruled, "that the government is immune from liability for the failure of AEC (Atomic Energy Commission) administrators and employees to monitor radioactivity more extensively or to warn the public more fully than they did." The court stated:

> The government deliberations prior to these decisions expressly
> balanced public safety against what was felt to be a national necessity,
> in light of national and international security. However erroneous or
> misguided these deliberations may seem today, it is not the place of the
> judicial branch to now question them.

This was a devastating blow to Haralson and his clients. They had worked so hard to prove the government's callous disregard for the health and safety of its citizens. They had directly connected the government's actions and omissions to the deaths by radiation-caused leukemia and cancers. Yet with the stroke of a pen, it all ended. When the U.S. Supreme Court subsequently denied review, the case of *Allen v. United States* was over.

Was it worth it? Haralson is adamant that it was. "A great deal of good and lasting significance came of the case," Haralson points out. "Congress passed a law permitting people to submit claims for deaths and be paid up to $50,000 — an insulting amount — but better than nothing. And at least the law gave official recognition of what happened to these people. These tragedies took place. Moreover, for the first time we exposed the government's misrepresentations to the public about the testing program and its safety. We added to the public's awareness about the hazards of radiation exposure. People came to understand, partially as a result of what we did, that the government does not always tell people the truth and that we must be ready to put what it says to the test."

Other attorneys deserving of mention for their important role in preparing the case include Ralph Hunsaker of Phoenix, Arizona; Stuart Udall, presently of Santa Fe, New Mexico; and MacArthur Wright of St. George, Utah.

The reported decision in this case, and the subsequent case history, can be found at *Allen v. United States*, 588 F. Supp. 247 (D. Utah 1984), *rev'd*, 816 F.2d 1417 (10th Cir. 1987) (precluding all liability), *cert. denied*, 484 U.S. 1004 (1988).

Dale Haralson

CHAPTER THREE

1985: The Case of the Undisclosed Drug Dangers

Access to Justice *Kenyon v. Hammer*

Access to Justice *Ueland v. Reynolds Metals Co.*

Medical Safety *Jane Doe v. John Smith, M.D.*

Access to Justice *Davis v. Graviss*

Product Safety *Bowen v. Jiffe Clorox Chem. Corp.*

Workers' Rights *Sabine Pilot Service, Inc. v. Hauck*

Winner
MacDonald v. Ortho Pharmaceutical Corp.
The Case of the Undisclosed Drug Dangers

Finalists for the 1985 Trial Lawyer of the Year Award protected people by improving standards of medical care and product safety, increasing access to the civil courts, helping personal injury victims receive full compensation, and establishing that an employer may not fire a worker for refusing to break the law. The winning case set an important precedent by holding a manufacturer of birth control pills responsible for failing to disclose the risk of a serious side effect directly to consumers.

Access to Justice

Kenyon v. Hammer

James L. Leonard and Kenneth P. Clancy

When Sharon Kenyon discovered in 1978 that she had been the victim of medical malpractice six years earlier, she and her husband William thought that they would still be allowed to file a lawsuit. After all, not only had they been unaware of the negligence, but there had been no realistic way for them to have learned of the mistake. It took a concerted effort by Phoenix, Arizona, attorneys James J. Leonard and Kenneth P. Clancy to ensure that the Kenyons had their day in court.

When Sharon Kenyon gave birth to a child in 1972, her doctor had committed an inexcusable medical mistake that would have tragic consequences many years later. Kenyon had Rh-negative blood; her newborn baby had Rh-positive blood. As any competent obstetrician knows, the doctor should have given Kenyon a drug called Rho GAM within 72 hours of delivery to counteract her body's immune response to the baby's Rh factor. However, Kenyon was not given the drug. As a result, six years later, her second baby was stillborn; the antibodies in Kenyon's immune system had destroyed the baby's blood cells.

At the time, the medical malpractice statute of limitations in Arizona was rigidly established at three years from the negligent act — without any clause stating that the statute would begin to run only after the victim learned, or should have learned, of the negligent act. Thus, it seemed that Kenyon had a suffered a terrible wrong without an available remedy even though, through no fault of her own, she was completely unaware that she had been the victim of malpractice during the earlier birth.

This apparent obstacle did not prevent attorneys Leonard and Clancy from championing the Kenyons' cause — despite the almost certain loss they would suffer at the trial and intermediate appellate levels — in the hope of achieving review by Arizona's Supreme Court. The attorneys' strategy succeeded. Leonard and Clancy argued to the state's high court that the statute's wording violated the equal protection clause of Arizona's Constitution because it discriminated against patients who were unable to discover their injury until after the three-year limitations period had run. The attorneys for the doctor countered that there was a compelling state interest for the wording of the statute, which was intended to discourage frivolous claims, promote settlement, and decrease the cost of litigation.

The doctor's argument did not impress the Court. The Court ruled that the ability to bring claims such as the Kenyons' is a fundamental right under Arizona's Constitution. The Court further noted that the statute of limitations for negligence claims had not accomplished the goals set forth by the defendant. Accordingly, the Kenyons were released from the statute's constraints and permitted to pursue their claim. For taking such a risky case to a successful conclusion, attorneys Leonard and Clancy were named as finalists for the Trial Lawyer of the Year Award.

The reported decision in this case can be found at *Kenyon v. Hammer*, 688 P.2d 961 (Ariz. 1984).

James L. Leonard

Access to Justice
Ueland v. Reynolds Metals Co.
J. Murray Kleist and Phillip Arnold

Eric Ueland worked as a lineman for the Seattle City Light Company when he suffered a tragic accident. Ueland was working with a crew stringing one-inch-thick high voltage cables. As was the usual practice, to pull the lines taut, the linemen used a device called a hydra-pull manufactured by the Pengo Hydra-Pull Corporation. While the crew was using the hydra-pull, the mechanism dropped a loop of cable that whipped out and struck Ueland, smashing him into a nearby utility truck. Ueland was left permanently incapacitated with severe mental and physical disabilities.

Ueland had two children who were now without their father's love, companionship, or guidance. Nevertheless, no cause of action existed in Washington for loss of parental companionship. That did not seem right to Seattle attorneys J. Murray Kleist and Phillip Arnold. They argued to the Washington Supreme Court that children should be able to sue in such cases. The defense argued that the issue was a matter for the state legislature, such suits would lead to court crowding, and the damages were too speculative. The defense also argued that permitting such claims would raise insurance rates.

The Court rejected all of the defendant's arguments and, recognizing a new cause of action, ruled that a child can indeed sue in the State of Washington for the loss of parental love, companionship, and guidance. The Court noted that to avoid overcrowding of the courts, such cases should generally be joined with the parent's injury claim. As to the argument about increased insurance rates, the Court reasoned that the compensation of a child who is affected emotionally is more important than insurance rates, especially in light of society's interest in having well-adjusted children. Since the children could have sued for wrongful death if their father had died, there was no reason to deny them compensation when their father's injuries were so severe that he could no longer interact with them or take any part in their upbringing.

The *Ueland* case ultimately settled for a significant sum shortly after the opinion came down. The case has often been cited for the proposition that a child has an independent right of action for loss of parental love and care when there is a tortious injury to the parent. Several other states have joined Washington in recognizing this cause of action.

The reported decision in this case can be found at *Ueland v. Reynolds Metals Co.*, 691 P.2d 190 (Wash. 1984).

J. Murray Kleist & Phillip Arnold

Medical Safety
Jane Doe v. John Smith, M.D.
Jean D. O'Malley

Jane and Jack Doe eagerly awaited the birth of their first child. (A court seal in the case prevents the disclosure of the couple's real names or the name of the defendant doctor.) Ten days before she was due to give birth, Jane Doe experienced excessive weight gain, edema, elevated blood pressure, and other complications of pregnancy. Concerned, she went to her physician Dr. John Smith. Her physician failed to properly diagnose her preeclampsia and toxemia, potentially fatal conditions. Nor did he admit her to the hospital or arrange for follow-up care. Somehow, the physician also failed to recognize that Ms. Doe was pregnant with twins. Things only got worse when it was time to deliver the babies. During the delivery, the doctor failed to take the necessary precautions when performing Ms. Doe's caesarean section.

Ms. Doe had a difficult and painful delivery on January 20, 1984. The twins survived, but Ms. Doe became fatally ill. She died four days later of Adult Respiratory Distress Syndrome (ARDS). In order for her husband to succeed in his medical malpractice and gross negligence claims, his attorney, Jean D. O'Malley of Washington, D.C., had to prove a causal connection between the preeclampsia and toxemia suffered earlier by Ms. Doe and the ARDS that eventually took her life. Such a link had never before been proven.

The case required O'Malley to research the frontiers of medical science. By using electron microscopy, she showed that a slide of Ms. Doe's tissues looked very similar to tissue slides of patients who had died of preeclampsia. Worldwide research of the medical literature also demonstrated a connection between preeclampsia and ARDS. O'Malley was also able to prove that Ms. Doe's medical records had been altered. For example, her blood pressure readings — which are critical in assessing preeclampsia and toxemia — had been changed.

Cornered with proof of the damages caused by his negligence, the physician settled for nearly $1 million. Although the settlement could not replace Mr. Doe's wife and the mother of his children, the money helped him to care for the twins. The medical community also benefited from O'Malley's research because she established a connection between ARDS and preeclampsia that had not been generally understood.

There is no reported decision on the merits in *Doe v. Smith*.

Access to Justice

Davis v. Graviss

William S. Bowman and Leslie M. Murray

Imagine suffering a serious injury and having doctors in utter conflict about how to treat it. That is what happened to auto accident victim Laura Davis. After receiving treatment for non-life-threatening injuries to her face and head, Davis appeared to be on the mend. Then she began to experience a clear, watery drainage out of her nose that was unlike anything she had experienced with a cold or the flu. Her doctors discovered that the liquid was cerebral spinal fluid that was leaking through a basilar skull fracture caused by the auto accident.

What to do for Davis posed a medical conundrum. Left untreated, Davis would risk suffering serious complications, such as meningitis, brain abscess, and other neurological problems. One doctor recommended surgery. A second doctor opined that the risks of surgery — paralysis, blindness, speech dysfunctions, seizures, and death — were even more grave. Unable to decide which course to take, Davis suffered emotional and psychological distress.

Louisville, Kentucky, attorneys William S. Bowman and Leslie M. Murray filed suit for the injuries Davis received in the auto accident and sought damages that would include the increased likelihood of future complications and Davis' mental distress. They obtained a jury verdict of $390,000, $157,500 of which was for the mental suffering caused by Davis' "between-a-rock-and-a-hard-place" medical condition. Although an intermediate appellate court had set aside the verdict, the Supreme Court of Kentucky ruled that the verdict should stand based on the increased risk of future injury and the mental anguish caused by Davis' condition. As a result of the hard work of attorneys Bowman and Murray, Davis was compensated for the injuries she sustained — both physical and mental.

The reported decision in this case may be found at *Davis v. Graviss*, 672 S.W.2d 928 (Ky. 1984).

Product Safety
Bowen v. Jiffe Clorox Chem. Corp.
John E. Shamberg

Young children are known to swallow things they shouldn't. One day, a toddler named Renee Bowen reached for a bottle of "Liquid Plum'r" drain cleaner that her mother had just poured down the kitchen sink. Unfortunately, a few drops remained in the bottle and the little girl swallowed them. The caustic, sodium-hydroxide-based liquid severely burned the child's esophagus.

The Bowen family retained attorney John E. Shamberg of Kansas City, Kansas to sue the manufacturer of Liquid Plum'r. The *Bowen* case was one of more than 20 similar cases handled by Shamberg and his partner, Lynn Johnson, of Shamberg, Johnson & Bergman, on behalf of children who accidentally ingested Liquid Plum'r or similar products. Shamberg argued in each of these cases that a household product must be safe for the environment in which it is used — including homes with little children who are likely to swallow the mixture.

Bowen, like the other cases, settled before trial. Renee Bowen is reported to be happy and doing well despite her injuries and the many surgeries she had to endure. The settlement helped to pay for the more than 200 medical procedures that the child received at Kansas University Medical Center. Three pediatric surgeons at the Center — Lucian Leap, M.D., Keith Ashcraft, M.D., and Tom Holder, M.D. — conducted animal tests and published a series of articles concerning the devastating injuries to the esophagus caused by ingesting minute amounts of a sodium-hyroxide-based drain cleaner. Their work, along with Shamberg's lawsuits, helped move the Food and Drug Administration and the Consumer Product Safety Commission to adopt more stringent child restraint closure and labeling standards for these products.

As a result of Shamberg's multiple lawsuits, the Clorox Company, which had purchased the original manufacturer of Liquid Plum'r, changed the formula to make the product more effective and less dangerous. Clorox also changed the drain cleaner's container. Liquid Plum'r now comes in child-resistant containers and has clearer warning labels. All of these changes have substantially reduced the risk of causing serious injuries to toddlers.

There is no reported decision on the merits in *Bowen*.

John E. Shamberg

Workers' Rights
Sabine Pilot Service, Inc. v. Hauck
Greg Thompson and Walter Umphrey

In Texas and many other states, non-union employees can be fired at their employer's discretion under the common law "at-will employment doctrine." Under this doctrine, an employee working without a contract has no protection against termination and can be fired for any or no reason. In the 1980s, several states, including Texas, created public policy exceptions to the rule, thanks to the groundbreaking work of attorneys Greg Thompson and Walter Umphrey of Provost, Umphrey, McPherson & Swearingen in Port Arthur, Texas.

Sabine Pilot Service fired Michael Hauck, a deckhand on one of Sabine's boats, for refusing to pump the boat's bilges into the water, as directed by his employer. Hauck refused to do as instructed because he had learned from the U.S. Coast Guard that pumping the bilges into the water was illegal. Thompson and Umphrey filed a wrongful termination suit on behalf of Hauck, claiming that the firing violated public policy because it is in the state's interest that employers not induce workers to break the law.

The defendant argued that there was no public policy exception in the State of Texas. However, Hauck ultimately prevailed in the Texas Supreme Court, which changed nearly a century of at-will employment rulings by creating a public policy exception. The Court held that an employee may sue for wrongful termination if he or she is fired solely for refusing to commit an illegal act. Thanks to the fine work of Thompson and Umphrey, employees in the State of Texas are no longer forced to choose between obeying the law and keeping their jobs. After the Texas Supreme Court's decision, the case settled for a confidential sum. *Hauck* has since been cited in hundreds of cases and secondary sources.

The reported decision in this case can be found at *Sabine Pilot Service, Inc. v. Hauck*, 687 S.W.2d 733 (Tex. 1985).

Greg Thompson

Walter Umphrey

1985 Trial Lawyer of the Year Award Winner
John F. Keenan
The Case of the Undisclosed Drug Dangers

W hat duty does a pharmaceutical company have to warn patients of the potential dangers and side effects of its prescription medications? Many might be surprised at the answer: generally, there is no duty to warn patients directly. As a general rule, a drug company's duty is to disclose the potential health risks associated with its products to doctors, not patients.

Doctors are then supposed to take these warnings into account, along with other facts about the medication and the patient's health condition, to determine whether to prescribe a particular drug. Once that decision is reached, it is the doctor's obligation to inform the patient of potential health hazards and side effects. The failure to provide an adequate warning could constitute medical malpractice, depending on the circumstances, if the drug adversely affects the patient's health. However, as long as the manufacturer properly disclosed the drug's risks to the doctor, the manufacturer can not be held liable to the patient for injuries caused by its prescription drugs.

That was the state of the law in Massachusetts when Carole D. MacDonald and her husband Bruce approached Worcester attorney John F. Keenan to represent them in a lawsuit against Ortho Pharmaceutical Corporation, the manufacturer of Ms. MacDonald's birth control pills. The MacDonalds had contacted Keenan because Ms. MacDonald had suffered a serious stroke as a result of taking the pills. The stroke had destroyed half of her brain's left hemisphere, leav-

What is public justice? Drug manufacturers warn consumers, not just doctors, of the dangers of prescription drugs.

ing Ms. MacDonald with a significant physical disability and speech impediments. Despite the serious nature of Ms. MacDonald's injuries, Keenan knew that the case would be difficult to win, even though proving causation would not be a problem.

Ms. MacDonald was in her twenties when she began taking the birth control pill. She had none of the known risk factors for stroke in young women: she didn't suffer migraine headaches; she didn't smoke; and she didn't have high blood pressure. But the possibility of a stroke was a known side effect of the kind of birth control pills taken by Ms. MacDonald, a danger against which Ortho had explicitly warned doctors, including Ms. MacDonald's.

Ms. MacDonald would later testify that she did not know that a stroke was one of the potential side-effects of Ortho's product. She also stated unequivocally that, had she known, she would not have chosen to use Ortho's birth control pills as her form of contraception.

For unknown reasons, Ms. MacDonald's OB/GYN never told her that the pills he prescribed could cause a stroke. The general warning label attached to Ortho's contraceptive pill dispensers warned, "The most serious known side effect is abnormal blood clotting, which can be fatal." However, there was no reference to the possibility of blood clots causing a stroke. The label complied with the then-existing regulations of the Food and Drug Administration (FDA), which did not require disclosure of a prescription drug's risks directly to the patient.

Adding to the complications in the case, the MacDonalds did not want to sue the prescribing physician for medical malpractice. This meant that Keenan could sue only Ortho for failing to warn consumers adequately about the possibility of a stroke. But the company had complied with all federal regulations regarding disclosure to the general public and had warned physicians about the risk of stroke. Under the law as it then stood, the MacDonalds' case could not be won.

Keenan was not deterred by the apparent hopelessness of his clients' desire to hold Ortho accountable for the injuries its drug had caused. "Despite the state of the law, I thought the case could be won," he says. "This was a time when the appellate courts were expanding tort theories of recovery. Those days are now sometimes called 'The Golden Age of Torts.' I thought the time and the case were right to move the law into a more consumer-friendly stance."

Keenan's theory involved the nature of birth control pills, how they generally come to be prescribed, and how these factors differed from other prescription medications. Most prescription drugs were, and are, selected for patients by doctors, not by patients themselves. Birth control pills were different, as Keenan saw it, because women often made the decision to use birth control pills prior to seeing their doctors. This is what had happened with Ms. MacDonald. She had gone to her OB/GYN asking for a prescription for "the pill." Thus, to Keenan, oral contraceptives were more akin to over-the-counter medications, which require explicit warnings to consumers about known health risks.

Keenan expected Ortho to fight hard to prevent oral contraceptives from being treated differently than other prescription drugs. This presented a potential problem. Keenan, of Wolfson, Dodson, Keenan & Cotton, was not part of a well-heeled firm. "I was essentially a sole practitioner," Keenan says. "While I was associated with other lawyers in a space-sharing arrangement, I would have to finance the case on my own. I knew it would be a real 'David versus Goliath' situation. But I believed I could make this a low budget production because the case would involve little factual development and would focus on the adequacy of Ortho's consumer warning under the law. For example, I wasn't going to have to bring in experts to prove that there was negligence in the manufacture or design, because there wasn't."

As expected, Ortho hired big corporate defense firms to handle the case, including one of the biggest firms in Boston and well-known New York lawyer to pursue appellate avenues. None of this deterred Keenan. "Perhaps it is my competitive nature, but I thought the long odds made it fun," he says.

Legal struggles against large corporations sometimes descend into "scorched earth" warfare, where the well-funded, corporate defense lawyers generally turn litigation into something out of Dante's *Inferno*. To Ortho's credit — and that of the company's defense lawyers — that disturbing pattern did not hold true in the *MacDonald* litigation."

"I didn't run into any discovery roadblocks," Keenan recalls. "There was no spitting contest, as so often happens. Even the two trials in the case were fairly fought and civility governed. The most unkind word said about my theory of the case was that it was 'simplistic,' and maybe it was."

This is not to say that the case was easy. When the first trial was held in February 1982, six years after Ms. MacDonald's stroke, Keenan had a predominantly male jury. Perhaps that was why the award in the first trial was disappointing. The jury awarded only $27,000 for Ms. MacDonald's injuries and nothing to her husband for loss of consortium or emotional injuries. But the jury made a crucial error when filling out the jury slips, requiring the judge to throw out the verdict.

In a second trial, held in April 1983, Keenan obtained a much better result. The jury awarded $800,000 for Ms. MacDonald's injuries and $50,000 for her husband's loss of consortium. When interest was added, the total exceeded $1.7 million.

Why the difference in jury awards? It was not in Keenan's presentation. The case had not changed materially in the year between the first and second trials. Keenan believes the key was a word not used often in those days — diversity. The second jury consisted of nine women and five men. Perhaps the women identified more with Ms. MacDonald than did the men of the first jury, or maybe they were able to bring a more empathic attitude to the couple's plight.

Before the champagne bottle could be uncorked, however, the judge granted a defense motion for a "judgment notwithstanding the verdict," ruling that, under Massachusetts law, Ortho had no duty to warn Ms. MacDonald directly that she risked a stroke when taking birth control pills. Keenan was disappointed, but understood there wasn't much else the judge could do under the circumstances.

There was no case law in Massachusetts to support Keenan's theory of the case, and the only other decisions from the federal appeals courts and other state courts were adverse to his position. Those courts agreed with the general rule that the pharmaceutical companies only had to warn the physician, not the consumer. Keenan appealed anyway.

Recognizing the importance of the case and the new question of law that it presented in Massachusetts, the state Supreme Judicial Court certified the matter for a direct appeal. The Court's landmark decision was everything Keenan had hoped for when he had agreed to represent the MacDonalds.

Concluding that birth control pills "stand apart" from other types of prescription drugs, the Court held that:

> ...the manufacturer of oral contraceptives is not justified in relying on warnings to the medical profession to satisfy its common law duty to warn, and that the manufacturer's obligation encompasses a duty to warn the ultimate user. Thus, the manufacturer's duty is to provide to the consumer written warnings conveying reasonable notice of the nature, gravity, and likelihood of known or knowable side effects, and advising the consumer to seek fuller explanation from the prescribing physician or other doctor of any such information of concern to the consumer.

In reaching its decision, the Court focused on who primarily decides to prescribe birth control pills for contraception:

> Whereas a patient's involvement in decision-making concerning use of a prescription drug necessary to treat a malady is typically minimal or nonexistent, the healthy, young consumer of oral contraceptives is usually actively involved in the decision to use "the pill," as opposed to other available birth control products, and the prescribing physician is relegated to a relatively passive role.

Another important difference between birth control pills and most other prescription drugs, the Court found, was in the nature of the follow-up care received by patients who take birth control pills. Whereas patients receiving prescriptions selected by the doctor may receive continual follow-up care, a birth control pill user receives renewals of her prescription on a yearly basis at her annual checkup. "Thus, the patient may only seldom have the opportunity to explore her questions and concerns about the medication with the prescribing physician," the Court reasoned, and the "patient cannot be expected to remember all the details [of any discussions or warnings] for a protracted period of time."

Having set the legal standard that applied, the Massachusetts Supreme Judicial Court turned to the adequacy of the warnings that Ortho had provided to Ms. MacDonald. Ortho had argued that the evidence presented to the jury had been insufficient to warrant the jury's finding that the warnings contained in the packaging were inadequate. Ortho had also argued that its warning had been in full compliance with FDA requirements. The Court ruled that, although FDA compliance was admissible as a defense to negligence, it "is not conclusive." The Court also ruled that a "reasonable warning not only conveys a fair indication of the nature of the dangers involved, but also warns with the degree of intensity demanded by the nature of the risk. A warning may be found to be unreasonable in that it was unduly delayed, reluctant in tone or lacking in a sense of urgency."

The Massachusetts Supreme Judicial Court reversed the trial judge's decision and reinstated the jury's verdict. The MacDonalds then received badly-needed compensation for the injury that Ms. MacDonald had suffered. Perhaps even more important, the case demonstrated that there are trial lawyers who will take great risks to litigate a "losing case" in order to make new law that will benefit the general public.

The reported decision in this case and the subsequent case history can be found at *MacDonald v. Ortho Pharmaceutical Corp.*, 475 N.E.2d 65 (Mass. 1985) (reinstating jury verdict), *cert. denied*, 474 U.S. 920 (1985).

John F. Keenan

CHAPTER FOUR

1986: The Case of the Deadly Tampon

Gun Safety *Kelley v. R.G. Industries, Inc.*

Government Accountability *Cole v. United States*

Drug Safety *Oxendine v. Merrell Dow Pharmaceuticals, Inc.*

Access to Justice *Pfost v. State*

Access to Justice *Wixted v. Pepper*

Access to Justice *Tabler v. Wallace*

Government Accountability *Malley v. Briggs*

Winner
O'Gilvie v. Int'l Playtex, Inc.
The Case of the Deadly Tampon

The finalists for the 1986 Trial Lawyer of the Year Award enhanced gun safety, fought for government accountability, battled for drug safety, and increased access to justice in numerous ways. The 1986 Trial Lawyer of the Year Award winners forced a tampon manufacturer to pay for the death of a woman whose tampon use resulted in a bacterial infection known as "Toxic Shock Syndrome." Their landmark success saved thousands of lives by prompting the manufacturer to remove the deadly product from the market.

Gun Safety
Kelley v. R.G. Industries, Inc.
Howard L. Siegel

"Saturday Night Specials," also known as junk guns and a criminal's best friend, were handguns that were manufactured so cheaply that they could be purchased for less than $100. They had short barrels that made them easy to conceal, but because they were so shoddily made, they were notoriously inaccurate and unreliable. These characteristics rendered them all but unusable in legitimate firearms activities, such as target shooting, hunting, and self-protection. In contrast, the junk guns seemed made-to-order for criminals and were often used in muggings, convenience store robberies, and murders. John Hinkley, Jr., used a Saturday Night Special when he attempted to assassinate President Ronald Reagan on March 30, 1981.

Howard L. Siegel of Rockville, Maryland, took on a manufacturer of the notorious Saturday Night Specials on behalf of Olen Kelley, who had been shot by a Saturday Night Special during a store robbery. R.G. Industries, a subsidiary of the German company Rohm Gesellschaft, had manufactured the gun. Siegel faced a problem in trying to hold the gun manufacturer liable for Kelley's injuries because guns are legal products with legitimate uses. Siegel argued, however, that because Saturday Night Specials were not appropriate for any legitimate use, their manufacturers should be strictly liable for injuries caused by the expected criminal use of their products.

Siegel's theory of liability was novel, and the case had to go up to the Maryland's highest court before Siegel won the right to sue on Kelley's behalf. The Court held that if a gun is a Saturday Night Special and is used in a criminal act, then the manufacturer and marketer can be held strictly liable for injuries resulting from the shooting. The Court then returned the case to the trial court to determine whether the gun used on Kelley was a Saturday Night Special.

Thanks to the Maryland Court of Appeal's decision, the insurance industry dropped its coverage of businesses involved in the sale and manufacture of junk guns. Not coincidentally, in 1986, R.G. Industries went out of business. Where decades of legislative initiatives had failed to dent the junk gun industry, an enterprising trial lawyer struck a blow against gun manufacturers that exhibited a reckless disregard for safety.

The reported decision in this case can be found at *Kelley v. R.G. Industries, Inc.*, 497 A.2d 1143 (Md. 1985).

Government Accountability
Cole v. United States
Jerry Shirley

Robert E. Cole served in the U.S. Navy aboard several submarines that were used during atomic bomb tests conducted by the United States in 1946 on the Bikini Atoll, in the central Pacific. Although Cole did not know it at the time, he, like thousands of other service personnel, was exposed to massive doses of ionizing radiation — a cause of cancer.

In 1981, cancer struck Cole and he died less than a year later. His family believed that the source of Cole's cancer was his exposure to atomic bomb-related radioactivity. They wanted to sue the federal government for wrongful death. Although the Federal Torts Claims Act (FTCA) permits suits against the United States, the federal government has sovereign immunity from suit for injuries received by uniformed personnel "incident to" their military service. This legal rule is known as the "*Feres* Doctrine." With few exceptions, the only avenue for recompense open to injured service personnel is through the Veterans Administration (VA).

When Cole's family approached attorney Jerry Shirley of Northport, Alabama, he did not encourage them to seek help from the VA. Instead, he developed an imaginative and bold strategy to get around the *Feres* Doctrine. Shirley argued that, although the government is immune from suit for injuries related to military service, the government nevertheless has a continuing duty to warn former service personnel of dangers to their health caused by in-service activities that are discovered *after* discharge.

The U.S. Court of Appeals for the Eleventh Circuit agreed with Shirley and rejected the application of the *Feres* Doctrine to Cole's death. It then returned the case to the trial court for further proceedings. In recognition of the important precedent he set, Shirley was then named a finalist for the Trial Lawyer of the Year Award.

Unfortunately, justice still could not be won for Robert Cole. In the end, the case met the same fate as that of the Trial Lawyer of the Year Award-winning case for 1984 — "The Case of the Atomic Downwinders." *Cole* was dismissed based on the "discretionary function" exception to the FTCA.

Even though the case was dismissed, Shirley's imaginative approach demonstrated a vital benefit that trial lawyers often provide to society. They help to create exceptions to legal rules that are inhospitable to the rights of injured individuals. Shirley's victory in the appeals court opened a door for veterans injured in service who would otherwise be barred from suing the federal government.

The reported decision in this case and the subsequent case history can be found at *Cole v. United States*, 755 F.2d 873 (11th Cir. 1985), *dismissed on remand*, 635 F. Supp. 1185 (N.D. Ala. 1986).

Jerry Shirley

Drug Safety
Oxendine v. Merrell Dow Pharmaceuticals, Inc.
Barry J. Nace

When Barry J. Nace of Washington, D.C., took on Merrell Dow Pharmaceuticals, he faced a formidable opponent with virtually unlimited resources. Despite this, Nace had convinced a jury in 1983 that Bendectin, an anti-nausea medication manufactured by Merrell Dow, caused Mary Oxendine to suffer a serious birth defect. (The beginning of this case is summarized in Chapter Two.)

Oxendine had been born with a shortened right forearm and only three fingers fused together on her right hand. The jury found that the Bendectin taken by Oxendine's mother during pregnancy had caused the birth defects and awarded Oxendine $750,000 in compensatory damages. However, the trial judge overturned the verdict, finding that the four types of evidence produced by Nace to show that Bendectin caused Oxendine's injury, when viewed separately, were insufficient to establish causation. The trial court refused to consider the cumulative effect of the evidence.

Undaunted, Nace appealed and sought to reinstate the jury's verdict. The appellate court ruled that the trial judge should have considered the evidence of causation as a whole when determining whether the jury could have reasonably reached its verdict. In the court's words, "like the pieces of a mosaic, the individual studies showed little or nothing when viewed separately from one another, but they combined to produce a whole that was greater than the sum of its parts." The appeals court reinstated the verdict and returned the case to the trial court to determine whether punitive damages were warranted. For his undaunting commitment to his client and his important contribution to the law, Nace was again honored as a finalist — this time, for the 1986 Trial Lawyer of the Year Award.

That, however, was not the end of the battle. After 10 more years of litigation, the verdict was ultimately thrown out, and judgment was entered for the defendant. Although Merrell Dow took Bendectin off the market shortly after the $750,000 jury verdict in this case, the Food and Drug Administration never mandated Bendectin's recall. As a result, Merrell Dow could still decide to reintroduce its anti-nausea drug in the U.S. market.

The later decision in this case can be found at *Oxendine v. Merrell Dow Pharmaceuticals, Inc.*, 1996 WL 680992 (D.C. Super. Ct. Oct. 24, 1996) (vacating jury verdict and entering judgment for defendant).

Barry J. Nace

Access to Justice
Pfost v. State
Joan B. Newman

The interests of big business are often antagonistic to consumers' rights. This conflict is reflected in the efforts of Corporate America throughout the country and in Congress to limit the right to civil jury trials, restrict punitive damage awards, and destroy contingency fees, among other things. This pro-business, anti-consumer campaign has a friendly-sounding name — tort reform. But the ultimate purpose of so-called tort reform is to stack the legal deck against injured individuals in favor of corporate and government wrongdoers.

That is exactly what happened when Montana passed a tort reform law called the "State Torts Claims Act." The purpose of the law was to cap damages caused by the state's negligence or other wrongdoing at $300,000, regardless of the extent of the harm caused to the victim. A limitation on the amount of damages recoverable in a civil action is, in essence, a limitation on an injured individual's right to obtain a full and meaningful remedy.

Richard Pfost learned the consequences of such unjust laws. One day, while driving his tractor down Interstate 90, he approached a bridge near Missoula, Montana. Unknown to Mr. Pfost, three accidents had previously occurred on this especially icy and dangerous bridge. Even though the State of Montana knew of the danger that the bridge posed to motorists, it failed to clean and repair the hazard, and failed to warn drivers of the danger. When Mr. Pfost drove onto the bridge, the ice caused him to lose control and he crashed through the side of the bridge. The accident left him a quadriplegic.

There was no doubt as to the state's liability. But there was real doubt as to whether Mr. Pfost would be justly compensated because of the $300,000 damages cap. He retained Joan B. Newman of Missoula, who filed two suits: one for damages caused by the state's negligence and one to declare the State Torts Claims Act unconstitutional. In a landmark decision in the second case, the Supreme Court of Montana ruled that the state was not entitled to special, partial immunity for the damages that its negligence causes. The Court stated that the damages cap was inherently unfair because it places "the burden of catastrophic damages not on the state whose agent caused them, but on the unfortunate person who received them." The Court voided the State Torts Claims Act as unconstitutional and permitted Mr. Pfost to proceed with his damages claim, unhindered by arbitrary limits on his recovery.

The reported decision in this case and the subsequent case history can be found at *Pfost v. State*, 713 P.2d 495 (Mont. 1985), *overruled by Meech v. Hillhaven West, Inc.*, 76 P.2d 488 (Mont. 1989).

Access to Justice
Wixted v. Pepper
Richard Myers

Those who provide essential services to people in need have tremendous power to coerce them into giving up important legal rights. In the practice of medicine, this power sometimes takes the form of requiring patients to sign contracts for services that contain "mandatory arbitration clauses." The result is that consumers often unknowingly waive their constitutional right to a jury trial to resolve a dispute with their physician, even if their physician commits malpractice or engages in some other form of wrongdoing.

Drs. William Wixted, Patrick Flanagan, and William Robinson ran an obstetrics clinic in Nevada. Before accepting patients for treatment, they required the women to sign a contract stating, among other things, that any civil dispute would be resolved through binding arbitration. Rhonda Pepper signed such a form before her doctor prescribed oral contraceptives. Eight months later, the birth control pills left her partially paralyzed.

When Pepper wanted to sue for malpractice, she discovered that she had unwittingly waived her constitutional right to have her case heard by a jury of her peers. Her attorney, Richard Myers of Las Vegas, took the issue up to Nevada's Supreme Court, which rejected the binding arbitration clause as unenforceable and permitted the lawsuit to proceed.

Since then, the high courts of several states and the U.S. Court of Appeals for the Ninth Circuit have cited the Nevada Supreme Court's decision with approval. The case has also been cited in more than 20 law review articles. Myers' persistence led to an important decision that protects the average patient.

The reported decision in this case can be found at *Wixted v. Pepper*, 693 P.2d 1259 (Nev. 1985).

Richard Myers

Access to Justice
Tabler v. Wallace
Peter Perlman

In the mid-1960s, three professional groups, the American Institute of Architects, the Associated General Contractors, and the National Society of Professional Engineers, successfully lobbied the State of Kentucky (and most other states) to pass a tort reform law known as "architects no-action statutes." These special statutes of repose banned individuals injured by the negligence of architects, engineers, and builders from recovering damages if the injury occurred more than five years after construction.

The Kentucky version of this special interest law almost ensnared the widow of William Wallace. Mr. Wallace was repairing an elevator in a hotel when he was crushed to death between the top of the elevator and the roof of the elevator shaft. The fatal accident was caused by the violation of building codes. The clearance between the top of the elevator and the roof was less than the minimum demanded by industry codes and safety standards. Thus, the builder and architect of the elevator shaft had been negligent. Nevertheless, because Mr. Wallace's fatal injury occurred more than five years after the building was constructed, it appeared that his widow would be cheated out of any remedy.

Mrs. Wallace retained attorney Peter Perlman of Lexington, Kentucky, to file a wrongful death suit. Perlman knew that, to obtain justice for Mrs. Wallace, he would first have to remove the obstacle posed by the state's "architects no-action statute." Perlman filed suit, arguing that the tort reform statute violated the equal protection clause of Kentucky's Constitution by giving special protection to a group of citizens that was not available to others. For example, a general builder, architect, and engineer could not be held liable under the law, but materialmen and others involved in a building's construction could be held liable — clearly an unfair circumstance. The statute also limited a victim's means of redress. For these reasons, Perlman argued, the statute was inherently unfair and provided unequal protection under the law.

The Supreme Court of Kentucky agreed with Perlman, declaring that the statute violated Kentucky's Constitution. The Court traced the constitutional ban on such "special legislation" to the Kentucky Constitutional Convention in 1890, where the framers expressed their aversion to providing certain groups with special favors. Thus, Mrs. Wallace was guaranteed her day in court.

After the Kentucky Supreme Court struck down the statute of repose, the case was returned to the trial court and assigned for a jury trial. Perlman won a verdict for Mrs. Wallace and the case settled on appeal in 1989.

The Kentucky Supreme Court's decision in this case is a landmark in the continuing fight against tort reform and has been frequently cited in connection with similar constitutional challenges around the country. As Perlman accurately notes, the decision "requires architects and builders to consider the long-term effects of their construction activities and shows that the justice system can meet the challenge of highly financed lobbies for the rich special interest groups."

The reported decision in this case and the subsequent case history can be found at *Tabler v. Wallace*, 704 S.W.2d 179 (Ky. 1985), *cert. denied*, 479 U.S. 822 (1986).

Peter Perlman

Government Accountability
Malley v. Briggs
Leonard Decof

The U.S. Constitution protects those accused of crimes from illegal law enforcement actions designed to obtain a conviction at the expense of individual rights. But what happens when judges or prosecutors intentionally undertake their duties in a blatantly unconstitutional way? They enjoy immunity, meaning that they cannot be held personally liable for their wrongdoing.

The same is not true of police officers, however, because they are not judicial officers. This became a key point of law to Louisa and Paul Briggs, who were awakened in the middle of the night by armed law enforcement officers who arrested and arraigned them on the charge of felony marijuana possession.

Mr. and Mrs. Briggs were unlikely drug defendants. Neither had a criminal record. Mr. Briggs, a real estate developer, was a member of the board of directors of a local bank and the former chairman of his town's chamber of commerce. Yet, when police officers heard two anonymous persons tell a drug suspect, who was being legally wiretapped, that they had seen Mr. and Mrs. Briggs smoking marijuana at a party in their home, a Rhode Island state trooper decided to lower the boom. He convinced a judge to issue an arrest warrant based on this scant evidence, notwithstanding the lack of probable cause. The issuance of the warrant led to the raid on the Briggses' home in the middle of the night. As a result of being busted in a drug raid, the couple's reputation was irreparably damaged.

After a grand jury refused to indict the couple, they sued the state trooper for violating their right under the 4th Amendment to the U.S. Constitution to be free from unreasonable search and seizure. The basis of the suit was that the officer knew he did not have probable cause to seek a warrant when he requested the judge's permission to arrest the couple. The trial judge, however, dismissed the case, ruling that the police officer could not be held liable for his actions because the judge who issued the warrant had absolute immunity from suit.

The Briggses' attorney, Leonard Decof of Providence, Rhode Island, appealed the dismissal and succeeding in obtaining review of the decision by the U.S. Supreme Court. The Court agreed with Decof's argument that the judicial immunity law should not be extended to police officers who violate constitutional rights. The matter was then returned to the trial court, where the Briggses had the opportunity to challenge and seek damages for the state trooper's actions.

The reported decision in this case can be found at *Malley v. Briggs*, 475 U.S. 335 (1986).

1986 Trial Lawyer of the Year Award Winner
Gerald L. Michaud and Mark B. Hutton
The Case of the Deadly Tampon

Tampons are supposed to make women's lives easier. But International Playtex's super absorbent tampons killed 23-year-old Betty O'Gilvie, who died of Toxic Shock Syndrome (TSS) in early 1983. The winners of the 1986 Trial Lawyer of the Year Award held Playtex accountable and forced the company to withdraw its deadly product from the market, preventing many more tampon-induced TSS deaths.

TSS is caused by common, and usually benign, bacteria that naturally inhabit a woman's vagina. Under certain circumstances, these bacteria can turn malignant by releasing toxic substances into the blood stream. The symptoms of TSS range from relatively mild, flu-like complaints to a severe, multi-system disease that causes high fever, rash, shock, vomiting, and diarrhea, followed by peeling of the skin during convalescence. The disease kills about five percent of those whom it afflicts.

What is public justice? Corporate wrongdoers that intentionally sacrifice lives for profits are forced to pay appropriate punitive damages both as a sanction for their past conduct and to deter similar conduct by them and others in the future.

During the late 1970s, the incidents of TSS skyrocketed. The Center for Disease Control (CDC) and others looked for answers. By 1980, two CDC studies firmly linked the onset of TSS with tampon use. Although about 10 percent of the cases did not involve tampons (including a few cases in men), of all the women who suffered TSS during menstruation, 99 percent were using super absorbent tampons.

But why the sudden increase of TSS in the late 1970s? Women had been using tampons for many years without widely suffering TSS. Had the disease itself somehow changed over time? No. After an investigation, it was clear that the cause and course of TSS remained unchanged. Had women somehow become more susceptible? No. There was nothing new to report on that front. What then? Surely something was different. Indeed, one thing was — the design of some tampons had changed. Many newer tampons had increased absorbency. It turned out that the greater the absorbency of the tampon, the greater the danger of TSS.

In 1980, the American College of Obstetricians and Gynecologists sent a letter advising its members to counsel patients that they should discontinue the use of super absorbent tampons. Also in 1980, two CDC studies showed that women who used Rely tampons (a super absorbent product using synthetic fibers) suffered TSS more often than women who used other brands. At about this time, a woman using Rely tampons during menstruation died of the disease. Proctor and Gamble removed Rely from the marketplace in September 1980. Then, in 1981, a research report called the "Tri-State Toxic Shock Syndrome Study" also linked TSS to super absorbent tampons. The study concluded that Playtex super plus and super tampons were in the highest risk category because, like the Rely tampons, they were made of synthetic fibers that were far more absorbent than cotton. In fact, women using these Playtex tampons were 15 times more likely to contract TSS than women not using Playtex tampons.

As the evidence of the danger of super absorbent tampons grew clearer, most tampons manufacturers took their high absorbency products off the market. Not Playtex. Sensing a market opportunity for itself, Playtex decided to, as an internal memo put it, "resist vigorously" the finding of the Tri-State Commission and use super absorbency as a marketing tool to convince women to buy Playtex tampons.

O'Gilvie's death from Playtex tampons was clearly avoidable. But at the time of her death, the extent of Playtex's disregard for the safety of its customers was not yet known. It would take a lawsuit and the dedicated efforts of Wichita, Kansas, attorneys Gerald L. Michaud and Mark B. Hutton to ferret out the truth and punish Playtex for its reckless and opportunistic behavior.

After O'Gilvie's bereaved spouse, Kelly, walked through the door of Michaud's law firm seeking assistance for himself and his two motherless children, Michaud assigned Mark Hutton to research the potential claim against Playtex. "When a product liability case comes in," Michaud says, "we begin by doing extensive research. It may be medical research. It may be legal research to see if there have been any other similar cases reported. Our firm had handled other toxic shock cases and Mark had become our expert on tampons.

It fell on his shoulders to build the foundation for the lawsuit." Michaud and Hutton would share the responsibilities at trial.

Satisfied that Playtex had much to answer for, the Law Offices of Gerald Michaud filed *O'Gilvie v. Int'l Playtex, Inc.* As is typical in cases against powerful and well-financed corporate interests, the discovery phase of the case was like running under water: a slow and arduous process in which it often seemed that little progress could be made. Eventually, Hutton was able to obtain key documents from Playtex. The documents demonstrated not only the company's knowledge of the danger of super absorbent tampons, but its irresponsible decision to use super absorbency as a selling point.

One of the key documents uncovered during discovery was a Playtex memo stating that super absorbency, advertised as the answer to tampon leakage, didn't really accomplish that task. The employee informed his superiors that the tampons were actually "over absorbent." The memo stated:

> In being obsessed with "absorbency" we lost sight of the fact that
> "leakage" complaints did not decrease as the tampon absorbency
> potentials were increased. Like the definition of a fanatic, "one redoubles
> his efforts because he has lost sight of his goals," we then converted
> our heavier weight tampons to PA [polyacrylate] fiber, providing
> even more absorbency.

In short, other than increasing market share, improving absorbency accomplished nothing but risked much.

Another key document in the case was a memorandum to a high-level Playtex executive that read, "For your eyes only, read and destroy. If the plaintiff's lawyers get this, it will go hard on us." The document in question did not involve TSS, but a lesser side-effect of super absorbent tampons. Still, Michaud believes that the document was vital to the case.

"It demonstrated a mindset," Michaud recalls. "It demonstrated to the jury that it wasn't a question of whether the company would act unethically. If it would destroy that document, which dealt with rashes, who was to say that it hadn't or wouldn't destroy documents dealing with the far more serious side effect of TSS? We had the documentation to prove that that was exactly what Playtex was capable of doing."

Michaud and Hutton were convinced that they had a winning case against Playtex. But tampon cases involving TSS that had been tried in other jurisdictions had not fared well. This was due to a deliberate industry strategy that repeatedly appears in product cases: settle the strong cases and impose confidentiality as a condition of recovery, then go to trial in the weaker cases or in cases involving weak attorneys. The purpose of the strategy is to limit litigation. By picking and choosing the cases to try or settle, the defense bar attempts to scare plaintiffs' lawyers out of the field.

Believing that such a strategy would work well again, and underestimating the strength of O'Gilvie's claim, Playtex's offer at the mandatory settlement conference was completely inadequate. Mark Hutton gave a figure beneath which the plaintiffs would not settle. Playtex put the squeeze on Hutton, who called upon Michaud for reinforcements.

"Mark called me at noon and asked if I could come down after lunch because Playtex was really beating on him," Michaud recalled with a chuckle. "He was being cast as the unfair litigator who would not budge to resolve a case reasonably. I told the defense attorney, 'Look, you have tried five cases [involving super absorbent tampons and TSS] and I know that all five of the plaintiffs' lawyers in those cases had a hard time finding the courthouse. This time you are going to face some lawyers who know how to try these cases.'"

The gauntlet was now thrown. There would be no compromise and no confidential settlement in this case.

In order for Mr. O'Gilvie to prevail, the jury would have to understand the workings of TSS, the reason why super absorbent tampons were so dangerous, the reckless disregard of Playtex, the extent of harm done to the O'Gilvie family, and the need to punish Playtex with punitive damages to deter future wrongdoing by Playtex and other companies willing to sacrifice the health and safety of consumers for larger profits.

During his opening statement, Hutton explained to the jury how he and Michaud would prove that Playtex had used the withdrawal of its competitors from the high absorbency tampon market to benefit itself, despite the known dangers to its customers. Using blow-ups as visual aids, Hutton informed the jury that Kimberly-Clark had removed its super absorbent tampons in 1980 and that Tampax had begun marketing an all cotton product. He then cut to the heart of the case:

What does International Playtex do? Nothing. They continue to market their high absorbency fiber tampon. Now, they're number one [in sales]; now in 1981, '82, '83, even today, they have the most absorbent tampon.

The void that was left after Rely was taken off the market, after Kimberly-Clark and Kotex changed their fiber, created an opportunity for International Playtex to have the most absorbent tampon....The evidence will show that consumers didn't know in 1981, '82, '83, and even today that International Playtex's tampon...creates the greatest risk of developing Toxic Shock Syndrome. By 1981, International Playtex had won the super absorbency war; they're number one....By 1981, International Playtex became the most dangerous tampon on the market.

Hutton also previewed some of the evidence that he and Michaud would present to the jury to prove that Playtex knew its marketing decisions would lead to the deaths of some of their customers:

In 1981 and 1982, the director of consumer affairs, Leonard Berger, has testified, and his testimony will be read to you, that in 1981 we [Playtex] knew of the deaths associated with our product. He knew in 1982. In 1983, he knew of deaths associated with the product, women using Playtex tampons. Then I asked him, "Could you predict more in 1984 [the year of Betty O'Gilvie's death]?" He said: "Possibly." This company knew as long as the fiber remains on the market there are going to be more deaths.

In addition to convincing the jury that Playtex knew of the dangers associated with its tampons, Hutton had to personalize the O'Gilvie tragedy. He told the jury that O'Gilvie was a mother of two children — Stephanie, age three at the time of O'Gilvie's death, and Kevin, age one. O'Gilvie's motherhood and career were just beginning. She was learning cosmetology and intended to work part time as a hairdresser. She hoped to later become a dental hygienist. But all that ended because she used Playtex super absorbent tampons.

"Toxic Shock Syndrome is an insidious disease," Hutton told the jurors. "It starts slow, it simmers, but once the bacteria begin to release the toxins, it gets into the system and it strikes fast. It's like a forest fire, spreads very, very fast....Heroic measures were taken to keep [Betty O'Gilvie] alive, but she died on April 2, 1983."

Playtex attempted to blame anyone and everyone for its legal predicament — anyone, that is, but itself. It claimed that O'Gilvie had not used Playtex products, an allegation soundly refuted at trial. It even tried to blame O'Gilvie for using a super absorbent tampon. A vague warning in the tampon package suggested that tampon use was associated with TSS, but failed to mention that the risk increased with the absorbency. In a last desperate act, Playtex accused the Michaud firm of suing Playtex, not because O'Gilvie had actually used Playtex tampons, but because the firm "had a theory" it wished to try. "That hurt my feelings," Michaud dryly retorted to the jury in his closing argument. "I might do a lot of things, but I am not dishonest."

As his closing argument reached a crescendo, Michaud told the jury a terrible truth:

> Rarely will you see arrogance and the lack of caring that you have seen in this case. People in that company who tried to get things done [getting the super absorbent tampon removed from the market] couldn't get it done, because Playtex was bent on one thing. Hey, Rely went off the market. Other manufacturers are making their tampons less absorbent. Here is a chance for us to capture the market and we'll promote our super absorbents and we'll capture the market even though we know that we are running the risk that we might kill literally thousands of women.

Michaud then spoke to the jury about the appropriate remedy in such circumstances and explained that punitive damages were required to "send a message":

> How do you send a message? If you sent a message of one million dollars back there, they would laugh at us. What is a million dollars when you have five hundred million? Doesn't mean much, does it? Drop in the bucket. They would say: Ha. Ha. That's not even a day's advertising. No, we have to get their attention....I want to say to you, you're the conscience of this community. You should return a just verdict you will be proud of. You can't come back and change this verdict five or ten years from now. So, I want to say something to you: You have more power as the finder of fact, you jurors, you eight people sitting here, than rarely anyone in their lifetime gets....You have a chance to make a decision that will affect a lot of people. You must exercise it wisely. In fairness to this defendant, you shouldn't do something unless it is justified. On the

other hand, you have it within your power, ladies and gentlemen of the jury, to save hundreds, nay, thousands of lives if you so choose.

The jury so chose: they awarded $1.5 million in compensatory damages (cut by 20 percent due to the comparative negligence of O'Gilvie's doctor) and $10 million in punitive damages. "The amount awarded was 100 times as much as Playtex ever offered in the case," Michaud says proudly.

That should have been the end of it — other than the expected appeal. But it wasn't. The trial judge, in a well-meaning but misguided attempt to transform the O'Gilvie tragedy into a public good, made Playtex an unusual offer. If it would remove its super absorbent tampons from the market, he would reduce the punitive damages to $1.35 million. Playtex lept at being rewarded for what the verdict would undoubtedly have forced it to do anyway. Michaud and Hutton appealed, as did Playtex.

The U.S. Court of Appeals for the Tenth Circuit affirmed the jury verdict and reinstated the full $10 million in punitive damages. The appellate court's ruling identified the problem with the trial court's approach:

> We are compelled to point out that the court's order subverts the goals
> of punishment and deterrence that underlie the assessment of punitive
> damages in Kansas. Far from punishing Playtex, the trial court here
> rewarded the company for continuing tortious conduct long enough to
> use it as a bargaining chip in the *remititur* proceedings. The possibility
> that other potential defendants would be able to reduce their liability
> for punitive damages in the same way, would encourage them to pursue
> the very behavior that the punitive award here was intended to deter,
> and thus would discourage voluntary cessation of injury-causing
> conduct. Such a result is simply untenable.

Michaud and Hutton's hard work not only helped the O'Gilvies to obtain justice for the tragedy they had suffered, but had helped to save thousands of lives. Playtex super absorbent tampons were removed from the market. Playtex also changed the package's warning language, using the very language that the trial lawyers' experts said they should have used. As a direct consequence, the danger posed by TSS to menstruating women was significantly reduced.

The reported decision in this case and the subsequent case history can be found at *O'Gilvie v. Int'l Playtex, Inc.*, 609 F. Supp. 817 (D. Kan. 1985) (reducing punitive damages award), *aff'd in part and rev'd in part*, 821 F.2d 1438 (10th Cir. 1987) (reinstating punitive damages award), *cert. denied*, 486 U.S. 1032 (1988).

Gerald L. Michaud

Mark B. Hutton

CHAPTER FIVE

1987: The Case That Bankrupted The Klan

Toxic Injury Prevention *Sterling v. Velsicol Chem. Corp.*

Access to Justice *Boyd v. Bulala*

Drug Safety *Blum v. Merrell Dow Pharmaceuticals, Inc.*

Religious Freedom *Wollersheim v. Church of Scientology*

Medical Safety *HCA Health Services of Midwest, Inc. v. Nat'l Bank of Commerce*

Access to Justice *Mahoney v. Carus Chem. Co.*

Religious Freedom *United States v. Aguilar*

Winner
Donald v. United Klans of America
The Case That Bankrupted The Klan

The finalists for the 1987 Trial Lawyer of the Year Award fought for victims of a chemical company's toxic waste dump, the right of medical malpractice victims to recover full compensation for their injuries, drug safety, religious freedom, competent nursing care for newborns, the protection of firefighters injured in the line of duty, and the rights of religious people who offer sanctuary to refugees. Civil rights attorneys Morris Dees and Michael Figures, as well as the Southern Poverty Law Center, were named Trial Lawyers of the Year for their innovative use of the civil justice system to put the oldest and largest branch of the Ku Klux Klan out of business.

Toxic Injury Prevention
Sterling v. Velsicol Chem. Corp.
Sid Gilreath

The illegal dumping of toxic waste poses a grave threat to environmental protection and public health. The dangers of this odious practice — and what can be done about it in a court of law — are reflected in this case.

In 1964, the Velsicol Chemical Company of Memphis, Tennessee, faced a dilemma when city officials ordered the company to stop pouring chemical byproducts from its pesticide plant into the city's sewers and dumps. Velsicol could have incinerated the material lawfully, but executives deemed that approach too expensive. Instead, the company purchased farmland in a secluded area of Hardeman County as a repository for its toxic waste. Between 1964 and 1973, Velsicol buried at least 300,000 fifty-five-gallon drums filled with toxic chemicals in trenches on the farm. Even worse, bulldozers working on the land often smashed the barrels open, spilling their chemical contents into the sandy soil and contaminating the water supply. Despite knowing about this contamination, Velsicol continued its toxic dumping. Indeed, Velsicol expanded the toxic dump site after a 1967 U.S. Geological Survey report exposed the dangers of the chemicals and the damage they had done to the water supply.

Fast forward to 1977: Daniel and Patsy Johnson are very alarmed. First, their daughter's "cold" simply will not go away; it deepens into a serious cough. Then something very odd occurs. The little girl throws up on the wooden kitchen floor. When Mrs. Johnson cleans up the area, she notices that the wood has been bleached white from the vomit.

The Johnsons were not the only local family battling illness. Their neighbors were suffering from headaches, nausea, and fatigue. Steve and Nancy Sterling, the Johnsons' next-door neighbors, noticed that their eyes burned when they showered, their skin frequently peeled, and dishes fresh from the dishwasher were covered with a white powder. There was also the constant smell of "bug spray" in the air. When their eight-month-old puppy went blind, the Sterlings decided that the time had come to get some answers.

The Sterlings called the Hardeman County Health Department, which tested the water for bacteria and reported that the water was safe. There may have been no dangerous bacteria, but the Sterlings knew something was wrong. They approached other government agencies, finally learning from an Environmental Protection Agency test that their water supply was contaminated with toxic chemicals, including carbon tetrachloride, chloroform, benzene, and trichlorothane. The Sterlings then retained Tennessee attorney John Wilder to file a class action against Velsicol. Shortly thereafter, at Wilder's request, trial lawyer Sid Gilreath of Knoxville, Tennessee, agreed to handle the case.

Although the number of plaintiffs exceeded 100, Gilreath tried the claims of five plaintiffs Judge Odell Horton had chosen as representatives for a round of test cases. Gilreath enlisted a team of experts to testify on the effects of toxic contamination. Eventually, more than 100 witnesses testified. It took the judge two years to complete a 500-page opinion, in which he wrote that Velsicol's dumping of toxic waste amounted to "gross, willful and wanton negligence." The judge awarded the plaintiffs the state's then-largest personal injury judgment: $12.7 million, which included $5.2 million in compensatory damages for the first five plaintiffs and $7.5 million in punitive damages to be divided among all 100-plus victims.

The decision in this case marked a breakthrough in toxic tort litigation because the court ruled that dumping chemical waste is an inherently dangerous activity. The landmark ruling has assisted attorneys nationwide in their efforts to hold companies responsible for the negligent disposal of toxic waste.

The reported decision in this case and its subsequent case history can be found at *Sterling v. Velsicol Chem. Corp.*, 647 F. Supp. 303 (W.D. Tenn. 1986), *aff'd in part and rev'd in part*, 855 F.2d 1188 (6th Cir. 1988) (remanding for recomputation of punitive damages).

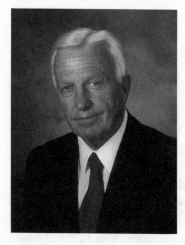

Sid Gilreath

Access to Justice
Boyd v. Bulala
William O. Snead, Rosemarie Annunziata,
and J. Randolph Parker

One of the prime targets of the tort reform movement is the right to a jury trial in civil cases, which is guaranteed in the Seventh Amendment to the U.S. Constitution. Many states have tried to limit this right by tying the hands of juries with damage caps. Limitations on damage awards prevent jurors from fully compensating victims for injuries that result from another's wrongful conduct. An epidemic of such laws swept the nation in the 1980s, during the so-called "medical malpractice crisis," when insurance companies massively raised the premiums that they charge doctors for errors and omissions policies. In Virginia, the legislature placed a $750,000 ceiling on malpractice damage awards — regardless of the damages actually suffered.

The problem with Virginia's damage cap was well-illustrated by the case of Veronica Lynn Boyd. Ms. Boyd was born a blind, mentally retarded quadriplegic with cerebral palsy due to the malpractice of her mother's obstetrician. The doctor, R.A. Bulala, apparently valued his free time more than the lives of the patients he was paid handsomely to serve. Ignoring hospital policy and standard medical practice, Dr. Bulala told the nurses working with him to wait until a newborn's head was clearly visible in the birth canal before calling him to attend the delivery. On the night that Ms. Boyd was born, two nurses attended her mother. The nurses lacked training in the emergency medical procedures necessary to deliver a healthy baby — and the doctor was not on the scene. In fact, Dr. Bulala did not even make it to the hospital in time to witness the birth.

The damages in the case were clearly greater than the artificial limitation imposed by Virginia law. Indeed, a jury awarded Ms. Boyd $8.3 million in damages. But the offending doctor then moved the court to reduce the damages to Virginia's $750,000 cap.

Trial attorneys William O. Snead and Rosemarie Annunziata, both of Fairfax, Virginia, and J. Randolph Parker, of Charlottesville, Virginia, literally made a federal case out of the damage cap law, arguing that it violated the right of civil litigants to unencumbered jury trials. U.S. District Court Judge James Michael agreed, ruling that the maintenance of the jury as a fact-finding body is of such historical and legal importance that an infringement upon it cannot be implemented without strict scrutiny by the judiciary. Applying that standard, Judge Michael found that Virginia's law did not pass muster. The court concluded that the award of damages was as much a jury function as the finding of liability and, therefore, the legislature could not interfere with the jury process by imposing limitations on jury trials. Accordingly, the court held that Virginia's damage ceiling was unconstitutional and reinstated the jury's $8.3 million award. This was the first case in which damage caps were held to be constitutionally suspect.

The case had an extensive history in the appellate courts after the trial court struck down Virginia's damage cap as unconstitutional and the plaintiffs' attorneys were honored as finalists for the Trial Lawyer of the Year Award. The U.S. Court of Appeals for the Fourth Circuit reversed, then certified several questions of state law to the Virginia Supreme Court. The state high court then ruled that, in cases involving obstetrical malpractice, it is permissible to have one damage cap for the mother and another for the child. The case was then returned to the trial court to determine the applicable interest. Finally, after approximately eight years of litigation, the case settled.

The reported decision in this case and its subsequent case history can be found at *Boyd v. Bulala*, 647 F. Supp. 781 (W.D. Va. 1986), *aff'd in part and rev'd in part*, 877 F.2d 1191 (4th Cir. 1989) (certifying questions to Virginia Supreme Court), *certified questions answered in* 389 S.E.2d 670 (Va. 1990) (upholding and applying statutory damages cap, excluding statistical evidence), *trial court judgment vacated in part*, 905 F.2d 764 (4th Cir. 1990) (ordering $850,000 judgment for plaintiffs).

Rosemarie Annunziata

J. Randolph Parker

Drug Safety
Blum v. Merrell Dow Pharmaceuticals, Inc.
Thomas Kline

How often do drug companies keep medicines on the market despite learning that they may pose a danger to consumers' health? The extent of the problem is not entirely known, but it is often a civil lawsuit, rather than government regulation, that brings such questions to light.

Since 1957, doctors had prescribed Bendectin as a treatment for morning sickness suffered by pregnant women. Evidence emerged that the drug caused birth defects. A spate of lawsuits followed questioning the drug's safety. By 1983, litigation over the safety of Bendectin was so rampant that the manufacturer, Merrell Dow Pharmaceuticals, Inc., removed the drug from the U.S. market — without, of course, admitting any wrongdoing. (See Chapters Two and Four re *Oxendine*.)

While Merrell Dow had been held liable for compensatory damages by 1987, the full extent of its misconduct had not yet been shown and it had never been held liable for punitive damages. That changed when attorney Thomas Kline of Philadelphia sued Merrell Dow on behalf of Jeffrey Blum. Blum had been born with club feet after his mother, Joan Blum, took Bendectin during her pregnancy. Kline demonstrated that Merrell Dow, a subsidiary of Dow Chemical, had made false reports to the Food and Drug Administration in 1963 regarding tests showing limb deformities in the fetuses of laboratory animals treated with Bendectin. The company did not disclose the existence of the alarming test results to the government until 1966. Even then, the company altered the results to attempt to play down the number of limb abnormalities linked to the drug. This evidence helped Kline prove a more direct relationship between the drug and the specific birth defects than had been previously demonstrated.

Kline used this evidence to obtain an award of $1 million in compensatory damages, plus $1 million in punitive damages against Merrell Dow. The case marked the first time that Merrell Dow was hit with punitive damages for the marketing of Bendectin.

After Kline was honored, the Blum case, like many other high-profile Bendectin cases, ultimately ended with the appellate courts overturning the jury's determination. The Pennsylvania Supreme Court reversed the $2 million verdict on the ground that a verdict of 11 (rather than 12) jurors was insufficient under the Pennsylvania Constitution. The case was retried in 1994. A jury of

12 then awarded the plaintiff $19.2 million. However, this verdict was also reversed — a result upheld by the Pennsylvania Supreme Court in 2000.

The later decision in this case and its subsequent case history can be found at *Blum v. Merrell Dow Pharmaceuticals, Inc.*, 626 A.2d 537 (Pa. 1991) (vacating jury verdict for plaintiffs), *after remand*, 705 A.2d 1314 (Pa. Super. Ct. 1995) (vacating second jury verdict for improper admission of evidence), *aff'd*, 764 A.2d 1 (Pa. 2000).

Thomas Kline

Religious Freedom
Wollersheim v. Church of Scientology
Charles B. O'Reilly

Religious freedom is one of the paramount liberties protected by the U.S. Constitution. The protection is important for all of us, but especially for religions that are deemed outside the mainstream. Too often, people who practice unconventional religions find themselves paying a high price for the pursuit of alternative faiths. At the same time, the First Amendment was not designed to permit alternative religious organizations the "freedom" to harass former adherents who have left the fold.

Larry Wollersheim had been a loyal member of the Church of Scientology for several years, but he began to question its teachings in 1971. The Church's response was to engage in an 11-year vendetta of harassing and bullying behavior. The activities of the Church's members destroyed Wollersheim's marriage, separated him from his young son, and ruined his business. As a result, Wollersheim suffered several emotional breakdowns.

When Wollersheim finally mustered up the courage to sever all ties with Scientology in 1981, he hoped that would be the end of the intimidation. But members of the Church continued to harass, threaten, and embarrass him. In desperation, Wollersheim fled California, assumed a new identity, and began anew in Colorado. He made new friends, opened a business, became engaged, and began to think that he could put the painful past behind him. Once again, however, members of the Church tracked him down and renewed the campaign of emotional harassment and intimidation. They undermined his professional efforts, broke up his engagement, and threatened his life.

Wollersheim turned for help to attorney Charles B. O'Reilly of Greene, O'Reilly, Broillet, Paul, Simon, McMillan, Wheeler & Rosenberg in Los Angeles. Despite the Church of Scientology's reputation for punishing its perceived enemies, O'Reilly took the case and sued the Church for damages.

During trial, attorney O'Reilly brought forward a number of former Scientologists who testified that the Church ran an Intelligence Bureau, the purpose of which was to plan and implement operations designed to incapacitate all potential threats to Scientology. O'Reilly proved that the Church had an official "Hit List" that singled out each individual deemed to be a "subversive person" or "SP" for short. Moreover, he demonstrated that all "SPs," including Wollersheim, were subject to the "fair game" policy, which allows Church members to engage in conduct designed to destroy the perceived enemy of the group. The policy was described as "thought reform," a process through which an individual's thought patterns are altered to Scientology's teachings.

During the case, O'Reilly was subjected to an unremitting campaign of intimidation and threats. Adding to the pressure, between 400 and 1,000 Scientologists surrounded the courthouse each day to protest the trial as a threat to religious freedom. It took full-time security guards posted throughout the trial to ensure the safety of the attorney and his client.

The Church defended its conduct and argued that the First Amendment provides absolute immunity from legal interference with religious beliefs. O'Reilly countered that tortuous conduct performed to carry out religious beliefs is properly subject to liability. The jury found that the tactics used by the Church of Scientology against those it perceived to be enemies were unacceptable and awarded Wollersheim $5 million in compensatory damages and $25 million in punitive damages. The amount of damages was reduced on appeal.

The later reported decision in this case and its subsequent case history can be found at *Wollersheim v. Church of Scientology*, 66 Cal. Rptr. 2d 1 (Cal. Ct. App. 1989) (affirming jury verdict in part and reversing in part), *cert. denied*, 495 U.S. 910 (1990), *cert. granted, judgment vacated, and case remanded*, 499 U.S. 914 (1991), *after remand*, 6 Cal. Rptr. 2d 532 (Cal. Ct. App. 1992) (reducing punitive damages to $2 million), *review dismissed*, (July 15, 1993), *cert. denied*, 510 U.S. 1176 (1994).

Medical Safety

HCA Health Services of Midwest, Inc. v.
Nat'l Bank of Commerce

Bernard Whetstone and Bud Whetstone

When HCA, a national hospital chain, purchased Doctor's Hospital in Little Rock, Arkansas, the new corporate administrator was inundated with requests to keep the nursery fully staffed so that newborns would receive constant nursing care. However, HCA reduced the pediatric nursing staff. As a result, babies were sometimes left unattended for significant periods of time.

Newborn James Talley was left alone in the hospital nursery in September 1992. After about 20 minutes by himself, the infant's breathing stopped. By the time he was found and resuscitated, Talley was profoundly brain damaged. He had gone approximately 15 minutes without oxygen.

Attorneys Bernard Whetstone and Bud Whetstone of Little Rock sued HCA on behalf of James Talley. They proved that it would have cost the hospital only an additional $70,000 per year per nurse to have someone in the nursery at all times. They also demonstrated that HCA was consistently two nurses short of proper staffing on the night shift. Instead of hiring two more nurses as urged by members of the pediatric ward — which would have cost a paltry $140,000 per year — HCA put every child born in the hospital at risk for a miniscule benefit to its bottom line. The jury awarded $1.85 million in compensatory damages to Talley, $777,000 to his mother, and $2 million in punitive damages.

The verdict prompted HCA to improve pediatric nursing staff levels throughout its chain of more than 1,000 hospitals, saving many newborns' lives and preventing many injuries. Bernard and Bud Whetstone were then honored for helping cause these life-saving changes.

Unfortunately, the Whetstones' victory on behalf of James Talley was short-lived. The court ordered a retrial and HCA eventually prevailed.

The later decision in this case and its subsequent case history can be found at *HCA Health Services of Midwest, Inc. v. Nat'l Bank of Commerce*, 745 S.W.2d 120 (Ark. 1988) (ordering new trial), *after remand*, 800 S.W.2d 694 (Ark. 1990) (affirming judgment for defendants).

Access to Justice
Mahoney v. Carus Chem. Co.
William J. Cook

Throughout the country, it is settled law that, if a chemical company causes a fire by recklessly storing highly flammable materials, it can be held liable for the resulting injuries. Until trial attorney William J. Cook of Westmont, New Jersey, sued Carus Chemical, however, firefighters in New Jersey were excluded from the right to seek compensation for the injuries they suffered in such a fire. A 1960 law known as the "Fireman's Rule" prevented injured firefighters from suing for injuries they incurred while fighting a fire.

The idea behind the Fireman's Rule was that firefighters assume the risk of injury because they knowingly engage in a dangerous profession where job-related injuries are foreseeable. Thus, under the Fireman's Rule, firefighters injured on the job would not be permitted to sue a property owner or the person who started the fire. The reasons for such a rule seemed so sound that several courts extended the rule to police officers injured by the foreseeable hazards of their profession.

However, should the Fireman's Rule apply when a fire is caused by wanton and reckless misconduct? Volunteer firefighter Thomas P. Mahoney was critically injured when a wall collapsed on him while he was battling a fire in a chemical plant. The fire broke out two hours after Carus Chemical accepted delivery of 180 barrels of potassium permanganate, a highly flammable powder.

To save money, Carus stored the powder in fiber, rather than metal, drums. Carus knew that this storage method was risky and had already decided to start using metal drums because of several fires caused by the improper containers. But instead of discontinuing use of the unsafe fiber drums immediately, Carus continued to use the defective storage cylinders until its supply was exhausted. Carus did not inform the chemical plant workers of the risk. Absent this reckless disregard of the public safety, Mahoney would not have been injured because there would have been no fire.

Mahoney's case tested the scope of the Fireman's Rule. Attorney Cook argued in the New Jersey Supreme Court that the rule should not apply in cases like Mahoney's because it would permit egregious wrongdoers to use the law as a shield against their reckless and wanton conduct. The high court agreed. By establishing an important exception to the Fireman's Rule, the case created a precedent that helped public servants nationwide to minimize unnecessary risks to their lives and to obtain just compensation for injuries that result from reckless conduct.

After the Court's decision, Carus Chemical paid a substantial sum to settle Mahoney's claim. The case also became the subject of an annotation at 62 A.L.R. 4th 703, published in 1988.

The reported decision in this case can be found at *Mahoney v. Carus Chem. Co.*, 510 A.2d 4 (N.J. 1986).

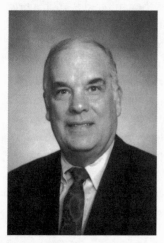

William J. Cook

Religious Freedom

United States v. Aguilar

James Brosnahan, Karen Snell, Ellen Yaroshevsky,
Steve Cooper, Robert Hirsh, William Walker,
Michael Piccaretta, A. Bates Butler, William Risner,
Nancy Postero, Thomas Hoidal, Professor Michael Altman,
and Paul Hoffman

Almost all finalists for the Trial Lawyer of the Year Award have won significant cases, established important precedents, or negotiated noteworthy settlements. In 1987, however, a large group of attorneys was honored with a nomination for a failed cause: defending the Sanctuary Movement.

Recall the turmoil in Latin America in the early 1980s, one of the last battlefields of the Cold War. In El Salvador and Guatemala, government-sponsored death squads roamed the countryside terrorizing and killing the citizenry. The ravages and terror of war destroyed national economies throughout the region. These terrors stimulated a mass migration of immigrants who fled north through Mexico and into the United States. The Immigration and Naturalization Service (INS) responded with increased border patrols and a policy of deportation that, for some refugees, meant almost certain death.

Members of the Sanctuary Movement, primarily religious workers, attempted to assist these refugees by opening their private homes and churches to save the refugees from deportation. The INS countered by launching a nine-month investigation of the movement, including undercover infiltrations of sanctuary organizations. In January 1985, these efforts culminated in indictments and prosecution for conspiracy and other crimes against 11 sanctuary workers.

The 13 trial lawyers named above pooled their talents to represent the 11 sanctuary workers accused of violating federal immigration laws. "The Sanctuary Trial" was held in Tucson, Arizona, between October 1987 and May 1988. During the trial, Judge Earl Carroll prevented any questioning of witnesses about the conditions that compelled the refugees to flee. Still, through skillfully constructed lines of questioning, the legal team gave the jury glimpses of the kinds of torture, murder, and fear that caused the migration north.

At one point, an illegal El Salvadoran refugee who faced imminent deportation begrudgingly took the witness stand for the prosecution. He testified that one of the defendants had sheltered him and his family. The refugee added softly, "She was the only person that offered me a roof over my head when I was most in need." When the prosecutor pointed at the same woman and asked the witness, for the purpose of identification, whether he recognized her, he replied, "With great love."

Because of their religious faith, the defendants believed that, no matter what the jury decided, their actions on behalf of the refugees were sanctioned by a power much greater than the U.S. government. Their faith gave them and their defense team comfort when the jury returned with guilty verdicts for eight of the 11 defendants. Those who were convicted received probation.

One of the defendants, a 61-year-old grandmother from Mexico, seemed to speak for all when she said, "I am a Christian woman and I have done what my religion teaches. I hope you, Your Honor, have a lot of accused like us."

Despite the loss in court, the Sanctuary Movement gained stature in the encounter. Favorable publicity resulting from the workers' acts of civil disobedience increased the number of people willing to join the Sanctuary Movement and spotlighted the terrors then occurring in Latin America.

The defense team was comprised of lawyers from a variety of backgrounds, many of whom left behind families and busy practices to represent the accused sanctuary workers for free. The team included James Brosnahan and Karen Snell of Morrison & Foerster in San Francisco; Ellen Yaroshevsky of the Center for Constitutional Rights in New York; Steve Cooper of the Neighborhood Justice Center in St. Paul, Minnesota; Paul Hoffman of the ACLU of Southern California; Arizona attorneys Robert Hirsh, William Walker of Stompoly & Stroud, Michael Piccaretta of Davis, Siegel & Gugino, A. Bates Butler of Butler & Stein, and William Risner and Nancy Postero of Keller & Postero; Thomas Hoidal of the Phoenix Federal Public Defender's Office; and Professor Michael Altman from the Arizona State University Law School.

The later reported decision in this case and its subsequent case history, can be found at *United States v. Aguilar*, 883 F.2d 662 (9th Cir. 1989) (affirming convictions), *cert. denied*, 489 U.S. 1046 (1991).

James Brosnahan

Ellen Yaroshevsky

Steve Cooper

Robert Hirsh

William Walker

Michael Piccaretta

William Risner

Michael Altman

1987 Trial Lawyer of the Year Award Winner
Morris S. Dees, Michael Figures
and the Southern Poverty Law Center
The Case That Bankrupted The Klan

When trial lawyer Morris Dees sued a white supremacist organization to collect damages for the lynching of Michael Donald, he came to depositions wearing a bulletproof vest and packing heat. In fact, Dees and his legal team had received so many credible death threats that the FBI warned him that he was the intended target of assassins.

Dees' enemies had a long and infamous history. Six Confederate veterans of the Civil War had created an underground white supremacist organization in 1865. They named their secret group the Ku Klux Klan (KKK), from the Greek word *kirkos*, meaning "circle." By 1867, the KKK had become a full-blown hate organization. Klansmen began terrorizing members of religious and ethnic minority groups, especially Catholics, Jews, and African-Americans. Over the next century, the KKK became increasingly powerful and dangerous, lynching hundreds of African-Americans in the North and South.

By the early 1980s, the KKK's ranks had shrunk to several thousand members. The KKK nevertheless remained violent and dangerous. However, thanks to the courage, determination, and legal creativity of a team of trial lawyers from the Southern Poverty Law Center (SPLC), one particular lynching resulted in the financial destruction of the United Klans of America (UKA) — the nation's oldest and largest organized branch of the KKK with chapters in 20 states.

What is public justice? Hate groups are held accountable for the damages they and their agents inflict upon their victims.

On March 20, 1981, 19-year-old Michael Donald said goodbye to his mother, Beulah Mae Donald, as he left her Mobile, Alabama, home to walk a few blocks to a corner gas station to buy cigarettes. As he was walking, a car pulled to the curb and a stranger asked him about the location of a local nightclub. When Donald approached the car to give directions, KKK member James

"Tiger" Knowles stuck a gun in his face and ordered him to get in. Knowles and fellow Klansman Henry Hays drove off with Donald in the back seat begging for his life.

The pair drove their randomly-selected victim to a remote spot and ordered him out of the car. Donald, sensing his impending murder, jumped Knowles and fought desperately for his life. The three struggled for the gun, which went off, but nobody was hit. The two Klansmen then slipped a noose over Donald's neck and cinched it tight. As Donald struggled for breath, Hays hit him repeatedly with a tree branch until all struggle ceased. To ensure that Donald was dead, Hays cut the young man's throat. The pair then shoved his inert body into the trunk of the car and drove back to Hays' house. The beaten and bloody body was strung up by the neck from a camphor tree across the street from the house, as Klan members gathered to drink beer and gloat. Meanwhile, two other Klansmen burned a cross on the grounds of the county courthouse.

The murder of Michael Donald was not easy to solve. After all, the only witnesses were the killers and they weren't about to turn themselves in. Others knew about the crime, but they, too, were Klansmen. Moreover, the group had concocted what it thought would be an airtight alibi — the night Donald was murdered, they were all together playing poker.

Mobile County law enforcement officials seem to have bought into the charade. They investigated the case as if the lynching had not been a hate crime. Indeed, despite the unequivocally racist imagery of a young African-American man hanging from a tree, District Attorney Christopher Galanos announced that racism did not appear to be a motive in the murder. Within days, law enforcement officers arrested three young white men for a crime they did not commit. Officials described them as "junkie types" who probably murdered Donald because they were "fired up on drugs." However, a grand jury refused to indict them because the evidence was so sparse. It looked as though the case would not be solved.

But Thomas Figures, an Assistant U.S. Attorney in charge of civil rights in the Mobile office of the U.S. Department of Justice, was not about to allow Donald's murderers to remain free. Thanks to his efforts, the FBI conducted a more intense probe that began to unravel the truth behind the lynching. The renewed investigation turned up enough evidence to convene a grand jury in May 1983, more than two years after the murder. The inquiry focused on the Klan members who attended the "poker party" at Hays' place, directly across the street from the tree where Donald's body had been strung up for viewing.

Finally, Knowles cracked. He confessed to the murder and agreed to testify against Hays in return for a life sentence. Hays would later receive the death penalty.

The murder convictions of the two killers were gratifying, but the full measure of justice had not yet been dealt. Dees, a co-founder of the nonprofit SPLC, sat in the gallery and listened as Knowles testified against his partner in crime. Knowles confessed that the reason for the lynching was a trial in Mobile in which an African-American man was accused of killing a white police officer. The jury was predominantly African-American. This fact embittered Knowles, Hays, and Hays' father, Bennie Jack Hays. The elder Hays held the title of "Grand Titan," the second-highest-ranking Alabama officer of the UKA. The three men plotted a lynching if the accused police killer was not convicted to express their disgust that African-American citizens were able to participate equally in juries. The murder was planned, Knowles said, to kill a black man and to "show the strength of the Klan…to show that they were still here in Alabama."

The night of the killing, Frank Cox — the "Exalted Cyclops" or leader of the Mobile Klavern of the UKA — along with Knowles and Hays borrowed a rope from Cox's mother and a gun from another Klan member. On the way back to Hays' house, the rope was tied into a hangman's noose that would later be cinched around their victim's neck. The group then watched the news to learn whether a verdict had been reached in the police killing case. They heard that the case had ended with a hung jury. That was when Hays and Knowles drove off, hunting for an African-American man to lynch.

Dees attended the criminal trial because he was interested in filing a civil lawsuit over the Donald murder. Dees promotes public justice by seeking to hold hate groups accountable in the civil justice system for their crimes. As a result, he and the SPLC have been the bane of the KKK and other hate groups for years. Now, with the convictions of Hays and Knowles, Dees wondered whether the UKA could be held accountable for the wrongful death of Michael Donald.

Michael Figures, the brother of the determined federal prosecutor Thomas Figures, served as the personal attorney for the bereft mother, Beulah Mae Donald. Mrs. Donald was a strong woman. To reveal the brutality of racism, despite the battered state of her son's body, she held an open-casket funeral. Dees discussed his idea of bringing a suit in the name of Michael Donald's estate. Mrs. Donald agreed. Dees and the SPLC then joined forces with Michael Figures to file a landmark civil suit.

Where had Dees come up with the idea of suing the hate group rather than merely the individuals convicted of the crime? "I was involved in suing the Committee to Reelect the President and the Republican National Committee in the wake of Watergate," Dees says. Dees had been George McGovern's head fundraiser and, in the early days of the Watergate investigation, he believed that the conspiracy was more widespread than the burglars who had taken the fall. He became one of the Democratic Party's attorneys in the case. "We immediately took the deposition of Watergate participants such as [H.R.] Haldeman, [John] Ehrlichman, [Maurice] Stans, and [John] Mitchell. We nailed down those people long before the tapes were discovered and John Dean turned." In the end, the case settled in the high six figures.

The question facing Dees in the *Donald* case was whether he could prove that the UKA's leaders had officially sanctioned the murder. Corporations and other organizations usually cannot be held responsible for the criminal acts of their members. However, Knowles had testified that the reason for the killing was "to show the strength of the Klan...to show that we are still here in Alabama."

Dees hoped that the legal team could parlay Knowles' statement into proof that the UKA had officially sanctioned the killing. If the trial lawyers could do that, they could obtain a very large judgment that the group probably couldn't pay — essentially putting the UKA out of business.

The KKK is a closed circle and it would require a deft touch to elicit its secrets. Believing that a velvet hand, rather than a bludgeon, would likely be the best approach, Dees decided to be "nice" to his adversaries.

How is one "nice" to a member of a Klan group? Surprisingly, Dees says it is not that hard. Though he in no way approves of their ideas or rationalizes their violence, Dees believes that many rank and file KKK members were themselves victims of hate. "Had some of these guys been members of a labor union or other benign group, rather than influenced by haters, they would probably not have gone wrong," Dees believes. "They are simply looking for some belonging and power in the world."

Dees' tactic paid off. He convinced former UKA member Johnny Matthew Jones to provide information. The police had not pursued Jones' testimony because they perceived him as mentally retarded. Dees believed otherwise and slowly ingratiated himself into the young man's confidence. Finally, Jones agreed to be interviewed. He told Dees that the local Klan chapter usually met at Bennie Hays' barn. He also recalled that the group discussed the idea of killing an African-American in retaliation for the failure of a predominantly

African-American jury to convict an African-American accused of killing a white police officer in Mobile. Jones said the original idea stemmed from Grand Titan Hays, who asserted that a "nigger ought to be hung by the neck until dead to put them in their place."

Ironically, Bennie Hays' edict would become the key to the case. In this regard, Dees' ability to be "nice" to KKK members proved to be a crucial factor. During the closing days of the criminal trial against Bennie's son, Henry, Dees spotted Bennie and his wife sitting forlorn in the back of the courtroom. He walked up to the couple and expressed his sorrow that their son was facing death row. That small bit of simple human kindness and courtesy would be responsible for breaking the case wide-open.

A few days after their brief exchange, Dees received a letter from the elder Hays, who wrote, "You talked very nice to me and my wife." Hays described Dees as "much different than I expected after being told what I had about you." The Grand Titan informed Dees that he wanted to straighten out his life. Hays was under indictment for arson; police suspected that he had torched his own house to raise insurance money to pay for his son's defense. As a sign of his good faith and contrition, Hays enclosed the official "Klavern charter" for the Mobile unit, issued in 1973, and signed by the national head of the UKA, Robert Shelton.

This was an exciting turn of events. Dees knew from testimony elicited during the original murder investigation that Bennie had possession of the UKA's scrapbook, book of rules, and regulation book. Bennie's decision to reach out to Dees indicated that the deepest secrets of the Mobile unit of the KKK could be exposed.

Dees visited Bennie and his wife, who were living in a trailer. Hays was bitter because he believed that the UKA's lawyers had abandoned his son. He was not willing to give Dees his files, but he did allow him to peruse them. Dees saw treasures in the file. How could he secure them?

Soon afterwards, Bennie was convicted for arson and jailed. Dees immediately issued a subpoena to Mrs. Hays for the records. He warned her that if she did not bring the documents or if she destroyed them, she could go to jail. She complied.

The records proved to be a bonanza. They included the Klan's secret constitution and painted a picture of the KKK as an organized hierarchy. The UKA branch was a paramilitary organization with Shelton as the commander-in-chief, Bennie Hays as the second in command of the Alabama chapter, and others named as officers of the chartered units. More important, the constitution stated explicitly that the local units' very purpose was to carry out the goals of the national organization to promote white supremacy. This discovery was a real breakthrough.

Still, Dees had to prove that the organization itself existed to further a criminal purpose. Dees turned to Gary Thomas Rowe, a former Klan member and FBI informant, who was then in a federal witness protection program. Through his connections, Dees communicated with Rowe and explained that his testimony could be crucial to the case. Rowe testified that Shelton had not only approved of violent attacks on African-Americans, but had personally led a bloody attack in 1961 against the civil rights organizers known as "Freedom Riders." Rowe described being called in 1965 by a high UKA official to "take a ride" to Montgomery, Alabama, with three other Klansmen, so they could find civil rights marchers to kill in the wake of a historic demonstration. While in Montgomery, the group murdered Viola Liuzzo, a white woman, as she drove marchers back to Selma, Alabama. With this testimony, Dees was encouraged that he could obtain a judgment against the UKA.

Knowles drove the last nail in UKA's coffin. Dees convinced the judge to permit the imprisoned Knowles to testify in person, promising that the SPLC would pick up the travel expenses and costs for the federal marshals, which amounted to more than $2,000 per day. "I wanted the jury to *feel* the murder," Dees recalls.

The realization and confession of what he had done had changed Tiger Knowles. He described the murder in excruciating detail. He characterized the lynching as a Klan killing, rather than a killing by members of the Klan. One reason for the murder, he said, was to send a message to the nation that the Klan did not want African-Americans to serve on juries. That is why Klan members burned the cross on the courthouse lawn. He testified that to ensure publicity, Henry Hays anonymously called a television station and informed the news desk that there was a body hanging from a tree. Knowles also made it clear that Bennie Hays, acting as a UKA official, sanctioned the murder. Beulah Mae Donald sat through the entire trial at the counsel table, only a few feet away from the men who had plotted her son's murder.

Just before the case was sent to the jury, Dees was called to Knowles' holding cell. Knowles, a joint defendant in the civil case, asked to make a closing statement to the jury. Dees describes the dramatic and emotional scene in his autobiography, *A Season for Justice*:

The young man who murdered Michael Donald addressed the jury: "Everything I said is true," Tiger Knowles began. "I was acting as a Klansman when I done this. I hope that people learn from my mistake. I've lost my family. I've got people after me."

Tears filled Knowles' eyes and I began to feel them well up in mine. Knowles pivoted and faced Beulah Mae Donald. "I can't bring your son back, but I'm sorry for what happened." He was sobbing now. Mrs. Donald rocked back and forth. "God knows if I could trade places with him, I would. I can't. Whatever it takes — I have nothing. But I will have to do it. And if it takes me the rest of my life to pay it, any comfort it may bring, I hope it will. I will."...There were no dry eyes [in the courtroom]. Knowles gave up trying to fight his own tears. "I want you to understand that it is true what happened and I am just sorry that it happened."

Beulah Mae Donald stopped rocking. "I forgive you," she said softly.

Dees and his legal team made history with this case. The all-white jury returned a verdict in a few hours, finding both the individual Klan members and the UKA liable for Donald's wrongful death. The jury awarded $7 million in damages. Mrs. Donald grabbed Figures' and Dees' hands. Her courage in facing her son's killers, along with the indomitable determination of her lawyers, bankrupted the UKA. As is their policy, Dees, Figures, and the SPLC took no fee for their representation, nor did they seek to be reimbursed for expenses and costs.

The only major asset that the UKA owned was a new 7,400 square-foot building. Six weeks after the trial, the deed to the property and the keys to the building were sent to Dees at the SPLC. Beulah Mae Donald was now its owner. Mrs. Donald liquidated the headquarters that hate built. The proceeds allowed her to move out of public housing and purchase a house — the first she had ever owned. Less than a year later, Mrs. Donald died, having left the world a better place for all her sorrow.

There is no reported decision on the merits in *Donald v. United Klans of America.*

Morris S. Dees

CHAPTER SIX

1988: The Case That Blew Apart Big Tobacco's Smokescreen

Government Accountability *Barrett v. United States*

Drug Safety *Graham v. Wyeth Laboratories*

Drug Safety *Ealy v. Richardson-Merrell, Inc.*

Auto Safety *Garrett v. Ford Motor Co.*

Toxic Injury Prevention *Ayers v. Township of Jackson*

Medical Safety *Jackson v. Power*

Workers' Rights *Millison v. E.I. du Pont de Nemours and Co.*

Government Accountability *Turner v. Dist. of Columbia*

Winner
Cipollone v. Liggett Group, Inc.
The Case That Blew Apart Big Tobacco's Smokescreen

The finalists for the 1988 Trial Lawyer of the Year Award sought public justice by promoting government accountability, safer children's vaccines and pregnancy drugs, auto safety, purer drinking water, higher standards of hospital care, and protection of abused children. The winning case, *Cipollone v. Liggett Group, Inc.,* was the first damages verdict by an individual smoker against a tobacco company. Although the breakthrough verdict would later be reversed on appeal, Big Tobacco's victory soon turned to ashes. Because of the *Cipollone* case, the public learned of internal documents harmful to tobacco defense strategies. The exposure of the industry's concealments and mendacity led to tremendous victories for public health in subsequent years.

Government Accountability
Barrett v. United States
Eugene R. Scheiman, Deborah Linfield, and Richard Kelly

New York trial attorneys Eugene R. Scheiman, Deborah Linfield, and Richard Kelly exposed the federal government's subjection of citizens to involuntary medical experiments involving the hallucinogenic drug mescaline. On December 2, 1952, Harold Blauer, distraught over his divorce, checked into the New York State Psychiatric Institute. In the second week of his treatment, doctors gave him a series of injections of mescaline — not because it would benefit his condition, but to fulfill a contract the Institute had with the U.S. Army Chemical Corps to conduct a medical experiment. The experiment's purpose was to "determine clinical effects on psychological behavior, including controls on normal human subjects necessary to evaluate the more profound changes expected in the behavior of psychiatrically liable subjects."

By the fourth injection, Blauer experienced body tremors, causing him to sit up and flop down again repeatedly. According to doctors' notes, Blauer was extremely agitated and resistant to treatment. On January 8, 1953, the fifth injection caused Blauer to lapse into a coma; within three hours, he died.

A malpractice case against the Institute led to a measly $18,000 settlement — half of which the federal government paid in secret. Blauer's family members did not know of the Army's involvement. They were misinformed that the death resulted from a reaction to therapeutic drugs.

Twenty-three years later, in 1975, the Secretary of the Army revealed that the Army had supplied the chemicals that caused Blauer's death and that these drugs were not at all therapeutic, but rather part of an experiment to develop chemical warfare agents. Elizabeth Barrett, one of Blauer's daughters, wanted to sue. She retained attorneys Scheiman, Linfield, and Kelly, who found a huge roadblock in the path of justice: the "exceptions" to liability under the Federal Tort Claims Act often make it impossible to sue the federal government. The Army used the Act to attempt to deprive Barrett of justice for her father's death, claiming that the statute of limitations had run out in 1956 — two decades before the Army admitted evidence of the conspiracy and cover-up — and that, in any case, the testing in which Blauer was killed was shielded from suit as a "discretionary function" that furthered national defense. The plaintiff's lawyers argued that no governmental immunity allows the Army to be so reckless as to kill innocent people in involuntary medical experiments.

The Army's defenses failed and Barrett was awarded $702,044. After Senior U.S. District Court Judge Motley's decision awarding damages, the federal government sought contribution from the State of New York. That matter was settled and the award paid, thus ending what the judge called "a sad episode in the conduct of the United States and a personal tragedy for an unsuspecting victim and family."

The reported decision in this case can be found at *Barrett v. United States,* 660 F. Supp. 1291 (S.D.N.Y. 1987).

Eugene R. Scheiman

Drug Safety
Graham v. Wyeth Laboratories
Ted Warshafsky and Andrew Hutton

Sometimes the hazardous side effects of drugs can be avoided if the manufacturer is willing to spend more money. Unfortunately, Wyeth Laboratories was not willing to that — and Michelle Graham was needlessly injured.

Two-month-old Michelle Graham was administered a DPT (diphtheria, pertussis, and tetanus) vaccination that caused terrible side effects leading to permanent brain damage. Michelle's parents retained Milwaukee, Wisconsin, attorney Ted Warshafsky and Wichita, Kansas, attorney Andrew Hutton to pursue justice on behalf of their infant daughter. The attorneys learned that Michelle's injuries could have been wholly avoided if the manufacturer of the drug, Wyeth Laboratories, had not discontinued the production of a safer, equally effective formula of DPT. They suspected the reason for the change was financial: the safer formula cost more to produce.

Wyeth Laboratories defended the case on the basis of federal preemption. Wyeth argued that because the Food and Drug Administration had approved the formula that had injured Michelle, then the fact of federal regulatory approval should prevent the Grahams from suing. But Warshafsky and Hutton demonstrated that the Food, Drug, and Cosmetic Act was never intended to preclude lawsuits for damages for harm caused by approved drugs. This opened the door for a trial on the merits.

At trial, Wyeth argued that it was not irresponsible to market a drug that carried some risk because the drug benefited the public by preventing epidemics. The trial lawyers countered that a safer formula existed which had the virtue of both preventing epidemics and posing far less risk to patients receiving the vaccines. The jury agreed, awarding $15 million in damages.

In addition to winning justice for their client, attorneys Warshafsky and Hutton successfully prevented Wyeth from retrieving all incriminating evidence that the attorneys had uncovered and disclosed in a public courtroom. Arguing against court secrecy, the attorneys prevailed upon the court to recognize the public's right to know. The U.S. Court of Appeals for the Eighth Circuit reversed the trial verdict based on an evidentiary issue involving defense expert witnesses. After one week of retrial, the case settled confidentially.

The reported decision in this case can be found at *Graham v. Wyeth Laboratories*, 666 F. Supp. 1483 (D. Kan. 1987).

Ted Warshafsky

Andrew Hutton

Drug Safety
Ealy v. Richardson-Merrell, Inc.
Barry Nace

Tenacious trial lawyer Barry Nace, honored in both 1984 and 1986 for his role in *Oxendine v. Merrell Dow Pharmaceuticals, Inc.,* resumed his courtroom battle with that company for manufacturing and marketing Bendectin as an anti-nausea drug for use by pregnant women. The drug helped ease nausea, Nace argued, but there was evidence that it also caused birth defects. In 1983, partially because of the work of attorney Nace, Merrell Dow had removed the drug from the U.S. market.

Removing the drug was one thing for Merrell-Dow; admitting the harm caused by Bendectin was quite another. Nace had won a $750,000 verdict that was overturned by the trial judge in the case of *Oxendine v. Merrell Dow.* Nace, however, convinced an appellate court to reinstate the verdict, leading to his 1986 nomination for the Trial Lawyer of the Year Award. Subsequently, the trial court rejected the verdict for a different reason, leading to another appeal.

Meanwhile, Nace fought Merrell Dow on behalf of Sekou Ealy, a boy born with arms of abnormal length, no thumbs, missing fingers, and an unbending elbow. Nace persuaded a jury that these injuries were attributable to Bendectin. The jury awarded $20 million in compensatory damages and $75 million in punitive damages against Merrell Dow. The trial judge set aside the punitive damages, but refused to throw out the compensatory award. In 1988, Nace was honored for this achievement.

Regretfully, this victory, too, was short-lived. The case was reversed on appeal, ending with a judgment for the defendant corporation. The appellate courts held that, regardless of what Nace had shown, the jury had found, and the trial judge had ruled, there was not sufficient evidence that Bendectin caused birth defects to allow the verdict to stand.

The decision in this case and its subsequent case history can be found at *Ealy v. Richardson-Merrell, Inc.,* 1987 WL 18743 (D.D.C. Oct. 1, 1987) (entering judgment on jury verdict, reducing damages award), *rev'd,* 897 F.2d 1159 (D.C. Cir. 1990) (ordering judgment for defendant).

Barry Nace

Auto Safety
Garrett v. Ford Motor Co.
Harold Sakayan, Sol Margolis, and Gerry Holtz

This legal trio held the Ford Motor Company accountable for deciding to value profits over lives and install lap belts without shoulder harnesses in the back seats of Ford Escort automobiles. The auto maker's decision saved it money, but cost 11-year-old Jimmy Garrett and his friend Chris Gaboury dearly. The boys were backseat passengers in an Escort involved in a head-on collision. Another boy riding in the front seat where he was protected by a three-point belt with a shoulder harness suffered only slight injury. However, the lap belts worn by Jimmy and Chris caused Chris' death and Garrett's permanent disability as a paraplegic.

Once again, a company tried to rely on a federal preemption defense to shield itself from a consumer lawsuit. Once again, the tactic failed. Reviewing the legislative history of the National Traffic and Motor Vehicle Safety Act, the plaintiff's attorneys demonstrated that the Act was intended to discourage unsafe designs, not immunize manufacturers who used them.

In the process of preparing their case, attorneys Sakayan, Margolis, and Holtz learned that European auto manufacturers had installed three-point seatbelts in their vehicles since the late 1960s. But U.S. manufacturers had decided not to follow suit based on a cost/benefit analysis. Indeed, the European version of the Ford Escort had the safer belts, while the U.S. version did not. The difference in cost? Only $12 per seat belt!

The jury was convinced of the righteousness of the cause, awarding Garrett $3.3 million in damages. The jury specifically found that Ford had acted negligently by failing to install rear shoulder harnesses and by defectively designing the seat belt.

The case settled during post judgment proceedings. Attorneys Sakayan, Margolis, and Holtz next petitioned the National Highway Transportation Safety Administration (NHTSA) to open an investigation into the safety hazard posed by Ford's belt design and issue a recall. NHTSA refused and closed the file. But Ford soon announced that it would install rear shoulder harnesses in its cars.

The reported decision in this case can be found at *Garrett v. Ford Motor Co.*, 684 F. Supp. 407 (D. Md. 1987) (denying preemption defense).

Gerry Holtz

Toxic Injury Prevention
Ayers v. Township of Jackson
Steven J. Phillips, Donald I. Marlin, Ivan B. Rubin,
and Arnold C. Lakind

Toxic dumping is a chronic problem in the U.S. This pervasive problem became a dangerous reality to the 300 residents of Jackson Township, a New Jersey community whose drinking water was contaminated by a municipal landfill. Not only did four trial lawyers ensure that the residents' medical needs would be met, but they also changed the status of toxic tort law.

The saga began in November 1978 when Jackson Township officials warned residents not to drink their well water and to limit their washing and bathing due to water contamination. The landfill-generated contamination had occurred as a result of Township negligence. Making matters worse, the chemicals found in the water caused cancer, kidney damage, mutations, alterations in genetic material, blood difficulties, reproductive anomalies, neurological injury, and skin irritation. Quite naturally, learning that they had used contaminated water for more than six years, residents lived in fear of health consequences to themselves, their children, and their pets.

The discovery of the tainted water led to a catastrophic breakdown of water services. At first, water was delivered to affected residents by tanker truck. Those who needed water had to take portable containers to water distribution centers and trek it back to their homes. Eventually, the Township dropped off water at its residents' property in 40-gallon barrels which weighed more than 100 pounds. The residents had to lug the barrels into their houses. The situation led to high levels of stress, depression, and health worries among the residents.

When attorneys Phillips, Marlin, Rubin, and Lakind attempted to remedy this injustice, they faced a significant legal impediment in the New Jersey Tort Claims Act's bar to recovery for pain and suffering or emotional distress. Realizing the injustice of so limiting recovery for these residents who had done nothing to contribute to their plight, the attorneys successfully argued that their clients would require frequent, specialized, and very thorough medical screening for early detection of diseases to which they had been put at greater risk. Moreover, the attorneys argued, Township residents had been denied the quiet enjoyment of their property — which represented diminution of a property interest, the recovery for which would not be barred by the New Jersey law. The case won the residents compensation on the order of $17 million.

Recovery for medical monitoring of victims exposed to toxic releases, even where no injury is manifest and where increased risk of illness is not quantifiable, represented a breakthrough in the law of torts. Thanks to trial lawyers Phillips, Marlin, Rubin, and Lakind, public and private landfill operators and mining and industrial companies can no longer count on the passage of time and tort law barriers to protect them from just redress.

The Superior Court Appellate Division, on appeal, reduced the value of the award to $2 million. The New Jersey Supreme Court subsequently reinstated the bulk of the verdict, awarding the clients $15.6 million. According to attorney Lakind, "The State of New Jersey now has rather stringent drinking water standards and frequent test requirements."

The reported decision in this case can be found at *Ayers v. Township of Jackson*, 525 A.2d 287 (N.J. 1987).

Donald I. Marlin

Ivan B. Rubin

Arnold C. Lakind

Medical Safety

Jackson v. Power

L. Ames Luce, Dan A. Hensley, Michael Cohn, and Leonard Schroeter

The case of *Jackson v. Power* closed a loophole that allowed hospitals to avoid liability for wrongdoing that occurred on their premises by using contract workers, rather than employees, to perform certain tasks. Through this loophole, hospitals and other institutions avoided liability for the negligence committed by these contract workers by invoking a legal rule that restricted recovery in such cases to the independent contractors themselves. Anchorage attorneys L. Ames Luce, Dan A. Hensley, and Michael Cohn, along with Seattle attorney Leonard Schroeter, successfully overcame this unfair limitation obtaining a $3.9 million settlement for a victim of hospital negligence.

In May 1981, 16-year-old Bret Jackson fell off a cliff while hiking in Alaska. He was airlifted to Fairbanks Memorial Hospital and taken to the emergency room shortly after midnight. Dr. Power, one of two emergency room physicians on duty at the time, failed to order certain medical procedures that would have disclosed Jackson's kidney injuries. This negligence caused Jackson to lose both kidneys.

Power was not an employee of the hospital, but of Emergency Room, Inc., an independent contractor that supplied physicians to the hospital's emergency room. Thus, even though the negligence occurred in the hospital E.R., the hospital invoked the "independent contractor defense," which would require the plaintiff to prove that the contractor was negligent *and* that the hospital was negligent in engaging or monitoring the contractor.

With genuine inspiration, the plaintiff's litigation team proved the independent contractor defense irrelevant. They showed that since the hospital was licensed as a "general acute care hospital," it was therefore under a statutory obligation to comply with state regulations requiring it to provide emergency care physicians on a 24-hour basis. Moreover, the hospital was accredited by the Joint Committee on Accreditation of Hospitals, which required it to comply with specified standards for supervision and maintenance of emergency care service. Indeed, the hospital's own bylaws called for a 24-hour staffed emergency room. This obligation, the attorneys successfully argued, was not subject to delegation. The hospital could contract out the labor, but not the responsibility.

The Alaska Supreme Court agreed with the lawyers' arguments, holding that public policy dictates that when a hospital operates an emergency room, it should not be allowed to shift liability to independent contractor physicians who staff the E.R. After the trial lawyers won this legal victory promoting hospital safety, the case settled.

The reported decision in this case can be found at *Jackson v. Power*, 743 P.2d 1376 (Alaska 1987).

Leonard Schroeter

Workers' Rights
Millison v. E I. du Pont de Nemours and Co.
David Jacoby and Joshua Spielberg

Trial lawyers David Jacoby and Joshua Spielberg of Haddenfield, New Jersey, prevented du Pont from avoiding responsibility for outrageous misconduct by hiding behind the Garden State's workers' compensation laws. For the first time in the U.S., a court held an employer fully accountable in damages for knowingly withholding medical information from its employees about health risks posed by asbestos.

At du Pont's Chamber Works and Repauno Plants in New Jersey, its corporate doctors provided annual physical examinations to its employees. For nearly 12 years, pursuant to corporate directives, company doctors gave employees a clean bill of health regardless of the actual results of their exams, even when x-rays disclosed the development of asbestos-related diseases. Under management directives, company doctors observed, but stayed mute, as the workers' health deteriorated. Meanwhile, du Pont's sham medical exams diverted its employees from seeking the genuine medical care that they sorely needed.

When the truth came to light, du Pont claimed that workers' compensation laws limited its liability. Despite the corporation's injurious policies, it claimed the wronged employees could not receive full redress at law, but rather, were only entitled to the limited benefits permitted under New Jersey's administrative workers' compensation system. If the argument held, then du Pont could limit its liability to less than $10,000 per worker.

Du Pont had reason to be optimistic. Under previous court rulings, the exception in the workers' compensation law that permitted lawsuits over an employer's wrongdoing had been limited to cases where the employer intentionally inflicted the harm. That limitation allowed employers to observe health and safety risks without lifting a finger to prevent injuries to workers. Accordingly, du Pont argued, since the company did not intend to inflict the asbestos-related injuries upon their employees, but merely observed the development of their employees' diseases, the workers could not hold the company accountable.

Trial lawyers Jacoby and Spielberg successfully argued that the case should go to a jury. The attorneys persuaded the court to expand the application of the exemption provision to include employers who "know" with "substantial certainty" that their conduct will result in injury to their employees. The trial resulted in a verdict for nearly $1.4 million in damages on behalf of six employees.

The New Jersey Appellate Division in 1988 and the New Jersey Supreme Court in 1989 upheld the verdict and damage award. In 1990, Jacoby and Spielberg settled a similar case confidentially on behalf of 300 du Pont employees. The cases promoted public justice by helping to deter ruthless, profit-minded employers from embarking on policies that harm employees.

The reported decision in this case and its subsequent case history can be found at *Millison v. E.I. du Pont de Nemours and Co.*, 501 A.2d 505 (N.J. 1985), *after remand*, 558 A.2d 461 (N.J. 1989) (affirming compensatory and punitive damages award).

David Jacoby

Joshua Spielberg

Government Accountability
Turner v. Dist. of Columbia
Joel Finkelstein

What happens when the government fails in its responsibility to enforce its own rules and regulations aimed at preventing child abuse? Attorney Joel Finkelstein of Washington, D.C., believed that government owes a "special duty" to child abuse victims and that, when government violates that duty, it should be liable to the victims.

In December 1982, Clara Turner lived with Keith Lynn Roddy, her daughters from a previous relationship, and their two sons — four-month-old Keith and two-year-old Lynn. After Roddy violently attacked Turner, she sought assistance from the local police. She left the home with her daughters under police protection. However, when Roddy demanded that his sons remain with him, the police refused to interfere.

About a week later, Turner's daughters reported that when they visited the apartment they found that Keith's diapers had not been changed, the toilet was stopped up, and there was no food. Then Roddy called Turner and threatened to kill her and the children if she did not return. She sought help from D.C.'s Child Protective Services (CPS), whose officials decided the issue was one of neglect rather than abuse. Therefore, instead of removing the boys immediately from Roddy's control, CPS referred Turner to a social worker who told her, "If I find neglect, I will return your children.... Don't call me, I'll call you." Yet he never gained access to the apartment and never sought the assistance of police to verify whether the children were cared for properly. Meanwhile, under Roddy's care, Lynn became malnourished and the baby Keith died of starvation and dehydration.

Attorney Finkelstein believed that D.C., and not just Roddy, should be held to account for this terrible tragedy. The District argued that unless the attorney could demonstrate that the District owed the family a "special duty," then it could not be held responsible. Finklestein argued that a special duty already existed because the language of the Child Abuse Protection Act prescribed "mandatory acts for the protection of a particular class of persons, rather than the public as a whole." The court agreed, ruling that D.C. was merely attempting to evade accountability. The case clarified the law, putting a government agency on notice that it cannot take for granted its duty to protect neglected and abused children.

The reported decision in this case can be found at *Turner v. Dist. of Columbia*, 532 A.2d 662 (D.C. 1987).

1988 Trial Lawyer of the Year Award Winners

Marc Edell, Cynthia Walters, and Alan Darnell
The Case That Blew Apart Big Tobacco's Smokescreen

Rose DeFrancesco Cipollone began smoking in 1942 as a 16-year-old high school student. She smoked because she saw movie stars smoking, and she wanted to be "cool, glamorous, and grown-up." Her cigarette of choice was the Liggett Group's Chesterfield brand, which she selected because advertising claimed it was "mild." By the end of 1943, she was smoking a pack a day.

Rose married Antonio Cipollone in 1947. When she became pregnant with her first child, she tried to quit smoking. However, she found that she was hooked and could not stop. Cipollone smoked an entire pack of Chesterfields while going through labor; her doctor supplied the cigarettes. Rose became a chain smoker, consuming between one and two packs a day.

In 1955, Rose switched from Chesterfields to another Liggett brand, L & M, because they were filtered and so she believed the filter would trap whatever was "bad" for her in cigarette smoke. She continued to smoke L & M's until 1968, when she switched to Virginia Slims, manufactured by Philip Morris, Inc. She switched because of advertising that associated the brand with beautiful, glamorous women and female liberation. She fell for the Virginia Slims advertising come-on, "You've got your own cigarettes now baby, you've come a long, long way."

By this time, Rose had developed a smoker's cough and had heard reports that smoking could cause cancer. She tried to cut back on her habit, but her addiction to nicotine was stronger than her fear of illness. Her husband repeatedly tried to persuade her to quit. She could not. Later, Rose would testify that

> *What is public justice? Companies that lie to consumers about the dangers of their products must pay for the injuries caused by those products.*

she believed the tobacco company assertions that there was no real proof linking smoking to cancer and that she believed tobacco companies "wouldn't do anything that was really going to kill you."

In the 1970s, in search of a safer cigarette, Rose switched to Philip Morris' Parliaments, based upon advertising from which she concluded that those cigarettes were safe or safer and because the filter was "recessed." In 1974, Cipollone's physician recommended that if she had to smoke, then she should switch to True brand cigarettes, manufactured by Lorillard, Inc. She switched, relying on True ads that indicated that True cigarettes were low in tar and nicotine, which reinforced her view that they were safe or safer than other brands.

Rose was diagnosed with lung cancer in 1981. Even after having been diagnosed with a catastrophic disease, she could not kick the habit. When her cancer required that one of her lungs be removed in 1982, she still smoked occasionally. She ceased smoking only after learning that her cancer was terminal. Cipollone died on October 21, 1984.

Smoking killed Cipollone and the lawsuit that resulted from her death eventually led to accountability for the tobacco industry. Although her case was eventually lost on appeal, her husband won an important victory when, for the first time in history, a jury rendered a monetary verdict against tobacco companies in a smoking related lawsuit. The case also blew apart some of Big Tobacco's smokescreen in the form of documentary evidence that served as a foundation for future cases that lead to industry liability.

New Jersey lawyer Alan M. Darnell was best known for prevailing against asbestos companies, an accomplishment which earned him the first Trial Lawyer of the Year Award in 1983. That same year, Darnell teamed with attorney Marc Edell and his colleague Cynthia Walters, two of the defense lawyers he had opposed in asbestos litigation. It was a creative and potent combination that pushed the tobacco defense lawyers beyond their well-honed abilities to obstruct, stonewall, and obfuscate justice.

Darnell knew that the tobacco companies would fight tenaciously, yet he had no idea of the extremes to which they would go to protect their clients' interests. "We were confronted by a wall of flesh," Darnell recalls. "There were times when two of us would be in a courtroom against more than 40 lawyers on the tobacco company side."

"Scorched earth warfare" does not begin to describe the defense effort that the trial lawyers faced. Defense lawyers, it must be remembered, are generally paid by the hour. It pays for them to make litigation complex, protracted, and expensive. A tobacco defense lawyer once bragged, in a quip reminiscent of

General George S. Patton's famous speech on how to win a war, "We won the case not by spending all of our money, but by making the other son of a bitch spend all of his."

The defense tactic was to win by attrition. Toward that end, the tobacco companies' lawyers made the case as grueling and exhausting as possible. Darnell estimates that the tobacco companies poured between $20-40 million into the costs of defense — not including attorneys' fees. Defense lawyers earned the "big bucks" for a reason: they were very good at their work. During the course of the litigation, the plaintiffs' lawyers endured hundreds of depositions, hundreds of motions, and so many interlocutory appeals that Darnell lost count of how many were actually filed.

"Everything was appealed; everything was fought over," says Darnell. "They deposed everybody that ever knew the Cipollones. They deposed their doctors. They deposed their family members. They deposed their neighbors. The depositions would last days and days. They worked Rose over so hard, they ran her so ragged, it affected her health. We wanted to take her deposition and put her on videotape. By the time we could do that, she was too sick. We had to hire an actress to read her testimony during the trial and all of the questions and answers were those that had been posed by the tobacco lawyers."

The tobacco company played the far-too-usual defense game of "hide the ball," obstructing the production of documents and/or hiding important evidence amid volumes of relatively inconsequential material. The attorneys and their paralegals spent week upon week reviewing documents, until their eyes were glazed. Such an ordeal would be extremely difficult even with today's computers and software programs, but this was the 1980s, before computerization made this tedious but necessary work easier. Just staying organized was an Augean task.

An important sidebar to the litigation was the struggle over whether the trial lawyers could tell the public about newly discovered — and damning — tobacco industry documents. This led to protracted litigation before a federal magistrate sympathetic to the tobacco industry's desire for secrecy, followed by U.S. District Court Judge Lee Sarokin's rulings favoring disclosure, and then by an appearance before the U.S. Court of Appeals for the Third Circuit, which took a friendlier stance toward Big Tobacco.

This tug-of-war began when the trial lawyers uncovered industry documents that belied the public posturing of tobacco company apologists. Defense lawyers sought a protective order mandating secrecy. They had labeled all of the "smoking gun" documents "confidential" and successfully urged the magistrate to restrict the use of the documents to the *Cipollone* case. But Judge Sarokin, citing the First Amendment, reversed the magistrate and entered an order that recognized the public's right to know about the material. The Third Circuit granted defendants a writ of mandate preventing the release of the documents and directing Judge Sarokin to "reconsider" his previous order.

Judge Sarokin reviewed the matter and accepted his duty to "abide by that mandate" while expressing deep concern that the "public interest" was ignored by allowing tobacco companies to maintain secrecy about the danger of their products. Still, the judge ruled that he had some leeway under the writ; he found that protective orders were "never intended to create barriers and discourage litigation against defendants. Good cause [for a protective order] was never intended to make other litigation more difficult, costly, and less efficient." Accordingly, Judge Sarokin, while not allowing the plaintiffs' lawyers to make the documents public, permitted the discovery to be used in "related" or "similar cases subject to the [confidentiality] terms of this order."

This common sense ruling, while keeping the public in the dark, meant that trial lawyers fighting the tobacco wars would not have to reinvent the wheel in each case. Even this was too much for the tobacco defense lawyers. They sought another writ of mandamus and sought to have the Third Circuit boot Judge Sarokin from the case based on his alleged refusal to abide by the higher court ruling. They failed but just barely. In a two-to-one ruling, the Court of Appeals refused the writ and permitted Judge Sarokin to remain on the case.

The trial lawyers had to separate the wheat from the chaff among the volumes of documents they reviewed as they prepared for trial. Because they did not have computers, the lawyers and their staffs had to physically divide the documents they intended to use in trial from those that were of lesser value. Documents that tended to prove the case were called "wild documents" by the legal team. Especially important documents were termed "Wow" documents — evidence that would compel an involuntary exclamation of "Wow!" from the reader. Actually, this was the polite term. The more common term for such vital evidence is a scatological profanity abbreviated as "H.S. documents." Among the most provocative documents was a memo describing cigarettes as "nicotine delivery systems." While this document would have little impact in *Cipollone,* its revelation would be of great benefit to trial lawyers pursuing other tobacco cases in years to come. H.S. indeed.

After intense wrangling, discovery fights, and multiple appeals, the case boiled down to whether the warning labels required by federal law served to inoculate the defendants from liability. The industry's cigarette label defense seems deeply ironic. When warning labels were first proposed, Big Tobacco fought them tooth and tong, watering down the labels to a vague caveat about danger to health rather than the specific alert that smoking causes cancer and other specific diseases. Now the defendants used these very labels as a fig leaf. They asserted that federal preemption defeated the claim that cigarette companies had failed to warn their customers adequately.

After a four-month trial, the jury awarded Rose Cipollone's surviving husband Anthony $400,000. The jury rejected the plaintiffs' fraudulent misrepresentation and conspiracy claims, possibly because tobacco defense lawyers had prevented disclosure of much key evidence. Nevertheless, the jury found that Liggett had breached its duty to warn Rose Cipollone of the dangers of smoking and violated express warranties before 1966. The jury decided that Rose bore 80 percent of the responsibility of the injuries she sustained from smoking.

The relatively low damage award, while disappointing, emboldened trial lawyers to bring more suits against Big Tobacco and to pursue public disclosure of tell-tale industry documents in the process. But the legal aftermath of *Cipollone* did not go smoothly for Anthony Cipollone or his lawyers.

The Liggett Group appealed its defeat. After a tobacco company victory in the U.S. Court of Appeals for the Third Circuit, the U.S. Supreme Court reviewed the case. In June 1992, the Supreme Court reversed the Third Circuit in part and affirmed in part. In an opinion by Justice John Paul Stevens, the Court ruled that the state law on failure to warn was preempted by the 1969 federal legislation that required warning labels to be put on cigarettes. However, the Court found that tobacco company advertising raised the issue of express warranty and that this part of the case could be retried. The Court also ruled that *Cipollone* could proceed at retrial on the claim that tobacco companies had fraudulently misrepresented the safety of smoking in advertising and public statements and on an additional claim that the tobacco companies engaged in a conspiracy to misrepresent the safety of cigarettes.

Even though the case could continue forward, the plaintiffs' legal team was exhausted, physically, emotionally, and financially. Anthony Cipollone had died; the plaintiffs would now be the Cipollone children, who were less than eager to invest many years of their lives in this high-risk, costly war of attrition. Moreover, the plaintiffs' team no longer had the resources to continue the struggle. Not only that, but the Third Circuit had removed Judge Sarokin from a related tobacco case, *Haines v. Liggett Group*, also mounted by Edell, Walters, and Darnell, and the judge had recused himself from *Cipollone*.

The exhausted team finally bowed out. They had nothing left to give. After years of effort, not to mention millions of dollars invested by the plaintiff firms, the tobacco companies ultimately paid not one dime in damages in *Cipollone*.

However, because Rose and Anthony Cipollone were willing to sue Big Tobacco, and because Edell, Walters, and Darnell willingly took on the most daunting of legal struggles, a new day was dawning. The *Cipollone* case would lead to an innovative approach to tobacco industry liability as states and health insurance companies sought to recover the staggering costs associated with paying for smokers' medical care. This, in turn, would lead to the high verdicts and global settlements of recent years. (See Chapters Sixteen and Seventeen.)

The key to this as yet unseen triumph — it cannot be overstated — was the document trail first blazed by lawyers Edell, Walters, and Darnell. For in the bowels of Big Tobacco's own archives would be found ample proof of what many suspected but which the tobacco companies had *known* for decades: that cigarettes are exceedingly dangerous and highly addictive. The fury Judge Sarokin expressed after reviewing volumes of tobacco documents *in camera* — an expression of human emotion that would cause the Third Circuit to remove him from the *Haines* case — eloquently presaged the wider outrage that was soon to come. Learning that tobacco lawyers had abused a tobacco-sponsored scientific institute to conceal the truth about tobacco behind a false shield of attorney-client privilege, Judge Sarokin demanded to know who was responsible:

> Who are these persons who knowingly and secretly decide to put the
> buying public at risk solely for the purpose of making profits and who
> believe that illness and death of consumers is an appropriate cost of
> their own prosperity!

In subsequent years, lawyers, judges, government regulators, and the general public would find out. It would not be pretty, but it would — at long last — bring an end to tobacco company hegemony over the American civil justice system.

Attorneys Darnell, Edell, and Walters thank attorney David Novak for his great assistance in this litigation. The reported decision in this case and its subsequent case history can be found at *Cipollone v. Liggett Group, Inc.*, 693 F.

Supp. 208 (D.N.J. 1988), *aff'd in part and rev'd in part,* 893 F.2d 541 (3rd Cir. 1990), *cert. granted,* 499 U.S. 935 (1991), *aff'd in part and rev'd in part,* 505 U.S. 504 (1992) (recognizing absence of preemption prior to 1969 federal statute, and statute's preemption of failure to warn claims, but no preemption of warranty, fraud, misrepresentation, and conspiracy claims).

Marc Edell

Cynthia Walters

Alan Darnell

CHAPTER SEVEN

1989: The Case That Unraveled the Ponzi Scheme
The Case That Preserved Proposition 103
The Case That Ended Perpetual Institutionalization in Texas

Human Rights *Rappaport v. Suarez-Mason,*
Martinez-Baca v. Suarez-Mason, and *Forti v. Suarez-Mason*

Product Safety *Elliot v. Brunswick Corp.*

Workers' Rights *McKay v. Ashland Oil, Inc.*

Medical Safety *Reilly v. Schneider*

Free Speech *Family Farmers for Prop. 9 v. J.G. Boswell Corp.*

Toxic Injury Prevention *Elam v. Alcolac, Inc.*

Co-Winners
In re Technical Equities
The Case That Unraveled the Ponzi Scheme

Calfarm Insurance Co. v. Deukmajian
The Case That Preserved Proposition 103

Texas Dep't of Mental Health and Retardation v. Petty
**The Case That Ended Perpetual
Institutionalization in Texas**

The 1989 Trial Lawyer of the Year Award finalists promoted human rights, improved product safety, vindicated a corporate whistleblower, put an end to serial medical malpractice, promoted freedom of speech, and helped clean up the environment. In an unusual twist, The TLPJ Foundation named two lawyers. Joe Cotchett of Burlingame, California, received the award for litigating two cases: first, he successfully sued accountants, lawyers, and other professionals who helped perpetrate a far-reaching investment swindle; and second, he worked *pro bono* to protect the constitutionality of Proposition 103, the California initiative that brought out-of-sight insurance rates under reasonable state regulatory control. James C. Harrington of Austin, Texas, shared the Trial Lawyer of the Year Award for pursuing justice for Opal Petty, a woman wrongfully committed in Texas mental institutions for half a century.

Human Rights

Rappaport v. Suarez-Mason, Martinez-Baca v. Suarez-Mason, and *Forti v. Suarez-Mason*

David Cole, Sandra Coliver, Paul L. Hoffman, Ellen L. Lutz, Clara A. Pope, Thomas J. Long, Sam Iffacharoff, Ralph N. Steinhardt, and Juan Mendez

A cadre of attorneys sought to hold Carlos Suarez-Mason, Commander of Argentina's First Army Corps from 1976 to 1979 and a brutal leader of that country's "Dirty War," accountable for the terror tactics that he orchestrated. He controlled all military and security forces in the Province of Buenos Aires, where his forces committed a multitude of human rights violations, including torture, rape, execution of political prisoners, and the kidnapping, or "disappearing," of thousands of people into secret detention centers.

After the downfall of his government, Suarez-Mason fled to California. A team of trial lawyers brought a series of cases against him on behalf of his victims. For the following three cases, the attorneys were justly acknowledged for their work on behalf of international human rights.

Forti v. Suarez-Mason: On February 18, 1977, Argentinean government officials, acting under orders of Suarez-Mason, seized members of Alfredo Forti's family from an airplane as they attempted to escape the oppression of their homeland. The Forti family, including five sons ages 8-16, was taken to a detention center and held incommunicado for nearly a week. The boys were then bound and blindfolded and released onto a Buenos Aires street. Mrs. Forti was put in a different car; she was never seen again. When the brothers inquired about their mother's fate, the Argentine government refused to confirm or deny that she had ever been detained.

The family sought relief against the former military strong man under the Alien Tort Claims Act, which allows non-citizens to file suit in U.S. courts against wrongdoers who violate "the laws of the nations." The Forti family initially found its path to justice blocked on the basis that "disappearances" were not universally condemned. However, by submitting affidavits from eight renowned legal scholars, the trial lawyers convinced the court that an international norm did condemn disappearance of persons as a human rights abuse. Consequently, the court ruled that the abduction of individuals by state officials or agents, followed by official refusals to acknowledge the abductions, constituted an act that could be punished under the Alien Tort Claims Act.

Martinez-Baca v. Suarez-Mason: Argentine attorney Horacio Martinez-Baca sued Suarez-Mason for ordering his arbitrary detention and torture. For four years, Martiniz-Baca was beaten on his feet, subjected to electrical shocks to his genitals, and pummeled on his head and chest until he collapsed. In a default judgment against the defendant, the plaintiff was awarded $1.17 million in lost income and $20 million for pain and suffering and punitive damages.

Rappaport v. Suarez-Mason: The litigation team's efforts culminated in this Alien Tort Claims Act suit on behalf of the wives of two men tortured and killed in prison and the siblings of a "disappeared" person. In a default judgment, the plaintiffs were awarded $60 million in compensatory and punitive damages.

These three cases helped to establish a common law permitting redress for international human rights abuses. Unfortunately, the plaintiffs have never been able to collect their judgments. Attempts to do so remain ongoing. Suarez-Mason's life, however, was made significantly more difficult by the publicity surrounding these cases. Argentina extradited him after he was sued in the U.S. He was pardoned in 1990. In 1996, he was charged with making an anti-Semitic remark — which is against Argentine law — and $1,500 of his assets were frozen. In December 1999, he was arrested again on charges of human rights violations for the theft of young children of the "disappeared." An Italian court convicted him in *absentia* of kidnapping and murder and sentenced him in *absentia* to life in prison.

Litigation team members included David Cole of the Center for Constitutional Rights in New York; Sandra Coliver of Human Rights Advocates in Berkeley, California; Los Angeles attorneys Paul L. Hoffman and Clara A. "Zazi" Pope of the ACLU Foundation of Southern California; Ellen L. Lutz of the Lawyers' Committee for Human Rights; Thomas J. Long of Morrison & Foerster in San Francisco; and Washington, D.C., attorneys Sam Iffacharoff of Gurerrieri, Edmund and James, Ralph N. Steinhardt of George Washington University School of Law, and Juan Mendez of Americas Watch.

A reported decision in the third case can be found at *Forti v. Suarez-Mason,* 694 F. Supp. 707 (N.D. Cal. 1988).

David Cole

Sandra Coliver

Ellen L. Lutz

Clara A. Pope

Sam Iffacharoff

Ralph N. Steinhardt

Product Safety
Elliot v. Brunswick Corp .
R. Ben Hogan, III

Fourteen-year-old Ashley Elliot and her teenage friends celebrated their initiation into an Alabama high school club by jumping from a lighted pier into the Tennessee River on July 24, 1982. As the girls plunged into the water, a teenage boy in a nearby speedboat pulled away from the pier. The boat fishtailed and its propeller struck Elliot four times, gashing her right leg and buttock, severing crucial nerves. She survived, but her injuries required multiple surgeries, leaving the teenager disfigured and faced with the possibility of future amputation.

Attorney Ben Hogan of Birmingham, Alabama, argued that her injuries could have been entirely prevented if the boat manufacturer, Mercury Division of Brunswick Corporation, had installed a safety device known as a "propeller guard" on the motor. Experts for the plaintiffs claimed that the guard was feasible and available and that it could have prevented many boat propeller injuries — all without materially impairing the performance or utility of pleasure boats.

Mercury's defense counsel argued that the judicial system was not qualified to analyze the "conscious" design choices made by the company. Mercury claimed that propeller guards would make boats more dangerous because guards cover a greater area of water than does an unguarded propeller and could arguably increase the likelihood of collision. The company stated that guards cause worse injuries at high speeds than do unprotected propellers.

Hogan countered by proving that practical and effective propeller guards had been available since 1978. At least one guard had been found to protect swimmers, enable boats to beach without damage to the propeller, and have no appreciable effect on steering or speed. The guard was so successful that by 1988 it was used by the U.S. Marines, U.S. Navy, U.S. Army, U.S. Coast Guard (USCG), and rescue services. Moreover, Hogan proved that if the relatively inexpensive guards had been in place, 80-90 percent of serious prop injuries in Alabama since 1979 could have been prevented.

Hogan revealed that Mercury had never instituted a research and development program to explore the potential for propeller guards and that its efforts in the field were essentially limited to the defensive measure of seeking to prove, when sued, that guards do not work or were flawed. The jury awarded $1.5 million in compensatory damages, and $3 million in punitive damages.

Unfortunately, after Hogan was honored for his achievement, the U.S. Court of Appeals for the Eleventh Circuit reversed the decision. Several federal courts have ruled that the Federal Boat Safety Act preempts people injured by unguarded boat propellers from suing the manufacturer. The issue is still being litigated in the courts.

Meanwhile, unguarded boat propellers continue to cause serious injuries and claim lives unnecessarily. At least 447 recreational boaters suffered injury and nine died as a result of being struck by a motor or propeller between 1995-1998, according to the USCG. However, the federal agency points out that the full extent of injuries caused by propeller guards is unknown due to under-reporting. For example, the USCG recorded only one propeller-related fatality nationwide in 1997. However, a 1998 study by the Texas Department of Health and the Texas Parks and Wildlife Department investigated injuries that resulted from propeller strikes in just four lakes during the peak boating season in the summer of 1997. The state agencies found 13 persons who sustained propeller-related injuries, including three who died. Based on a comparison of these findings with those of the USCG, the study concluded that "severe boat-propeller related injuries may be more common than previously reported."

The later decision in this case and its subsequent case history can be found at *Elliot v. Brunswick Corp.*, 903 F.2d 1505 (11th Cir. 1990) (reversing jury verdict and ordering judgment for defendant), *cert. denied*, 498 U.S. 1048 (1991).

R. Ben Hogan, III

Workers' Rights
McKay v. Ashland Oil, Inc.
John McCall, David Tachau, Kenneth Robinson, and Anthony Fitch

Whistleblowers provide an essential check and balance to the abuse of government and corporate power. Maybe that explains why they are so viciously attacked by those who prefer secrecy and silence to public accountability — and why whistleblowers often need the assistance of legal counsel.

Ashland Oil vice presidents Bill E. McKay, Jr., and Harry D. Williams both objected when their company decided that bribery was the best way to access a new oil reserve in Oman. But the company "invested" $29 million in an African chromium mine controlled by a powerful official of Oman in exchange for access to Omani crude oil.

McKay's and Williams' complaints about the transaction, which eventually amounted to $46 million in payments, led the Securities and Exchange Commission (SEC) and Congress to investigate the Omani *quid pro quo.* Ashland settled with the SEC without admitting guilt by agreeing not to bribe overseas officials in the future. Soon thereafter, Ashland fired McKay and Williams.

Convinced that they lost their jobs because of their principled opposition to corporate crime, the two hired Louisville, Kentucky, attorneys John McCall and David Tachau of Brown, Todd & Heyburn, and Kenneth Robinson and Anthony Fitch of Donahue, Ehrmantraut & Montedonico. The four attorneys, outraged at the treatment of their whistle-blowing clients, launched a brilliant and aggressive litigation campaign. Not only did they sue Ashland and some of its officers and executives for wrongful termination, but also for violating the Federal Racketeering Influenced and Corrupt Organizations Act (RICO). Specifically, they charged that Ashland engaged in a pattern of illegal interstate activity to obtain oil in the late 1970s and early 1980s that led to the dismissals of McKay and Williams. Ashland's defense was that its past business practices were commonplace.

The jury found that Ashland's payments were bribes and that the former vice presidents had been fired for failing to acquiesce in this unlawful conduct. It awarded the plaintiffs $69.5 million. This was more than double the amount that the plaintiffs had requested and was among the largest verdicts ever in Kentucky. Ashland appealed, but then settled for $25 million.

There is no reported decision on the merits in this case.

John McCall   *David Tachau*   *Kenneth Robinson*   *Anthony Fitch*

Medical Safety
Reilly v. Schneider
Larry S. Stewart, David Bianchi, and Gary Fox

Trial lawyers came under attack in the 1980s for causing the medical malpractice insurance crisis by supposedly bringing frivolous lawsuits against innocent
doctors. That charge resonated with the public, particularly with physicians
complaining loudly and publicly about abrupt and draconian hikes in their
malpractice insurance premiums. The ugly truth is that malpractice exists, and
with the medical profession unable or unwilling to police itself adequately,
civil justice is often the only recourse for and deterrent to wrongful medical
conduct. Miami attorneys Larry S. Stewart, David Bianchi, and Gary Fox, who
successfully sued orthopedic surgeon Dr. Aaron Schneider and Humana
Hospital of St. Petersburg, Florida provided this necessary service.

In March 1981, Dr. Schneider traveled to Hawaii to observe three Posterior
Lumbar Innerbody Fusion (PLIF) surgeries. The PLIF is a delicate and complex
back procedure undertaken only by the most skilled surgeons. On the basis of
this observation, and with no hands-on experience in the procedure, Dr.
Schneider returned to St. Petersburg and set himself up as an expert on PLIF.
He began conducting "back seminars" in which prospective patients were
sold on the operation as a good remedy for their back pain. He even wheeled a
former patient in to the room, had her get out of a wheelchair, and walk as if
he were a religious healer. Only instead of a "healing from God," seminar
attendees were told that the miracle was PLIF.

Dr. Schneider applied to Humana Hospital for permission to perform the
surgery. He also required special tools for the procedure. He obtained both
after two quick meetings with the hospital's review committee, which never
investigated his experience or competency to perform the procedure. The committee's main concern was financial: the hospital required Dr. Schneider to
hold the hospital free and harmless from any damage awards awarded to
injured patients.

In the following years, Dr. Schneider performed a number of unnecessary
and unwarranted PLIF procedures and related surgeries. He also performed
the procedure at the wrong levels of the spine.

In a bizarre twist, Dr. Schneider obtained material for bone pegs, which he
used in the procedure to fuse vertebrae, by creating a macabre "bone bank."
According to his own testimony, he purchased hip bones from the local
morgue, brought them home where he cut them up in his garage, then hosed

them off in his yard with a garden hose, "double bagged them," and stored them in the kitchen freezer. Repeatedly, he left these bone pegs protruding into patients' spinal canals and nerve roots. Patients were left in excruciating pain, with major nerve damage, significant disability, and impotence.

Nothing was done to stop the carnage until attorneys Stewart, Bianchi, and Fox began filing lawsuits. On behalf of six former patients, the lawyers uncovered and exposed the outrageous conduct of Dr. Schneider and Humana Hospital. They obtained more than $7 million in verdicts on behalf of the victims. As a result, Dr. Schneider no longer performs the PLIF procedure. The case also led to an investigation by the State Department of Professional Regulation.

There is no reported decision on the merits in this case.

Larry S. Stewart

David Bianchi

Gary Fox

Free Speech
Family Farmers for Prop. 9 v. J.G. Boswell Corp.
Ralph Wegis

Attorney Ralph Wegis is a nationally known legal warrior against the pernicious corporate strategy of curbing individual freedom of speech by filing actions known as Strategic Lawsuits Against Public Participation (SLAPP). Wegis helped pioneer a potent antidote to the SLAPP — the "SLAPP-back suit."

A small group of California farmers supported the building of the Peripheral Canal, which would have brought increased water from the Sacramento River Delta to the agricultural region of California's Central Valley. The issue was before California voters in an initiative known as Proposition 9, a measure adamantly opposed by the J.G. Boswell Company, an agricultural corporate giant.

"Family Farmers" entered the campaign with gusto, printing advertisements in several California newspapers stating that Boswell and another agricultural corporation opposed Proposition 9, because it would benefit small farms. The farmers asserted, "If the small farms go out of business, Boswell and Salyer will be able to dominate California agriculture, setting prices where they want them."

In response, J.G. Boswell Co. sued the group, naming as defendants three farmers and 1,000 "John Does." By listing so many unspecified defendants, the corporation intended to send a message that others who joined the Family Farmers would do so at their own legal peril. The company charged that the Family Farmers' ad accused the company of price fixing.

The SLAPP worked. Contributions to the farmer's group immediately dried up, and it ceased all campaign operations. Insurance companies for the individual farmers threatened to terminate coverage, warned them to cease all political advocacy, and levied a 50 percent deductible on future claims. Formerly vocal on water issues in the Central Valley, the farmers were suddenly silent.

The libel suit was eventually thrown out in court. But attorney Wegis of Bakersfield, California's Klein, Wegis & Duggan wanted to press the issue of free speech even further. So he filed a SLAPP-back suit, which became known as the "David v. Goliath case." The plaintiffs argued that the company's original claim was not filed based on the merits of the case, but to use the legal system to gag the farmers. The jury agreed. It awarded $13.5 million in actual and punitive damages, sending a resounding message that the powerful misuse of the legal system to stifle political debate is at their own peril.

There is no reported decision on the merits in this case.

Ralph Wegis

Toxic Injury Prevention
Elam v. Alcolac, Inc.
Lantz Welch

Alcolac, Inc. fired up its Sedalia, Missouri, plant in May 1978 to produce chemicals used in plastics, cosmetics, soaps, and textiles. Immediately, the company's neighbors noticed noxious odors. Soon far more serious problems became obvious. Chemical and soap residues leaked from the plant and "foam storms" up to 20 feet high blew across neighborhoods. Health problems abounded, ranging from nose, eye, and respiratory tract infections to liver and nervous system ailments. The citizens first complained to government at the local, state, and federal levels. Receiving no meaningful assistance, they turned in desperation to trial lawyer Lantz Welch of Kansas City, Missouri.

Welch faced enormous problems. While residents were undoubtedly suffering, he needed to pinpoint which of the numerous chemicals discharged from the plant were causing which specific health complaints. Moreover, proving that the discharges caused the injuries and going head-to-head with extremely well-financed corporate defense lawyers would be not be easy, considering that Welch had a small law office.

Welch's first task was to bring in reinforcements. Welch filed suit on behalf of 31 Sedalia residents with the help of local lawyers Timothy Brake and Grant Davis of Lantz Welch; J. Kirk Rahm of Rahm & Rahm; Charles Fairchild, Jr., of Fairchild, Fairchild and Beal; and J.R. Hobbs of Linde, Thornson, Lanworthy, Kohn & Van Dyke.

The trial took four and a half months with testimony and evidence adduced from 165 witnesses, hundreds of documents, and tens of thousands of recorded transcript pages. Expert testimony covered a wide range of issues, including environmental medicine, epidemiology, immunology, industrial hygiene, internal medicine, pharmacology, and toxicology. At the conclusion of the trial, the jury awarded $200,000 in compensatory damages and $43 million in punitive damages. The trial judge, however, ruled that a new trial on damages would be required. Both sides appealed.

On March 14, 1989, the Missouri Court of Appeals affirmed the finding of liability and in a landmark 371-page ruling laid down a roadmap for prosecuting future toxic tort cases. The evidence, the Court found, clearly proved that the company was "reckless and utterly indifferent to the rights of plaintiffs." The matter was returned to the trial court for retrial. After further litigation, Alcolac went out of business.

The reported decision in this case and its subsequent case history can be found at *Elam v. Alcolac, Inc.*, 765 S.W.2d 42 (Mo. Ct. App. 1988), *cert. denied*, 493 U.S. 817 (1989).

Lantz Welch

1989 Trial Lawyer of the Year Award Co-Winner
Joseph W. Cotchett
The Case That Unraveled the Ponzi Scheme

When unscrupulous financiers, aided by well-known and respected accountants, lawyers, and banks, con consumers into purchasing worthless stock, the consequences to individual investors can be devastating. That's what happened in the Technical Equities scam.

Harold Stern, founder and former Chief Executive Officer of Technical Equities, smooth-talked thousands of people into investing their savings in his high-flying real estate investment firm from 1976 through 1985. Stern's business plan was modeled after the classic con known as a "Ponzi scheme." Named after Charles A. Ponzi, who cheated hundreds of investors during the 1920s, the investment scam is often effective because it seems to investors that they are earning huge returns very quickly.

However, the returns do not come from good investing or business successes, but from other investors who have also been promised high returns. In other words, Victim A is paid a return on his or her investment by part of the money invested into the scam by Victim B, who in return is paid money as a return on investment by the funds of Victim C and so on. Having done very well for themselves, the early victims, now feeling confident in the "investment," often increase the size of their investments and, wishing to share their opportunity with others they care about, may also bring their friends and relatives into the scheme.

Soon, the Ponzi business is really raking it in. Meanwhile, the promoter milks the sweet deal for all it is worth: he or she lives it up on other people's money, socks money away in secret bank accounts, and buys property. Eventually the "business" can no longer maintain regular payments to investors and the empty shell collapses of its own weight — or the con artist skips town

> *What is public justice? Accountants, lawyers, bankers, and other professionals are held accountable when they help further fraudulent investment schemes.*

— leaving cheated victims with nothing to show for their dreams but empty bank accounts and broken lives.

Stern masterminded a Ponzi scheme that ran wild for several years in Northern California under the name of Technical Equities Corporation (TEC). Stern, an attorney and accountant, began his nefarious scheme by establishing an investment club as an offshoot of his tax preparation business, which eventually became Stern Management Associates (SMA).

"Stern staffed the fledgling company with bookkeepers who were still students at San Jose State University," Cotchett wrote in his book *The Ethics Gap*, in which he describes the case. "They were cheap, hungry, and didn't know enough to ask questions. They were also good window dressing, giving SMA a fully staffed look at a fraction of the cost of real bookkeepers. Illusion would prove to be Harry Stern's most enduring quality."

Stern eventually outgrew SMA and formed TEC, which bought and bled small manufacturing firms of their credit and equity, and left them dead in a file. Here's where the Ponzi scheme came into play: instead of buying the firms with cash, Stern paid in TEC stock and notes. Then Stern went to his pool of investors and sold them the company or real estate, leaving himself as the trustee to manage all the assets. That left Stern in control of all of the assets of the new company, plus the cash the investors paid to buy the business at his recommendation. Finally, Stern borrowed to the hilt, using these assets as collateral.

Some of the nation's most respected financial institutions lent their names in support of TEC as referral sources for investors. Referrals came from such trusted companies as Security Pacific National Bank, the accounting firm of KMG Main Hurdman, the brokerage firm of Bear Sterns and Co., and Bank of the West. With such solid financial entities backing Stern, it is no wonder so many investors fell victim to fraud.

For years, Stern took in money and assets and borrowed against them. It was a sweet deal for him — and an unmitigated disaster for individual investors. When the scheme finally collapsed, auditors could not account for

$100 million in investors' funds. While he did serve a few years in prison, Stern never paid back a dime of the money he bilked from his investors.

When investors approached trial lawyer Joseph W. Cotchett of Cotchett, Pitre & Simon for help, he decided that the major companies who had lent their good names to the support of TEC should pay the price, not the cheated investors. He sued Stern and TEC, which declared bankruptcy. Cotchett also sued Security Pacific Bank, KMG, Bear Sterns, and, as he puts it, "too many lawyers to list," in one of the largest fraud cases California had ever known.

Usually such cases take years. Cotchett realized that his clients, many of whom were elderly, did not have that kind of time. Two of the cheated victims, Bob and Thelma Scott, died by double suicide because Bob had been defrauded of the money to pay for Thelma's nursing home care. To hasten public justice Cotchett demanded a trial within 90 days, as was permitted under the California Code of Civil Procedure. This bold and innovative move caught the defense lawyers by surprise.

"It was pandemonium when I came up with that motion," Cotchett recalls with a chuckle. "The day I filed the papers, my phone rang off the hook from defense lawyers saying, 'Joe, why are you doing this?' One lawyer even complained that his billing would be impacted adversely."

But Cotchett was not in the business of padding corporate defense lawyers' bank accounts. The trial lawyer wanted to obtain redress for investors without the usual obstructionism, obfuscation, or endless delays.

A jury heard evidence on how seven "test clients" — from among the 600 consumers Cotchett represented — were swindled. The three-month trial involved more than four million documents. This was one of the first trials in which a lawyer used computer-operated document projections in the courtroom, a technological breakthrough that has since become commonplace.

The defrauded investors received a compensatory damage award of $6.8 million plus a punitive damage award of $147 million against TEC for the seven test cases — the largest punitive damage award in California until that time. However, TEC had no money. Therefore, what counted was obtaining redress from the institutional defendants. Reading the handwriting on the wall, before trial, several banks and brokerage houses settled for $60 million. The subsequent cases against the banks, attorneys, brokers, and appraisers settled for almost 100 cents on the dollar. In the end, most of the investors got nearly all their money back.

Cotchett's efforts provided badly needed redress for defrauded investors and spurred further investigations into similar frauds throughout the state and nation. On the downside, alarmed by Cotchett's deft use of the California Code of Civil Procedure to gain a swift trial, business forces lobbied the legislature to amend the statute to permit preferential setting of a trial date only if the moving party demonstrates that the *health* of a 70-year-old or older plaintiff is such that a preference is necessary to prevent prejudice to the party's interest in the litigation.

"They called it the Cotchett Amendment," the lawyer says ruefully. Apparently, some powerful corporate players did not appreciate Cotchett's pandemonium-causing maneuver as much as his consumer clients did.

There is no reported decision on the merits in this case.

Joseph W. Cotchett

1989 Trial Lawyer of the Year Award Co-Winner
Joseph W. Cotchett
The Case That Preserved Proposition 103

I f the Technical Equities fraud case had been the only lawsuit that Joe Cotchett handled in 1989, he would have richly deserved honors as one of the nation's top trial lawyers. Yet he also fought successfully to save the consumer-friendly Proposition 103 from a powerful and concerted attack by the automobile insurance industry.

The passage by California voters in 1988 of Proposition 103 was a watershed event in the relationship between consumers and auto insurance companies. The measure, a reaction to inflated automobile and casualty insurance rates, infuriated an insurance industry that was used to having its way with state insurance regulators. The initiative's pro-consumer provisions included a mandated 20 percent discount for good drivers; a 20 percent rollback on rates since November 1987; a requirement that insurance rates be based on driving records instead of residence; and transformation of the state office of insurance commissioner to an elective, rather than an appointed, post.

Proposition 103 received more than 50 percent of the vote, despite the fact that its grassroots proponents, led by Ralph Nader's Voter Revolt Project, had a campaign budget of only $2 million to defeat the insurance industry's $70 million effort to stifle rate reform.

What is public justice? Courts respect the right of voters to approve initiatives that protect them from unfair business practices.

However, the insurance industry did not let the battle end when Proposition 103 passed. Arguing that the initiative violated due process of law because it would improperly take money out of their pockets, insurance companies predicted catastrophic consequences for both carriers and the insurance-buying public and fought to have the initiative declared unconstitutional. When they filed suit, the California courts stopped Proposition 103 from taking effect.

Cotchett realized that the defense of Proposition 103 was in trouble because of a lack of resources to battle against the concerted attack by the deep-pocketed insurance industry. So he agreed to work *pro bono,* alongside other attorneys, including Proposition 103 author Harvey Rosenfield and Professor Karl Manheim of Loyola Law School. The team had to work fast. Because it was a constitutional challenge, the litigation went directly before the California Supreme Court.

"It was a massive effort," Cotchett recalls. "We had to dig through millions of insurance company documents at the Department of Insurance. We only had a few months' time to put in what was essentially years' worth of work. We would practice law during the day and then work on the case until midnight, putting the briefs together. It was a nightmare, but it had to be done."

The case was also highly political. The Court was primarily Republican and often voted pro-business. That meant Cotchett had to lead a public relations battle as well as conduct an intense appellate litigation.

"The real world of law is often as politically oriented as it is about the law," Cotchett says. "We had to be sure and put out there in as public a fashion as we could that the voters had passed this measure, that it would be wrong for the decision to be narrowly based on some minor technicalities, as urged by the insurance companies. We also argued that the constitution did not protect any right of the insurance industry to gouge the public. So, we put the political banner out there and waved it high."

Cotchett argued the case before the California Supreme Court in March 1989, only four months after the election. The Court issued its unanimous ruling on May 9, 1988, in favor of the pro-consumer initiative. Based on a balancing test that weighed the burden on the insurance industry against the benefit to the commonweal, all but one minor provision, which the court ruled was severable from the balance of the measure, was left intact. Insurance companies that found the new law too onerous could cease selling insurance in California or apply for relief from "confiscatory" rates by showing how the rate cuts might prevent them from earning a "fair and reasonable return." The Court stated, "In view of these safeguards, we conclude that...the provisions of Proposition 103 relating to the setting of insurance rates, and procedures for adjustment of rates, do not on their face deprive insurers of due process under the state or federal Constitutions."

That ruling would not end the legal contest over Proposition 103, but it was probably the most important legal victory on the road to the initiative's eventual implementation.

The reported decision in this case can be found at *Calfarm Insurance Co. v. Deukmajian,* 771 P.2d 1247 (Cal. 1989).

1989 Trial Lawyer of the Year Award Co-Winner
James C. Harrington
The Case That Ended Perpetual
Institutionalization in Texas

Opal Petty was a shy, troubled 15-year-old girl in 1934, when her father committed her to a Texas mental hospital. Although there was no adequate evaluation or explanation of why her father and the State shut her away, Petty would remain institutionalized, unnoticed and without due process, for more than half a century.

Over the years, the State's diagnoses of what allegedly ailed Opal varied wildly from schizophrenic and mentally ill to not mentally ill, from mentally retarded to not mentally retarded. No one considered releasing her, nor did she receive a legal hearing to determine whether the State had a right to hold her. The State provided Petty no rehabilitative treatment during this time, but put her to work in an institutional laundry for a nominal weekly wage of two dollars. The forced confinement without proven cause and the compulsory drudge work without reasonable compensation meant that essentially, her labor amounted to peonage.

Petty was liberated from her bleak existence by her nephew Clint Denson and his wife Linda Kaufman who first learned of her existence through a casual reference at a family reunion picnic. The news that Denson had a long-lost aunt stunned him. He and his wife found Petty at the San Angelo State School in San Angelo, Texas. When the couple first visited Petty, they were shocked and dismayed to see her abysmal living conditions. Petty, whose hair was matted and filthy, wore ragged clothing and even her purse had patches. Worse, she was living with patients far below her intellectual level. Denson told the *Austin American-Statesman* that he was appalled that institution officials "weren't even aware she could read or write." Denson and Kaufman learned this significant fact only when Opal began reading a magazine to them.

> *What is public justice? The state is barred from using mental hospitals to confine people who are not mentally ill.*

Opal began to correspond with her newly found family, complaining of her lonely life and asking to come home. Due to their intervention and the recognition by Texas officials that Opal did not require institutionalization, she was released to a group home and soon was living with Denson and Kaufman.

Petty and her family consulted with attorney James C. Harrington, then the Director of the Texas Civil Liberties Union in Austin, Texas. Harrington and co-counsel Deborah Hiser of Advocacy Inc., filed a claim for damages on behalf of Opal and a class action lawsuit on behalf of other wrongfully institutionalized mental health patients held without regular legal review to determine whether their forced confinement was justified.

Harrington was disgusted at what his investigation unearthed. "Electric shock treatment was pretty standard," Harrington says. "And the patients were living in these big dorms, by which I mean just big rooms with beds in them. There was a tremendous amount of sexual abuse going on, and a lot of physical abuse by the guards. The food was terrible, there was no air conditioning. They were kept locked up in their units. It was just awful."

Texas officials fought the suits, in Harrington's words, "tooth and nail." "They mounted every discovery block they could think of to delay the case," Harrington says. "I believe they even intentionally 'mistrialed' the case when the State's trial lawyer spoke loudly about federal government checks Opal received — loud enough for the jury to hear — during a bench conference. In my entire career, I never saw anything like it. The judge was fit to be tied, but it worked effectively to delay the case."

When the case proceeded again to trial, a psychiatrist testified that Petty should not have been hospitalized for more than six months for depression. The doctor also testified that she had developed "institutionalization syndrome" from the poverty and bleakness of her environment and that this caused her to withdraw, lose cognitive skills, communication abilities, and motivation. Therefore, her forced confinement caused symptoms that led to personality difficulties which, in the minds of those responsible for her, justified her further confinement.

On May 2, 1989, a Travis County jury awarded Opal $505,000 in damages against the Texas Department Mental Health and Retardation to compensate her for 52 years of forced confinement (37 in state hospitals and 15 in state schools), during which she never received a legal review to determine whether she belonged in forced care. The publicity generated from the trial and the related class action changed Texas law. No longer would hospitalized mental health patients be confined involuntarily without regular legal review. These changes led to the release of other patients who had been confined for many years without legal review. For example, one woman was released into a nursing home after spending 50 years behind hospital walls without legal review.

Petty's $505,000 verdict did not survive. The trial court reduced the award to $250,000 under the Texas Tort Claims Act (TTCA), a "tort reform" measure that capped the State's liability for damages. The State appealed even the reduced damage award all the way to the State's highest court.

On December 31, 1992, the Texas Supreme Court affirmed the verdict, as reduced by the trial court. Petty used the money to build a small house on her nephew's property.

The later decision in this case can be found at *Texas Dep't of Mental Health and Retardation v. Petty*, 848 S.W.2d 680 (Tex. 1990) (affirming judgment against state).

James C. Harrington

CHAPTER EIGHT

1990: The Case of the Indentured Mental Patients

Human Rights *Domingo v. Republic of the Philippines*

Government Accountability *Taylor ex rel. Walker v. Ledbetter*

Toxic Injury Prevention *Dow Chem. Co. v. Alfaro*

Government Accountability *Rastello v. City of Torrance*

Workers' Rights *United Steelworkers of America v. Phelps Dodge Corp.*

Winner
Orr v. Sonnenburg
The Case of the Indentured Mental Patients

The finalists for the 1990 Trial Lawyer of the Year Award fought for human rights and workers' rights, protected the safety of children, stood steadfast against American corporations dumping toxic waste in other countries, and exposed police misconduct. Trial Lawyer of the Year Award winners Terrance Smith and Anthony DeBonis proved that Indiana's mental hospitals were essentially treating patients as indentured servants, forcing them to work for the State without compensation.

Human Rights
Domingo v. Republic of the Philippines
Michael E. Withey

In 1981, labor activists Silme Domingo and Gene Viernes were gunned down in the streets of Seattle. One month earlier, the pair had successfully lobbied the International Longshoremen's and Warehouseman's Union (ILWU) to pass a resolution condemning the Marcos regime and establishing a union task force to monitor brutality against labor unions in the Philippines. Three local Filipino gang members were convicted for the murders, but the families of Domingo and Viernes suspected that the Marcos regime had instigated the killings. They approached Seattle attorney Michael E. Withey, who represented ILWU Local 37 and was a friend of the victims. Withey vowed to hold Marcos accountable.

In 1982, Withey filed suit against Marcos, his wife Imelda, and a list of their operatives in the U.S. and the Philippines, alleging that the Marcos government had ordered the killings as part of a broad conspiracy to "surveil, harass and intimidate" Marcos' political opponents residing in the U.S. This marked the beginning of an eight-year struggle for justice.

Withey was so committed to the cause that, for two years, with the assistance of the Committee for Justice for Domingo and Viernes, he ceased private practice to investigate the murders. The investigation ultimately pieced together a complex series of events that climaxed in the killings, exposing a 14-year program to track and neutralize anti-Marcos activists in the United States. Trial Lawyers for Public Justice assisted in the investigation.

The case was tried in November 1989. Withey laid out the extraordinary evidence he had developed. The dramatic high point of the trial came in a videotaped deposition of Ferdinand Marcos himself, taken in Hawaii before his death. In the deposition, Marcos admitted that he operated an intelligence network in the U.S., but he claimed it was nonviolent. However, in response to specific questions about his connections to and control over his operatives, Marcos asserted his Fifth Amendment privilege against self-incrimination.

After a three-week trial, the six-member jury reached a unanimous verdict in less than a day's deliberation, finding that Ferdinand and Imelda Marcos had conspired to murder Silme Domingo and Gene Viernes. The damage award exceeded $20 million. After the verdict, the prosecutor's office investigated and brought charges against Marcos ally Tony Baruso for conspiring to commit the murders. Withey testified at Baruso's criminal trial, which resulted in a life sentence for Baruso.

The reported decision in this case and its subsequent case history can be found at *Domingo v. Republic of the Philippines,* 694 F. Supp. 782 (W.D. Wash. 1988) (denying motion to dismiss), *appeal dismissed,* 895 F.2d 1416 (9th Cir. 1990).

Michael E. Withey

Government Accountability
Taylor ex rel. Walker v. Ledbetter
Don C. Keenan

Georgia social workers removed one-year-old Kathy Jo Taylor from her mother's home in 1982, based on her grandmother's reports of child abuse. The baby girl was not placed with her grandmother, but with strangers — and the state made no effort to determine whether the grandmother's home would be a suitable environment.

Less than a year later, Taylor's foster mother shook her, beat her, and threw her to the floor because she soiled her diaper. The infant lapsed into a coma.

Taylor's family approached Atlanta attorney Don C. Keenan for help. Taking the case *pro bono*, Keenan saw an opportunity to protect other similarly situated children throughout the state. He filed suit in U.S. District Court in Atlanta in February 1984, asserting that children have a constitutional right to proper oversight and protection when in state custody. The complaint contended that the State of Georgia should be held accountable for failing to place Taylor with her family and for not properly screening her foster mother.

The court dismissed the case, ruling that state agencies were immune from suit for failing to take action. A three-judge panel of the U.S. Court of Appeals for the Eleventh Circuit affirmed the decision. Keenan petitioned for, and the court granted, an *en banc* hearing. The Eleventh Circuit *en banc* panel then ruled that the state had violated Taylor's civil rights by failing to protect her. It also agreed with Keenan's argument that state regulations governing cases such as Taylor's did not satisfy due process requirements. The court, therefore, opened the door to suits against state officials by children injured in the foster care system.

The State of Georgia settled the case and signed a consent decree changing the state's entire foster care system. The agreement prohibited the corporal punishment of foster children, required caseworkers to give first priority to placing foster children with relatives, established screening procedures for foster parents, and promulgated a minimum standard of oversight between case workers and foster children.

The reported decision in this case can be found at *Taylor ex rel. Walker v. Ledbetter,* 818 F.2d 791 (11th Cir. 1987) (*en banc*), *cert. denied,* 489 U.S. 1065 (1989).

Don C. Keenan

Toxic Injury Prevention
Dow Chem. Co. v. Alfaro
Charles Siegel

Every year, American chemical manufacturers ship to developing countries thousands of tons of toxic chemicals and dangerous products that are banned in the U.S. The process is called "dumping." Knowing that they are not injuring Americans and that foreigners usually cannot sue in U.S. courts, companies often disregard the potential damage that their dumped products can cause. Unlike U.S. courts, the courts in most other countries do not award punitive damages, have weaker product liability standards, and rarely provide jury trials for civil matters. As a result, many companies treat injuries and deaths in developing companies as mere costs of doing business.

Dallas attorney Charles Siegel represented 30 Costa Rican farmers who claimed that they became sterile due to exposure to a pesticide banned in the U.S., but sold abroad by Dow Chemical and Shell Oil. Domestic production of the pesticide, known as DBCP, ended in 1977 when it was linked to sterility in American chemical plant workers. But Dow Chemical and Shell Oil, two of the largest producers of DBCP, continued to sell their remaining stocks of the pesticide to Standard Fruit of Costa Rica, a subsidiary of Dole Fresh Fruit Company, for use in Central America.

A Costa Rican toxicologist linked an increased incidence of sterility and other conditions in banana workers to the use of the pesticide. He brought it to the attention of Dallas attorney Russell Budd, who realized that Costa Rican courts would provide the workers with little, if any, compensation. Budd filed suit in Florida state court, then contacted Siegel to search for other possible American venues in which to file suit.

Siegel filed suit in both California and Texas state courts, considering them the least likely to dismiss the claims on the basis of forum *non conveniens*. The defendants succeeded in removing both the Florida and California cases to federal courts and getting the cases dismissed on forum *non conveniens* grounds. Although the Texas case was initially removed to federal court, the federal judge remanded it back to state court because Shell Oil's corporate headquarters and Dow Chemical's largest manufacturing plant were in Texas. Like the federal courts, the Texas trial court dismissed the case on the basis of forum *non conveniens.*

Siegel appealed, invoking a 1913 Texas statute which, he argued, opened up the courts to plaintiffs injured by Texas corporations in other jurisdictions. The Texas Court of Appeals agreed with Siegel, as did the Texas Supreme Court in a 5-4 decision. Siegel's victory helped to hold these and U.S. corporations accountable for their wrongdoing overseas.

The reported decision in this case and its subsequent case history can be found at *Dow Chem. Co. v. Alfaro*, 786 S.W.2d 674 (Tex. 1990), *cert. denied*, 498 U.S. 1024 (1991).

Charles Siegel

Government Accountability
Rastello v. City of Torrance
Browne Greene, Brian Panish, and Timothy Rastello

Near midnight on August 30, 1984, Torrance, California, Police Sergeant Rollo Green was returning home after a night of heavy drinking. While driving home, he struck 19-year-old Kelly Rastello's motorcycle, killing the young man. Even though the investigating police officers found Sergeant Green disoriented and smelling of alcohol, he was not arrested or charged.

In an outrageous attempt to turn the victim into the cause of the tragedy, members of the Torrance Police Department told Rastello's parents that their son had been speeding and had run into the back of Green's truck. Suspecting a cover-up, Kelly Rastello's older brother, Timothy Rastello, a partner with the law firm of Holland & Hart in Denver, retained Browne Greene and Brian Panish of Greene, Broillet, Taylor & Wheeler in Los Angeles to uncover the truth. It took the attorneys five years to obtain justice for the Rastello family.

The City of Torrance fought the wrongful death claim vigorously, filing 10 separate motions to dismiss. The City objected to nearly every document requested and continually stonewalled during the more than 100 depositions taken by the plaintiffs. The most significant discovery battle arose over the plaintiffs' request to research the police department's internal affairs records to determine whether its officers had engaged in a pattern of covering up police misconduct. This battle was fought all the way to California's Supreme Court, which ordered the City to give plaintiffs access to the closely guarded records. Greene and Panish not only prevailed in their protracted discovery battle, but obtained sanctions against the defense attorneys, who were fined $37,500 for perjury, contempt of court, and misuse of discovery.

The evidence obtained by Greene and Panish proved that Sergeant Green's drinking problem was well known within the department. In fact, his supervisor had brought him to an Alcoholics Anonymous meeting a month before the fatal accident. Four months later, a gas station attendant had reported Sergeant Green for drunk driving after the officer had offered the attendant money for sex. Yet Green's colleagues never charged him, nor did his supervisors ever discipline him for his drinking problem.

The plaintiffs' investigation showed that Sergeant Green had been drinking for almost seven hours before the motorcycle accident and had driven away from the collision, returning 15 minutes later. The plaintiffs' investigation also showed that the officers on the scene protected Sergeant Green by concealing damaging evidence, failing to run a routine sobriety test, and neglecting to call the California Highway Patrol or the L.A. County Sheriff's Office. The senior officer at the scene used an unrecorded radio channel to communicate with the watch commander instead of a standard taped channel. Other officers falsified witnesses' testimony and falsely recorded skid marks, which would have pointed to Green's liability.

Most shocking, however, were the internal affairs files, which demonstrated that Sergeant Green's case was just one part of an appalling pattern of police misconduct and cover-ups. For example, the City had covered up the fact that one of its lieutenants had sexually molested his stepdaughter for several years and the City had let several officers off the hook for gang-raping a woman. The records also revealed blatant examples of police department discrimination against African-Americans and members of other minority groups.

Attorney Greene, in his closing argument, asked the jury to send a message to other police departments nationwide — and send a message they did. Outraged by the evidence of multiple cover-ups of abuses and wrongdoing by Torrance police officers, the jury awarded $375,000 against Sergeant Green on the wrongful death claim; $5.525 million against the City of Torrance, the Chief of Police, and six police officers involved in the cover-up; and an additional $137,000 in punitive damages against the Chief of Police and five officers. The verdict led the City Council of Torrance to take steps to ensure greater accountability, measures followed by other municipalities. The appellate court affirmed the verdict.

In an ironic twist, Sergeant Green later suffered a loss of the same kind that he had caused the Rastello family. A drunk driver killed Green's son, who was riding his motorcycle. According to attorney Panish, the merciful John Rastello, whose son Green had killed, went to the grieving father "to provide him with support in dealing with the loss of his son…to forgive Green and help someone in need."

There is no reported decision on the merits in *Rastello*.

Browne Greene   *Brian Panish*   *Timothy Rastello*

Workers' Rights
United Steelworkers of America v. Phelps Dodge Corp.
Michael McCrory

Arizona is a "right to work" state, where unions are not encouraged. This was especially true of the copper industry, one of Arizona's largest employers during the 1980s. In 1983, 20 unions, led by the United Mineworkers of America, called a strike against Phelps Dodge Corporation after it refused to agree to a contract signed by three other mines in the state. In an attempt to break the strike, the company aggressively recruited out-of-state workers and refused to bargain.

The union retained attorney Michael McCrory of Washington, D.C., to pursue the strikers' civil rights claims. What the lawyer thought would be a three-week engagement turned into a five-year struggle, requiring McCrory to move to Arizona. He eventually represented more than 30 striking miners' families, charging that Phelps Dodge had used local law enforcement as a private army to break the strike.

The litigation involved extensive discovery with more than 100 depositions and innumerable discovery disputes. The trial court dismissed Phelps Dodge from the suit on a motion for summary judgment, but the Pima County Sheriff's Department remained a defendant. At trial, McCrory presented more than 30 specific incidents demonstrating that strikers were being charged on the slightest ground while "scabs" — workers who crossed the picket line — were free to act with impunity. For example, when a scab broke a striker's jaw with a rifle butt, he was released on his own recognizance and fined only $35.

The jury found that law enforcement officers had arrested two plaintiffs without probable cause and awarded them $181,850. McCrory then appealed the earlier dismissal of Phelps Dodge from the case. He prevailed at an *en banc* appellate hearing before the U.S. Court of Appeals for the Ninth Circuit, which reinstated the case against the mining company. These claims subsequently settled.

While litigating this case, McCrory was also pursuing other civil rights cases on behalf of strikers. He won cases for false arrest and for wrongful tear-gassing. In the end, McCrory won more than $1 million for the striking mineworkers from state and local police agencies. McCrory's victories sent a strong message that workers have a right to strike without fear of retribution from law enforcement officers.

Other attorneys who deserve recognition for their important work in these cases include Gerald A. Pollock and Sherry L. Teachnor for their assistance at trial and Jeff Freund, Bruce Lerner, and Patricia Pollack of Bredhoff & Kaiser in Washington, D.C., for their assistance in appealing the dismissal of Phelps Dodge to the Ninth Circuit.

The reported decision in this case and its subsequent case history can be found at *United Steelworkers of America v. Phelps Dodge Corp.*, 865 F.2d 1539 (9th Cir. 1989) *(en banc), cert. denied,* 493 U.S. 809 (1989). The reported decision in a related civil rights action can be found at *United Steelworkers of America v. Milstead,* 705 F. Supp. 1426 (D. Ariz. 1988).

1990 Trial Lawyer of the Year Award Winners
Terrance L. Smith and Anthony DeBonis, Jr.
The Case of the Indentured Mental Patients

P atients in mental hospitals are among the most overlooked and for-
gotten people in our society, but are often in need of the greatest care
and attention. The case of *Orr v. Sonnenburg* presented the question of
whether mental hospital patients should be compensated for compulsory labor
performed during their institutionalization.

Between 1970 and 1975, patients in Indiana state mental institutions were
required, often under threat of punishment, to perform menial tasks such as
laundry, building maintenance, scrubbing floors, barber-beautician services,
canteen duty, cleaning toilets, cooking, housekeeping, and other essential
institutional tasks. The institutions saved millions in salaries by not paying
these patients for their labor.

Indiana attorneys Terrance L. Smith and Anthony DeBonis, Jr., of Smith &
DeBonis fought a 16-year battle to reform the state's mental hospitals. Smith
believed that forcing patients to work without pay constituted a significant
violation of their rights. He filed suit in
May 1974 on behalf of more than 8,500
hospitalized mental health patients, seeking just compensation for these patients.

What is public justice?
The State cannot force
patients in its mental
hospitals to work at
the hospitals without
compensation.

Throughout its history, the case was
a roller coaster of successes and setbacks.
In 1976, Smith won summary judgment
based on the federal Fair Labor Standards
Act (FLSA). But, barely one month later,
the U.S. Supreme Court decided *National
League of Cities v. Usery*, a ruling adverse
to *Orr* because it held that the FLSA could
not constitutionally be applied to state and municipal employees.

Smith then went back to the drawing board and pleaded six different theories of recovery, including a renewed claim under the FLSA, four other claims
alleging unjust enrichment and violations of the Federal Civil Rights Act (42
U.S.C. § 1983), the Thirteenth Amendment to the U.S. Constitution (which
bars involuntary servitude), the Indiana Constitution, and a statute known as
the Indiana Patient Remuneration Law.

In 1978, after Smith obtained certification of the case as a class action, he once again obtained summary judgment. However, in a reversal that presaged a pattern, the judgment was overturned on appeal based on procedural defects in the class certification process. The problem involved the appointment of attorneys across the state as guardians *ad litem* for members of the class; Smith would have to locate each member of the class.

As discovery in the case proceeded, Smith was faced with continuous delay tactics and obstruction by the state. "When I started getting into the records, they really fought us," Smith recalls. At first, the state would release only the patient numbers of the class members. Separate court orders were then required to obtain first the names, then the addresses, of the class members. After four years of delay, the trial court threatened the state with significant sanctions. Finally, Smith obtained the names of class members and the nature and extent of the work each had performed.

Smith launched a full-scale investigation. "I hired private investigators, who interviewed more than 100 people," he says. "What we found was consistent across the board, whether the commitment was voluntary or not, whether insurance was paying the bill or they were public welfare cases. People were working about eight hours a day without any compensation or reduction of their bill."

To handle the enormous amount of data, Smith developed one of the earliest specialized computer programs to track the many class members and calculate their damage claims. Smith and his colleagues logged thousands of miles as they traveled across the state, interviewing former patients and witnesses and compiling more than 20,000 pages of documents.

In 1985, the case received an unexpected boon — the U.S. Supreme Court reversed its prior decision in *National League of Cities*, permitting FLSA claims by state and municipal workers, which would include patient-workers in state mental institutions.

In 1987, Anthony DeBonis joined Smith's firm and immediately began working on the case, too. At trial in the spring of that year, Smith and DeBonis presented a compelling case using videotaped and live testimony. One patient testified that she went from electro-shock therapy to typing memos, once receiving an award as the hardest worker — a $10 gift certificate to an ice cream parlor. Another patient recounted having to work full days scrubbing floors, even though she had a broken wrist in a sling. Other patients described being forced to work under the threat of losing personal privileges or, in some instances, being subjected to electro-shock therapy for refusing to donate their labor. Numerous patients from each of the state's 10 mental institutions testified. It became clear that the State of Indiana had systematically subjected its mental health patients to forced labor in each of its mental institutions.

State officials justified these labor practices as "therapy." Dr. Otis Bowen, Indiana's governor in the early 1970s, rationalized the system as a form of compensation for free room and board and a way to defray the costs of care. Smith and DeBonis rebutted the defense by demonstrating that the work assignments were not part of a therapy program and that the real purpose behind the practice was to skirt state statutes and reduce the Department of Mental Health's workforce.

The plaintiffs' presentation convinced the special judge assigned to the case. On November 17, 1987, he ruled that the plaintiffs had performed 8,735,891 hours of uncompensated labor for the state during the relevant time frame. The judge ruled that each patient should receive $1.60 per hour for the compulsory labor, plus $1.60 per hour for prejudgment interest. Based on these figures, the court awarded the class almost $28 million in damages and $5.6 million in attorneys' fees and costs, and set aside another $2.5 million to compensate counsel for future work on appeals.

On August 7, 1989, the Indiana Court of Appeals substantially affirmed the decision, but did not permit prejudgment interest. The key issue on appeal was whether the patients' labor was in the form of "general services" or "particular services." Under the Indiana Bill of Rights, all state citizens may be forced to perform general services, that is, "services which an individual owes to the government and for which the individual can demand no compensation." Examples of such general services include serving on a jury and testifying as a witness. In contrast, particular services are not required of every citizen. Applying these legal distinctions to the facts of this case, the court found that the work performed by the patients "must be characterized as particular services." Thus, the patients were entitled to the compensation awarded by the trial court, absent the prejudgment interest, leaving the judgment at $13.977 million.

After Smith and DeBonis were honored for their commitment and achievements, the Indiana Supreme Court wrote a bitter end to this story. It reversed the decision and instructed the lower courts to dismiss all counts. The Court held that the U.S. Supreme Court's reversal of *National League of Cities* did not apply retroactively and that, as a result, the FLSA minimum wage requirements did not apply to the plaintiffs in this case. It ruled that the State's defense of the plaintiffs' work as "therapy" was "a matter of genuine dispute," that the unjust enrichment claim failed because the patients lacked an expectation of payment, and that the Thirteenth Amendment had not been violated because the compulsory labor was not akin to a form of "civic duty."

Illustrating its callous attitude toward this tremendous injustice, the Indiana Supreme Court said:

> The State's demand was not unreasonable. The work requirement was reasonably related to the patients' hospitalization. The plaintiff class was, in many ways, the direct beneficiary of its own labor. The plaintiffs performed tasks that improved their daily lives. Had the State required every patient to cook his own food and wash his own clothes, the connection between each patient and the benefit of his labor would have been undeniably clear. Although the State's decision to divide the tasks, specialize the labor and take advantage of economies of scale somewhat blurs the connection, the connection remains quite real.

Smith and DeBonis sought review by the U.S. Supreme Court, aided by Trial Lawyers for Public Justice and Harvard University Law School Professor Laurence Tribe. The Court denied *certiorari*.

Smith considers the ruling "one of the great travesties by any Supreme Court" and believes that the "sole purpose" of the Indiana Supreme Court's ruling was to protect the state's finances.

Despite a very painful loss, Smith and DeBonis are proud of their work on behalf of Indiana's hospitalized mental health patients. Smith says, "We put in so many hours of effort and advanced so much in costs, I don't want to count it. At one point, the state offered us a settlement that would have put money in our pockets, but given our clients only a few cents on the dollar off their bills. Of course, we turned it down. We were in it for the benefit of the clients and that is who we were going to advocate for, win or lose."

The reported decision in this case and its subsequent case history can be found at *Orr v. Sonnenburg,* 542 N.E.2d 201 (Ind. Ct. App. 1989), *rev'd sub nom. Bayh v. Sonnenburg,* 573 N.E.2d 398 (Ind. 1991) (ordering judgment for state defendants), *cert. denied,* 502 U.S. 1094 (1992).

Terrance L. Smith

CHAPTER NINE

1991: The Case of the Cheated Workers

Workers' Rights *Buenrostro v. Washington State Apple Advertising Comm'n*

Workers' Rights *Strom v. Boeing Co.*

Civil Rights *Berhanu v. Metzger*

Government Accountability *Huerta v. San Francisco*

Government Accountability *American Baptist Churches v. Thornburgh*

Auto Safety *Johnston v. General Motors Corp.*

Winner

Gavalik v. Continental Can Co.; Amaro v. Continental Can Co.; and *McLendon v. The Continental Group, Inc.*

The Case of the Cheated Workers

The finalists for the 1991 Trial Lawyer of the Year Award promoted public justice for people who sometimes find it difficult to find an advocate. The nominees for this year represented migrant farm workers, employees subjected to electromagnetic pulse radiation, an Ethiopian student who was bludgeoned to death by racist skinheads incited by a white supremacist group, a 61-year-old grandmother beaten by San Francisco police, refugees seeking asylum, and General Motors auto owners endangered by safety defects. The Trial Lawyer of the Year was honored for his 10-year successful struggle, with the help of an ace legal team, to protect steelworkers from a Byzantine corporate scheme to strip them of their pension rights.

Workers' Rights
Buenrostro v. Washington State Apple Advertising Comm'n
Paul Stritmatter

Migrant farm workers endure grueling work, low compensation, and insecure lives with no benefits. Adding to their difficulties, migrant farm workers sometimes fall prey to fraud and are the victims of abuse — often without a meaningful or effective remedy.

Thanks to the efforts of Hoquiam, Washington, attorney Paul Stritmatter, a group of cheated farm workers received justice. In the summer of 1987, a radio advertisement campaign ran in the Southwest on both English and Spanish stations. While mariachi music played in the background, the Washington State Apple Advertising Commission (WSAAC) trumpeted a call for workers:

> A very important message for all farm workers who want to earn
> *good money!* The largest crop of apples in the history of the State of
> Washington is being harvested now! They need forty-five *thousand* farm
> workers…They are paying *good money!* All eligible farm workers come
> registered under the new immigration laws *free!* Don't wait any longer
> …*Earn good money…*Go to East Washington State *this very day!*

The ad worked. Thousands of farm workers rushed to the freedom and opportunity of Washington State in September 1987. But instead of finding abundant work, they discovered that the harvest was actually quite small. Indeed, there were enough local workers available to conduct the entire harvest without outside help. The ads, however, kept running and did not cease until the Governor of Washington personally asked the WSAAC to end the campaign.

By that time it was too late. More than 3,000 farm workers were stranded in Washington with no means of support. Many were sleeping in the streets, under bridges, or out in the open air. The migrant workers were in a desperate plight; they had no money, no jobs, no food, no access to health care — and no way to get home. The migrants quickly created a huge strain on an already overburdened social welfare system.

In October 1987, Daniel Ford and Becki Smith, attorneys with the Seattle-based Evergreen Legal Services, filed a class action suit against WSAAC and its advertising agency, McCann-Erickson, charging fraud and negligent misrepresentation, and seeking injunctive and monetary relief. When a trial judge threw out everything except the claims for damages, the legal aid lawyers turned to Trial Lawyers for Public Justice and its lead counsel, Paul Stritmatter. Aided by Ford, Stritmatter took the case from there.

Stritmatter faced a daunting task. His clients were more than 800 extremely poor, mobile farm workers, many of whom spoke little English. He faced a powerful foe — a quasi-governmental commission with deep-seated economic power overseeing one of Washington State's most lucrative industries. Worse, Stritmatter faced significant community antagonism, making a fair trial a remote prospect.

Stritmatter's first move was to request a change of venue. The case had been filed in Seattle, but the defendants had successfully obtained a change of venue to Chelan County — the heart of apple country. Unless he could remove the case to a less hostile locale, the suit was as good as dead.

Stritmatter commissioned a private survey, conducted in April 1989, to demonstrate that his clients could not receive a fair hearing in Chelan County. The survey disclosed significant local prejudice against migrant farm workers. Moreover, a large number of potential jurors had a financial stake in the outcome of the litigation. Stritmatter convinced the judge to move the case to Spokane County.

Even though the forum was friendlier, Stritmatter still faced an unfriendly opponent. During the next several years, the WSAAC tried to have the class decertified. The Commission also attempted to persuade the Court that each member of the class would have to prove that he or she had individually relied on the ad as the sole reason for traveling to Washington State — an impossible task, considering the numbers involved, the logistics, and the totality of the circumstances.

When WSAAC's arguments failed and the trial approached, the case settled for $617,000. It was the largest settlement ever obtained for migrant farm workers in Washington State. Any funds not collected by individual class members were earmarked for the educational, medical, housing, or childcare needs of migrant farm workers in the state.

For his outstanding advocacy on behalf of the poor and powerless farm workers of Washington State, attorney Paul Stritmatter was named a finalist for the 1991 Trial Lawyer of the Year Award.

In addition to Ford, Smith, and Stritmatter, the litigation team also included Seattle attorneys Mary Alice Theiler of Gibson, Douglas, Theiler and Drachler, and Ted Spearman of Webster, Mrak & Blumberg.

There is no reported decision on the merits in this case.

Paul Stritmatter

Workers' Rights
Strom v. Boeing
Michael E. Withey

Washington State was the site of another important case in 1991 — this one involving a corporate powerhouse, the Boeing Company. Robert Strom had served as a loyal Boeing employee for 23 years when the company sent him to work as a technician in its electromagnetic pulse (EMP) radiation group in 1983. While performing that work, Strom was continually exposed to high doses of EMP radiation, one of the types of radiation emanating from nuclear explosions. Boeing was testing the effects of EMP for the U.S. Department of Defense, searching for ways to protect sensitive military electronics from being knocked out or damaged by EMP radiation.

Strom did not worry about his repeated exposure because Boeing assured him and the hundreds of other employees in the EMP group that exposure was entirely safe. Strom did not question the frequent medical exams conducted by the company because such precautions were normal in several different sections of Boeing. He did wonder, however, why the company doctors took so many samples of his blood.

Then tragedy struck. In 1985, Strom came down with an extremely rare and lethal form of leukemia. Believing his illness was connected somehow to his exposure to EMP radiation, Strom filed a workers' compensation claim. Then Strom found documents proving that part of what Boeing was doing in its EMP work was testing *whether exposure caused leukemia or other adverse health effects in humans.* In short, Strom and his fellow workers were being used involuntarily as human guinea pigs.

Strom sought legal help, but no one would take on the Seattle-based Boeing Company. Finally he contacted Trial Lawyers for Public Justice, which recruited Michael Withey of Seattle's Schroeter, Goldmark & Bender to serve as its lead counsel. In June 1988, undaunted by the "800 pound gorilla" status of Boeing in Washington State or by the novelty and complexity of the issues, Withey filed a class action suit against Boeing, Boeing Medical Services, and Lovelace Biomedical and Environmental Research Institute. The class action suit charged the defendants with conducting human experimentation on Strom and his 700 fellow employees without their informed consent. The suit also contended that Strom's illness was a direct result of his exposure to EMP radiation.

Boeing first denied the charges. However, after CBS-TV aired a "60 Minutes" program with a lead segment on the controversy, the company began to change its tune. In a company newsletter, Boeing executives contradicted their court position by admitting having conducted medical research on EMP employees. Yet Boeing still contended that its conduct was proper.

In August 1990, after a discovery period characterized by corporate obfuscation and obstructionism, the case was set for trial. But before the courtroom doors swung open, the company settled. While not admitting to any wrongdoing, Boeing paid Strom over $500,000. In addition, Boeing agreed to provide Strom's co-workers with up to ten years of annual medical exams overseen by an independent medical administrator and pay $200,000 in a class fund to be utilized by the administrator in fulfilling the terms of the settlement. The settlement provided that, if other class members fell ill, they would be free to sue Boeing for compensation.

Strom donated a large part of his settlement to the creation of the Robert C. Strom Foundation, which supports research, educational seminars, publications, and litigation — continuing the study of electromagnetic radiation begun as a result of the Boeing litigation.

For his precedent-setting work, Michael Withey was named, for the second time, as a finalist for the Trial Lawyer of the Year Award. (See Chapter Eight.)

Withey's TLPJ team included his law partners Leonard Schroeter and Murray Kleist of Seattle; William Rossbach of Rossbach & Whiston in Missoula, Montana; Herbert Newberg of Philadelphia; and TLPJ Executive Director Arthur H. Bryant.

There is no reported decision on the merits in this case.

Michael E. Withey

Civil Rights
Berhanu v. Metzger
Morris Dees

Morris Dees, the anti-hate group crusader and co-founder of the Southern Poverty Law Center (SPLC) in Montgomery, Alabama, was again honored by TLPJ in 1991 for his zealous advocacy of civil rights. TLPJ had previously named Dees as Trial Lawyer of the Year in 1987 for successfully holding the United Klans of America liable for the lynching of a man in Mobile, Alabama. (See Chapter Five.) This time, Dees was honored for his success in taking on the White Aryan Resistance.

Tom Metzger and his son John founded the White Aryan Resistance (WAR) and ran this white supremacist group from Metzger's home in Fallbrook, California. As the host of a notorious cable television show and publisher of the WAR newspaper, Metzger spewed hatred and vitriol against people of color.

Dees contended that this hatemongering led to the murderous 1988 actions of three neo-Nazi skinheads who beat Ethiopian student Mulugeta Seraw to death with a baseball bat in Portland, Oregon. In October 1989, Dees and attorneys from the Anti Defamation League of B'nai B'rith filed suit against the Metzgers, WAR, and two skinheads on behalf of Seraw's uncle, the executor of the dead man's estate. The suit charged the white supremacists with wrongful death and conspiracy to violate Seraw's civil rights.

In order to hold Metzger accountable, Dees had to prove that the murderers carried out their crime with the encouragement and assistance of the Metzgers. The trial was made more difficult by Metzger's choice to act as his own lawyer. Metzger turned the trial into a circus, cross-examining himself and charging the Portland police with inspiring the killing. He even claimed that the skinheads somehow acted in self-defense.

But Dees, in his calm, patient, and persistent style, presented a devastating case. He showed how the killers' gang received the WAR newsletter, which featured comics depicting the killing of blacks and Jews. He distributed examples of other WAR propaganda, including manuals for identifying and "eliminating" so-called enemies of the white race. Most tellingly, Dees produced a tape of a Metzger telephone message saying that it may have been the skinheads' "civic duty" to kill Seraw.

In fewer than five hours, the jury sent Metzger and WAR a powerful message about racist rage: it ordered the defendants to pay the survivors of

Mulugeta Seraw $12.5 million. Metzger immediately declared himself bankrupt. As he had previously done with the United Klans of America, Dees seized all of Metger's known bank accounts and forced him to sell his house. The authorities even took the WAR post office box into receivership to collect the money coming in from WAR's lucrative mail order network.

Once again, Morris Dees innovatively used the civil justice system to draw the line against hate. For his extraordinary work, Dees was named, for the second time, as a finalist for the Trial Lawyer of the Year Award.

Other attorneys deserving of mention for helping Dees in the discovery and litigation were J. Richard Cohen of SPLC; Elder M. Rosenthal of Rosenthal & Greene in Portland, Oregon; and Richard E. Shevitz of Hopper, Wenzel & Galliher in Indianapolis.

The later reported decision in this case and its subsequent case history can be found at *Berhanu v. Metzger*, 850 P.2d 373 (Or. Ct. App. 1993) (affirming jury verdict), *review denied*, 865 P.2d 1296 (Or. 1993), *cert. denied*, 511 U.S. 1106 (1994).

Morris S. Dees

Government Accountability
Huerta v. San Francisco
Arthur C. Johnson

Eugene, Oregon, attorney Arthur C. Johnson grappled with another form of organized brutality — the kind sometimes perpetrated by police. United Farm Workers of America activist and 61-year-old grandmother Dolores Huerta was leading a San Francisco demonstration against President George H. W. Bush, Sr., during the 1988 presidential campaign, when police tactical squads began to sweep the crowd away from a hotel entrance. As the police closed in from all sides, the 5-foot-2-inch Huerta found herself trapped and was struck repeatedly by officers for failing to disperse. Huerta was so badly hurt by the beating that she almost died.

When San Francisco officials refused to take action, Johnson filed suit in the U.S. District Court, charging the city with civil rights violations under U.S. Code Section 1983 for ratifying the actions of the police. Video tapes of the demonstration taken by local TV station KRON clearly showed the police officer in question beating Huerta, striking her at least eight times, not the two times claimed by the city. With the videos incontrovertibly proving that the police officer acted improperly, Johnson was halfway home.

Proving the city's liability was more difficult. Johnson analyzed an enormous mass of documentary evidence, looked into the San Francisco Police Department's training policies, and researched the disciplinary history of the offending officer. Johnson learned that while citizens had twice sued the officer, alleging wrongful assault, he had never been disciplined. Johnson also showed that after the Huerta beating, documents urging the officer to receive counseling had been removed from his personnel file.

The city eventually paid Huerta $825,000. Even more important to Huerta, the settlement achieved substantial reforms in the law and police practices in San Francisco. For example, the San Francisco Police Department crowd control manual was completely rewritten to include, among other things, provisions limiting how and when officers may use batons. Thereafter, officers who violated the new policies were subject to discipline, including suspension or dismissal. Officer Fred Lau, who worked extensively on rewriting the crowd control policies, later became Chief of Police.

Thanks to Arthur Johnson, justice was obtained for Huerta and for the people of San Francisco, an extraordinary achievement by any measure.

Others deserving mention for their roles in this case include Huerta's personal attorney Dianna Lyons and Michael Phillips, Claudia Ingram, and research assistant Mardel Skilman, all of Johnson's firm. George Riley, then an assistant city attorney responsible for the defense of Huerta's claim, also helped achieve the reforms.

There is no reported decision on the merits in this case.

Arthur C. Johnson

Government Accountability
American Baptist Churches v. Thornburgh
Marc Van Der Hout

San Francisco was also the site of an important case holding the government accountable for discriminatory immigration policies. Each year, thousands of refugees flee from oppression, exploitation, and egregious violations of human rights in their home countries, seeking political asylum in the U.S. To prevent political considerations from clouding decision-making on asylum requests, Congress passed the Refugee Act of 1980, which prohibits the Immigration and Naturalization Service (INS) from considering nationality when reviewing asylum applications.

Unfortunately, during the 1980s, INS generally ignored the Act. Those seeking asylum from countries deemed friendly to the U.S. — particularly those from South America and Central America — were usually refused refuge. On the other hand, people fleeing from oppression in communist countries often received a more sympathetic reception.

San Francisco trial lawyer Marc Van Der Hout stood against this illegal and unjust approach to processing asylum applications. He took his stand while President Ronald Reagan's administration vigorously tried to break the back of the sanctuary movement. The Reagan Administration strategy included routine denial of asylum applications from Latin American countries. In 1984, the Center for Constitutional Rights (CCR) filed the case of *American Baptist Churches v. Thornburgh* in federal District Court, seeking an order preventing the discriminatory reviews of asylum requests from Latin Americans. The case also sought to prevent the prosecution of sanctuary workers.

Van Der Hout, an immigration lawyer and president of the National Lawyer's Guild, agreed to serve *pro bono* as co-counsel, primarily dealing with the immigration issues. He continued in that status until 1988, when the sanctuary plaintiffs' case was dismissed. That left two immigrants, representing a broad class of litigants, still in the case. Suddenly, Van Der Hout found himself as the lead counsel in a case with explosive political and social ramifications.

Undaunted, Van Der Hout energetically set about proving that the government's treatment of the asylum-seekers violated the Refugee Act of 1980. The INS demonstrated why it had a reputation for litigating cases to the hilt. Van Der Hout and his legal team fought off not one, not two, but three separate INS attempts to have the case thrown out of court. The plaintiffs' lawyers also poured through thousands of asylum applications at dozens of federal facilities throughout the country. They did this research in order to prove that a discriminatory pattern worked against refugees from countries such as Guatemala, El Salvador, and Honduras. This extensive search, aided by a crack team of attorneys, proved that the United States only granted asylum to three percent of Salvadorans and less than one percent of Guatemalans during the previous ten years. In contrast, the asylum rate for refugees from countries such as China and the Soviet Union was as high as 76 percent. More to the point, Van Der Hout unearthed a "smoking gun" memo from 1987 directing INS field offices to give preference to Nicaraguans seeking asylum. Not coincidentally, at this time the U.S. adamantly opposed the Nicaraguan government to the point of financing the Contras, a controversial rebel force opposed to the Nicaraguan communist regime.

These successes culminated in marathon negotiating sessions, including several 16-hour meetings and a final nine-hour conference call, leading to a triumph for justice. Under a settlement finalized in January 1991, the government agreed to reopen more than 150,000 Salvadoran and Guatemalan claims denied during the previous ten years. An additional 500,000 Guatemalan and Salvadoran refugees received work authorizations and were permitted to remain in the U.S. pending adjudicating of their claims.

Other attorneys deserving mention for their vital roles in this case include Lucas Guttentag of the Immigrants' Rights Project of the American Civil Liberties Project in New York; Morton Stavis, Frank E. Deale, and Ellen Yaroshevsky of CCR; and James Garrett, Michael L. Zigler, and Lori A. Schechter of Morrison & Foerster.

The reported decision in this case can be found at *American Baptist Churches v. Thornburgh*, 760 F. Supp. 796 (N.D. Cal. 1991) (approving class action settlement).

Auto Safety

Johnston v. General Motors Corp.
Jere Locke Beasley

Demonstrating the depth and scope of cases handled by Trial Lawyer of the Year Award finalists, Jere Locke Beasley of Birmingham, Alabama, was honored for important work advancing auto safety. The case involved a Chevrolet pick-up truck driven by Ford Lewis, accompanied by his grandson, seven-year-old Bart Johnston. Lewis came to a stop sign and duly stopped. He then began to execute a left turn. Suddenly, the truck stalled. A logging truck was bearing down on Lewis' vehicle; the truck driver braked hard, but failed to stop. The collision killed young Bart.

Beasley sued General Motors (GM), alleging that Lewis' brand new pickup was defective and that the defect caused Johnton's death. The suit centered on a computer chip sensor called a PROM, which regulates the amount of air entering the engine. Beasley argued that an incorrectly calibrated PROM caused the stall that led to the fatal accident.

GM fought back with all of the energy and intensity its lawyers could muster. However, documents unearthed in discovery showed that GM engineers were aware that the PROM, as installed, would cause "hesitation, sags, and stumbles" in pickups accelerating from a stop. Beasley also proved that GM consciously chose not to issue a public recall and replace the defective parts. Instead, in a "silent recall," the company sought to surreptitiously replace PROMs in more than 9,000 pickups when the vehicles were brought in for regular service. Not only did the company know of the problem, it chose to keep its customers in the dark about the potential danger. Worse, it undertook this course after conducting a study that showed that a full recall would cost the company $42 million.

The jury was suitably outraged by GM's conduct in permitting a known defect to remain in its trucks and found that the faulty PROM was the cause of the accident. After only an hour and 15 minutes of deliberation, the jury awarded $15 million for wrongful death and $75,000 to Lewis for his injuries. It was a good verdict that, of course, could never make up for the tragic death of a young boy. On appeal, the Supreme Court of Alabama affirmed the judgment, but reduced the punitive damages award to $7.5 million.

The later reported decision in this case can be found at *General Motors Corp. v. Johnston*, 592 So. 2d 1054 (Ala. 1992) (affirming jury verdict in part, reducing punitive damages by half).

Jere Locke Beasley

1991 Trial Lawyer of the Year Award Winner
Daniel McIntyre
The Case of the Cheated Workers

B etween 1975 and 1980, Continental Can Company laid off 400 workers at its West Mifflin, Pennsylvania, plant as part of a corporate-wide scheme designed to rid the corporation of union employees who were close to retirement age. The point of the enterprise under the company's "liability avoidance program" was simple and cruel: to prevent these senior workers from qualifying for their pension benefits. The United Steelworkers of America, AFL-CIO, negotiated these "magic number" pensions in 1971 and 1977 to assist older workers hit by layoffs. To qualify, employees had to work for Continental for 20 years and the sum of their age and years of service had to be at least 60. When qualified workers were laid off, Continental was required to pay a regular pension plus a $300 monthly supplement until the worker reached age 62.

Utilizing an advanced computer program, the company investigated ways to eliminate its future "magic number" liability. Continental would draw a line on its seniority roster and fire everyone below that line by a predetermined date, so that the corporation could lay off older employees mere months — and sometimes only days — before they attained their "magic number" and the vested pension that came with it.

> *What is public justice? Corporations either keep their promises to their workers or are forced to do so.*

The company told its employees that they would be rehired in a short time. The laid-off employees believed this promise because the can manufacturing business was seasonal and the workers had endured periodic layoffs over their years of service. Because the employees believed that they would soon be recalled, many did not seek alternative employment. Indeed, other companies sometimes refused to hire laid-off Continental Can Company employees on a permanent basis because there was an expectation that the workers would soon return to their previous employer in order to qualify for their pensions.

Meanwhile, the Continental Can Company had a computer with a red light that would literally flash a warning if a senior worker were about to be rehired inadvertently.

In 1980, the layoffs came to the attention of Daniel McIntyre, an assistant general counsel to the United Steelworkers of America (USA). With help from other union attorneys, McIntyre filed suit in 1981 against Continental in Pittsburgh federal court. McIntyre and his team charged the company with violating the federal Employmee Retirement Income Security Act (ERISA) by laying off workers for the purpose of denying them their pension rights.

McIntyre did not know it when the suit was filed, but he had just embarked upon a difficult journey that would take more than a decade to complete. It was a path that would lead through five separate courts across the country and would result in suits involving 3,900 Continental employees at 45 of the company's plants nationwide.

At first, McIntyre did not know that the layoffs were part of what was essentially a conspiracy. But in 1982, an attorney in Alabama representing workers at another Continental plant unearthed a startling piece of evidence: the "BELL User Manual." BELL was a backward acronym for "Let's Limit Employees' Benefits." This was the manual for Continental's computer program that had been designed to determine who should be laid off to eliminate workers nearing the "magic number."

McIntyre should have seen this document previously. After all, he had asked the company to turn over all documents related to the layoffs at the Pennsylvania plant. Perhaps realizing that the "BELL User Manual" provided a smoking gun in the lawsuit, the defendants had "failed" to comply with their duty to disclose this important piece of evidence — proof that the layoff decisions were designed explicitly to strip workers of pensions they would otherwise earn.

Utilizing the information gleaned from the BELL document, as well as numerous other probative documents, McIntyre worked with trial lawyer H. Tim Hoffman of Oakland's Hoffman & Lazear to bring a similar suit in Los Angeles in 1982.

In 1983, Bernie Kleiman, general counsel to USA, called in Chicago lawyer Robert Plotkin, who was experienced in labor law and class actions. Kleiman asked Plotkin to become lead counsel for a new case in federal court in Newark, New Jersey, that would become a nationwide class action.

Plotkin and McIntyre put together a first-rate team of lawyers to handle the national class action litigation. McIntyre left the union to pursue the case as a private practitioner and he brought in Hoffman, who was already familiar with the Los Angeles case. Hoffman was then District Counsel for the steel-workers' union. Plotkin introduced a fourth team member, attorney Rose Wehner from his Chicago firm, Plotkin & Jacobs. Wehner would prove indispensable in organizing and retrieving documents necessary to prepare for depositions and cross-examinations.

McIntyre remained personally involved in the three different cases ongoing from East Coast to West. This required him to crisscross the country at a furious pace, coordinating the voluminous discovery and trial preparations. One day the legal team had five depositions in five cities across the country.

Continental Can's lawyers engaged in a "scorched earth" legal strategy. The company resisted discovery at every turn, withholding crucial documents from their production responses, and launched two countersuits against McIntyre and the United Steelworkers of America. Continental Can's legal minions went one step further: they attacked McIntyre personally, insulting his legal ability and maliciously and falsely labeling him a drunk. At one point in the New Jersey litigation, McIntyre obtained a court order preventing opposing counsel's "abusive conduct at depositions." Making matters more depressing, the defendants were awarded summary judgment in the Los Angeles case, a decision later reversed on appeal.

The Pittsburgh case was the first to come to trial, with Roslyn Litman of Pittsburgh's Litman, Litman, Harris, Brown & Watzman as lead counsel. Despite damaging documents unearthed by McIntyre and Litman, the judge ruled in 1986 that the "desire to prevent further employees from attaining eligibility benefits" was only one factor behind the layoffs, and thus ruled that ERISA had not been violated. Oddly, the judge accepted that the well laid out "liability avoidance program" was never the official policy in Pittsburgh.

Flush with victory, Continental Can made a modest offer of settlement. But the plaintiffs' team resisted. They *knew* their clients had been victimized in a most egregious fashion and were not about to allow a setback — as damaging as it was — make them quit now. The team prepared to appeal.

Meanwhile, the struggle continued on other fronts. Hoffman took the Los Angeles case to a bench trial in 1986. Finally, the company's executives were forced to either lie in front of a judge or admit, as the documentary evidence amply demonstrated, that the company designed a system to save money by denying workers their pensions. As the admissions of wrongdoing mounted, Continental Can decided that discretion was the better part of valor. After judgment on liability, the company settled for $7.5 million to avoid facing a trial on damages. Soon, 400 workers cheated of their pensions were being paid and McIntyre received his first compensation since going private in 1984.

The news soon got better. A document uncovered in the Los Angeles case proved that the company had made false assertions in the Pittsburgh case. The crucial document proved that in May 1980, the executive office in Pittsburgh had received a presentation that detailed the "rather dramatic results" the pension avoidance program had produced at the Pennsylvania plant. This document had not been disclosed in the Pittsburgh case, and the disclosure of the document proved to be the turning point. In February 1987, the Third Circuit unanimously reversed the trial judge's ruling, ruling that the company had violated ERISA not only in Pittsburgh but *nationwide*.

With Continental Can dealt such seemingly lethal blows, McIntyre expected the matter to resolve expeditiously. The company had other ideas. The company continued its slash and burn tactics and its campaign of personal vituperation, accusing the attorney, among other *ad hominem* attacks, of being "driven by greed" and of misrepresenting facts.

Because the Third Circuit definitively found Continental in violation of ERISA, the only remaining issue in the New Jersey litigation was whether the workers laid off would have lost their jobs in any event without the existence of the illegal plan. This was the key moment. What happened here would materially impact thousands of other Continental Can workers.

Judge H. Lee Sarokin in Newark federal court heard the case. McIntyre and Hoffman impeached a slew of Continental officials, including the company's former CEO, with the company's own documents. McIntyre's cross-examination of the defendant's expert witnesses, who opined the layoffs would have happened liability avoidance plan or no liability avoidance plan, was also handled deftly.

"We were living like monks in a Newark apartment building," recalls Hoffman. "All we did was eat, sleep and read, preparing for depositions and cross-examinations."

"Dan went to the library and checked out a bunch of books on the most arcane information about pensions," says Plotkin. "There was a particular expert witness that he really prepared to cross-examine."

Under McIntyre's withering cross, Continental Can's key expert witness admitted to receiving $2.2 million for his testimony. However, he could not account for why the company dismissed so many senior workers — apart from the plan to deny pension rights.

"At the end of Dan's cross-examination, this fellow was sitting in the witness chair with his elbows on his knees and his head hanging," says Plotkin.

In ERISA litigation, the corporate defendant puts on its defense first. In the end, the plaintiffs' attorneys had built such a powerful case that they never called a live witness. Relying on cross-examination and documents alone, the trial lawyers established a direct link between the dismissals of the workers and the company's desire to keep their pensions for itself.

"I was shocked at the depth of their self-righteous belief that they could do something morally wrong — taking money from retirees — and think it was all right," says Hoffman.

In 1987, Judge Sarokin blasted the company's arrogance, ruling that the avoidance of pension liability scheme so permeated the corporate culture that it materially impacted all layoff decisions. Indeed, Sarokin agreed with McIntyre that the unethical corporate conduct raised serious questions that "far transcend the legal issues presented by the case."

Next came the damage phase of the trial. At the urging of Judge Sarokin, both sides submitted arguments to a special master for arbitration. Plotkin's partner, John Jacobs, joined the team for the settlement phase. Finally, after 10 years of travail, personal insult, and more than 14,000 hours of work, Continental agreed to settle for $415 million to compensate its fired employees. It was the largest recovery for workers from a single ERISA case in U.S. history. The settlement permitted those workers who were closest to vesting when laid off to receive between $100,000 and $200,000 apiece — enough to materially improve the quality of their retirements.

Once again, David had defeated Goliath. McIntyre's indomitable spirit and the exemplary work of the litigation teams materially improved the lives of his thousands of clients and sent corporate America a clear message: do not steal the retirement security of longtime, loyal workers. For his extraordinary contributions and singular presence in all three of the pension fund cases, McIntyre was named the 1991 Trial Lawyer of the Year.

In addition to McIntyre, Kleiman, Plotkin, Hoffman, Wehner, Litman and Jacobs, other attorneys deserving recognition for their important roles in the *Continental Can* cases include Thomas Betz of Pittsburgh's Litman, Litman, Harris, Brown & Watzman; Chicago sole practitioner Robert Allison; and Susan Haerr and Jonah Orlofsky of Chicago's Plotkin & Jacobs.

There was no reported decision on the merits of the Los Angeles case, *Amaro v. Continental Can Co.* The reported decisions in the Pittsburgh and New Jersey cases, and their subsequent case histories, can be found at *Gavalik v. Continental Can Co.*, 812 F.2d 834 (3d Cir. 1987), *cert. denied*, 484 U.S. 979

(1987); *McLendon v. The Continental Group, Inc.*, 660 F. Supp. 1553 (D.N.J. 1987), *affirmed*, 908 F.2d 1171 (3d Cir. 1990), *after remand*, 802 F. Supp. 1216 (D.N.J. 1992) (approving class action settlement), *affirmed without opinion*, 22 F.3d 302 (3d Cir. 1994), *cert. denied*, 513 U.S. 973 (1994).

Daniel McIntyre

John G. Jacobs

H. Tim Hoffman

Robert Plotkin

Rose Wehner

Roslyn Litman

CHAPTER TEN

1992: The Case of the Ten-Dollar Lawyers
The Case That SLAPPed Decom Back

Civil Rights *Brooks v. Francis, Brooks v. Kemp,* and *Brooks v. State*

Workers' Rights *Howe v. Varity Corp.*

Insurer Accountability *Golden Rule Ins. Co. v. Smith*

Civil Rights *Kraszewski v. State Farm Gen. Ins. Co.*

Co-Winners
Nat'l Ass'n of Radiation Survivors (NARS) v. Walters
and *NARS v. Derwinski*
The Case of the Ten-Dollar Lawyers

Tanner v. Decom Medical Waste Systems, Inc.
The Case That SLAPPed Decom Back

The finalists for the 1992 Trial Lawyer of the Year Award fought for racial justice on death row, protection of employees' health care benefits, insurance coverage of HIV-positive patients, and women's equal employment opportunities. The co-winners of the 1992 Trial Lawyer of the Year Award battled in two different cases for veterans' rights to access the civil justice system and the First Amendment right to protest a medical waste company's wrongdoing.

Civil Rights
Brooks v. Francis, Brooks v. Kemp, and *Brooks v. State*
Stephen Bright

Protecting against racial discrimination in the criminal justice system is crucial to the creation of a just society. This issue is most urgent in capital death cases, where defendants are disproportionately minority and indigent with no money to afford adequate counsel and where appointed counsel are too often unable or unwilling to mount a thoroughly professional defense.

Attorney Stephen Bright understood these issues of institutional racism as director of Atlanta's Southern Center for Human Rights. Bright was one of the few attorneys in the Deep South willing to take on capital murder cases involving poor people of color. He also taught new attorneys how to litigate capital cases in order to expand and deepen the pool of legal talent.

Bright's commitment to protecting the rights of these defendants resulted in an extended struggle to save the life of an African-American named William Anthony "Fats" Brooks, who had been sentenced to death by an all-white jury in Muscogee County Superior Court in 1977 for the kidnapping, robbery, rape, and murder of a 23-year-old white woman named Jeannine Galloway. After Brooks' court-appointed lawyers failed on the direct appeal of his case, Bright and attorney George Kendall, both of whom practiced law in Washington, D.C., agreed to take over as Brooks' *pro bono* legal counsel. The attorneys filed writs of *habeas corpus.* The day before Brooks' scheduled execution date — January 13, 1983 — the U.S. Court of Appeals for the Eleventh Circuit granted Brooks a stay of execution. Soon thereafter, the lawyers persuaded the Court of Appeals to overturn the conviction based on faulty jury instructions, which unconstitutionally shifted the burden of proof.

The State of Georgia reindicted Brooks in 1987. State Senator Gary Parker, a black attorney whose district included part of Muscogee County, and Southern Center attorney Ruth Friedman joined Kendall, who now worked with the NAACP Legal Defense Fund, on the defense team led by Bright. The attorneys had three main objectives. The first, which would prove crucial to the outcome, was to ensure that Brooks' fate was decided by a representative jury that included African-Americans, since prosecutors often attempted to skew justice against black defendants by empanelling all-white juries. They also sought a change of venue and strove to prevent the case from being retried as a capital crime.

The lawyers succeeded only in their first objective, obtaining a jury with eight African Americans and four whites. The jury found Brooks guilty of the crime. But during the penalty phase of the trial, Bright showed the jury crucial evidence that Brooks' previous attorneys had failed to introduce at the first trial, including proof of the severe abuse Brooks suffered throughout his childhood. After deliberating for only an hour, the jury decided that Brooks would spend the rest of his life in jail rather than receive the death penalty.

News of the re-trial and verdict gained nationwide coverage, including an article in *Time* magazine on racial disparities in death sentences. Muscogee County featured prominently in the article. The media attention prompted Congress to hold hearings on the Racial Justice Act, which would have required prosecutors to show race-neutral reasons for any racially disproportionate use of the death penalty. Bright, Parker, and Southern Christian Leadership Conference President Rev. Joseph Lowery testified on the legislation before a subcommittee of the House Judiciary Committee. Bright succinctly prefaced his remarks to the subcommittee stating, "We're tolerating things in our judicial system that we wouldn't tolerate in any other area of our society."

The reported decisions in this case and its subsequent case history can be found at *Brooks v. Francis,* 716 F.2d 780 (11th Cir. 1983); *Brooks v. Kemp,* 809 F.2d 700 (11th Cir. 1987); *Brooks v. State,* 395 S.E.2d 81 (Ga. 1989), *after remand* 415 S.E.2d 903 (Ga. 1992) (affirming sentence of life in prison).

Stephen Bright

Workers' Rights
Howe v. Varity Corp.
Vance K. Opperman, Andrea J. Kaufman,
H. Richard Smith, and Steven K. Gaer

Massey-Ferguson, the country's largest manufacturer of farm and industrial equipment, and its Canadian parent company, Varity Corporation of Toronto, tried to cancel its retirees' health plans through a rigged corporate restructuring that transferred its pension obligations to a new, Canadian-based corporate entity called Massey Combines Corporation. To allay the fears of employees and retirees about the restructuring, Massey Combines' president, Ivan Porter, sent a letter to the affected employees and retirees promising that their "pay levels and benefits will remain unchanged." However, Massey Combines lasted 22 months before it was taken into receivership — the Canadian equivalent of bankruptcy. A Canadian court ordered the receiver to liquidate all assets of the company and to terminate all health benefits. As a self-insured corporation, Massey Combines had no resources to provide employees with any severance package.

Desperate retirees, having lost their pensions and health benefits, approached Des Moines attorneys H. Richard Smith and Steven K. Gaer of Ahers, Cooney, Dorweiler, Haynie, Smith & Allbee. Believing the case had merit, knowing it would require a class action approach, and aware that most other large firms in Des Moines had at one time or another represented Massey-Ferguson, Smith and Gaer sought help from attorneys Vance K. Opperman and Andrea J. Kaufman of the Minneapolis firm of Opperman, Heins & Paquin.

The trial lawyers fought the case in both the American and Canadian courts. When the arduous discovery process ended, the attorneys had proof that on the day that Massey Combines opened, it only had $15,000 in liquid assets and an inventory of over-priced farm equipment, compared with a crushing debt of $300 million (Canadian). Varity had merely stripped off its profit-sucking divisions and its retirement health plans and folded them into a company born to die. Varity executives apparently cared little that this shell-game maneuver, which they called "Project Sunshine," could ruin the retirement security of 4,000 loyal employees.

The jury trial began in Des Moines on August 26, 1991, with U.S. District Judge Donald E. O'Brien presiding. The company argued that the restructuring was legitimate and that Massey Combines was now separate and distinct from Varity. Yet the trial lawyers proved that there were significant ties which bound the companies together and that the reorganization scheme was a sham designed, at least in part, to cheat the retirees out of their just and hard-earned retirement benefits.

The most damning evidence against Varity and Massey-Ferguson came in the form of testimony from a business acquaintance of Varity chairman Victor A. Rice. The witness testified that Rice had bragged at Chicago's Union League Club during a trade association meeting that he had just scored a "major financing coup" which would enable him to "unload all his big losers" into a new unit — Massey Combines. Varity's attorneys did not call Rice to the witness stand to deny that he had made the statement.

The jury found the companies liable for compensatory and punitive damages totaling $33 million against Varity Corporation and $3 million against Massey-Ferguson.

The later reported decision in this case and its subsequent case history can be found at *Howe v. Varity Corp.,* 36 F.3d 746 (8th Cir. 1994) (affirming judgment for plaintiff class), *opinion clarified,* 41 F.3d 1263 (8th Cir. 1994), *cert. granted,* 514 U.S. 1082 (1995), *affirmed,* 516 U.S. 489 (1996).

H. Richard Smith

Insurer Accountability
Golden Rule Ins. Co. v. Smith
Tom Owens and Scott Hendler

The Golden Rule Insurance Company cancelled the insurance coverage of David T. Smith, an HIV-positive gay man, when he applied for coverage for AZT drug therapy for his disease. The insurance company claimed that Smith had materially misrepresented his health status in several categories when he had applied for coverage one-and-a-half years earlier. Smith believed he had answered all of the insurance company's questions honestly and to the best of his ability, considering the wording of the queries. Moreover, he had sought the help of a health care professional in filling out the application.

Dallas attorneys Tom Owens of Akin, Gump, Hauer & Feld and Scott Hendler of Baron & Budd took Smith's case *pro bono*, defending against the policy cancellation and seeking a declaratory judgment that the policy remained in effect. Owens and Hendler built Smith's defense around three key points. First, the case was about discrimination against an HIV-positive person, not any alleged misrepresentation. Second, Smith made no misrepresentation about HIV, since there had been no question on the application about HIV status, but only a question about whether Smith had a "blood abnormality." Smith's immune system evaluation had found his blood count to be within normal ranges. Third, Smith had not intended to deceive in his responses to ambiguously worded questions.

The trial was hard fought, with both sides scoring telling points in front of the jury. Nevertheless, the verdict vindicated Smith; the jury found that he had not attempted to deceive Golden Rule. U.S. District Court Judge Sidney Fitzwater issued a judgment that the company remained bound to its contractual commitment to provide up to $1 million in health insurance benefits as long as Smith paid the premiums.

Golden Rule filed a notice of appeal to challenge the trial court's ruling and an award of attorney's fees. Then the case settled for a confidential amount. Mr. Smith continues to live and work in Dallas, Texas, and is covered by a $1 million health insurance policy.

Co-counsel Lisa Blue of Baron & Budd also deserves recognition for her important work in jury selection in this case.

There is no reported decision on the merits in this case.

Tom Owens *Scott Hendler*

Civil Rights
Kraszewski v. State Farm Gen. Ins. Co.
Guy Saperstein

Oakland, California, attorney Guy Saperstein of Saperstein, Mayeda, Larkin & Goldstein mounted a 13-year class action suit charging that the State Farm Insurance Company discriminated against women in its hiring and promotion practices. In the end, an historic settlement was achieved that not only garnered damages for the plaintiffs, but also shattered a glass ceiling that had been holding back women at the insurance company.

The tale of this historic precedent began in the mid 1970s when three women filed claims against the company with the Equal Employment Opportunity Commission (EEOC) after State Farm refused to allow the women, who were already clerical employees, to transition into sales. Every time the women had applied for sales, State Farm refused them for various reasons, such as their lack of experience or college degrees, or a supposed company policy not to encourage transfers from operations into sales. Yet men who had the same "disqualifications" had successfully entered the State Farm sales force. Indeed, two of the women had found sales positions with competitors of State Farm, proving in their minds that the refusal to transfer was thinly-veneered gender discrimination.

When the EEOC failed to resolve the matter and gave its permission for the women to sue, Saperstein filed suit in federal court. Saperstein believed there were hundreds, if not thousands, of women who had been turned away from sales positions due to gender discrimination.

State Farm went into the usual corporate rope-a-dope maneuver of obstructing discovery and attempting to run out the clock. They almost succeeded. Having denied under oath in discovery that records were kept of sales applicants' aptitude tests, the matter went to trial. But then, in the middle of the trial, State Farm's obstructionism was unintentionally undermined by one of the company's own witnesses.

The witness, an employee in State Farm's research division, was trying to support the company's claim that the number of women interested in sales agent trainee positions was exceedingly low compared with the number of positions available. The witness referred to the number of women who had taken the company's aptitude tests.

Saperstein interrupted. He asked the witness to repeat what he had just said. The researcher confirmed that the company had a database in its Bloomington, Illinois, headquarters that stored all sales applicants' aptitude scores.

Saperstein expressed outrage. Here was crucial evidence that he had requested during discovery, but which State Farm had denied existed. Judge Thelton W. Henderson was livid. He granted the attorney's request for a remedial discovery period of one week and imposed a then record-high $430,000 sanction against State Farm for discovery abuse. State Farm never contested the sanctions. With the additional evidence adduced, Saperstein's victory was complete. Judge Henderson found State Farm liable for sexual discrimination in its recruitment, selection, and hiring of sales trainees.

State Farm offered $13 million for a global settlement. Saperstein held out for individual trials of the estimated 60,000-70,000 women against whom State Farm had discriminated. After 90 trials and 75 settlements, State Farm realized that individual trials would take years. The case settled for $157 million — then the largest employment discrimination settlement in U.S. history. Combined with the individual settlements and trials, State Farm's gender bias cost it $245 million in damages, not counting its defense costs. Each class member received on average $200,000 to compensate her for the company's egregious wrongdoing.

"More important than the money," says Saperstein, "pursuant to the consent decree negotiated following the trial, State Farm instituted new selection practices, which have increased the hiring of women sales agents from less than one percent, when the case began, to more than 50 percent every year since 1992."

The reported decisions in this case and its subsequent case history can be found at *Kraszewski v. State Farm Gen. Ins. Co.*, 38 Fair Empl. Prac. Cas. (BNA) 197 (N.D. Cal. 1985) (general liability); *Kraszewski v. State Farm Gen. Ins. Co.*, 912 F.2d 1182 (9th Cir. 1990) (expanding back pay award), *cert. denied*, 499 U.S. 947 (1991).

Guy Saperstein

1992 Trial Lawyer of the Year Award Co-Winner
Gordon P. Erspamer
The Case of the Ten-Dollar Lawyers

W hat if you wanted an attorney to represent you and the law prevented any attorney from charging more than pocket change for his or her services? The real world impact of such a law would make it nearly impossible to find a lawyer. The law would effectively deny access to justice.

Such a law is impossible in the U.S., you say? Think again. Until the advocacy of San Francisco attorney Gordon P. Erspamer, such a law existed. In the name of protecting veterans from unscrupulous attorneys, lawyers representing veterans in matters before the U.S. Veterans Administration (VA) could charge no more than $10 for their services.

In 1862, Congress passed a law limiting attorneys' fees in matters involving veterans and the government. At first the fee cap was $5, approximately one month's pension payment. Congress raised the fee cap to $10 shortly after the Civil War, and it remained in place for the next 129 years. The purpose of the fee limitation was not to deprive the veterans of their legal rights or to skew veterans' proceedings in favor of the government. Rather, Congress designed the fee cap to protect veterans, who were often uneducated, from unscrupulous attorneys and to ensure that pension recipients would never have to share

What is public justice? The government cannot deprive Americans of their rights to petition for redress and due process by effectively preventing them from hiring lawyers.

their benefits with lawyers. This was also why the procedures for processing veterans' claims were kept simple and informal: no lawyers were wanted or needed. It was a system that worked reasonably well for a time.

Fast forward to 1946, the beginning of the Cold War. Earnest G. Erspamer, the man who will become Gordon Erspamer's father, is a survey officer aboard the *USS Bowditch* near the Bikini Atoll in the Central Pacific during the atomic bomb tests. Erspamer's test site duties required him to enter the water of the lagoon only days after an atomic bomb detonation in the very area. "It was very dangerous work," Gordon says. "But he was in the military and you do what you are told."

Erspamer was exposed to dangerous levels of radiation. He became ill and filed a claim in 1947 when he left the service. That claim went nowhere. Neither did his later claim as an atomic veteran when he developed leukemia, a disease blamed by the Erspamer family on exposure to radiation. (Three other people on Erspamer's team at Bikini also developed cancer in later years.)

In 1982, Gordon Erspamer was a young associate at the San Francisco law firm of Morrison & Foerster, a large corporate and business firm with a strong commitment to *pro bono* work (one of the prime factors that induced Gordon to accept his position). Gordon represented his father *pro bono* in the senior Erspamer's claim for veteran's benefits as a result of his leukemia. After his father died of his disease, the lawyer continued the case on behalf of his mother. He soon concluded that the $10 attorney fee cap was effectively preventing many veterans from obtaining justice and was directly responsible for the profound difficulties atomic veterans had in successfully presenting claims for service-related benefits before the VA.

Erspamer's conclusion would force him to confront the power and majesty of the federal government. The VA, which prided itself in its non-adversarial system of processing claims for service related benefits, was not about to change its system voluntarily. The VA maintained that veterans already received able assistance from veterans' service organizations. Yet the Erspamer family had learned that filing a claim based on harm caused by radiation exposure was an infinitely complex matter that required the assistance of an attorney. According to attorney Erspamer, cases in which *pro bono* attorneys aided atomic veterans had a 2,500 percent greater chance of obtaining benefits for the veteran or family than when the applicants acted on their own behalf or were represented by veteran's service organizations.

Erspamer's interest in atomic veterans' issues induced him to submit a request to his firm's *pro bono* committee, which gave him permission to mount a constitutional attack on the $10 fee cap. The expected budget for the entire case was estimated to be $100,000. Erspamer and his firm didn't know it, but they were about to embark on a 12-year knock-down-and-drag-out-no-holds-barred contest against the federal government. The battle would ultimately cost the firm more than $3.5 million in attorneys' time and costs.

Erspamer filed his case in the U.S. District Court for the Northern District of California. He based his constitutional challenge on the rights to petition the government for redress and due process guaranteed, respectively, by the First and Fifth Amendments to the U.S. Constitution. Erspamer's opening move was to apply for a preliminary injunction preventing the government from enforcing the $10 cap during the litigation.

On June 12, 1984, Judge Marilyn Hall Patel granted the request. The U.S. Supreme Court permitted welfare recipients to retain attorneys, she noted, because "the right to be heard would be in many cases, of little avail if it did not comprehend the right to be heard by counsel."

The judge emphasized the complicated procedural requirements of prosecuting a veteran's claim to justify an injunction against the fee cap. Veterans initially present their claims to one of the approximately 58 VA regional offices where a rating panel made up of a medical specialist, a legal specialist, and an occupational specialist, makes an initial determination as to whether the claim should be granted or denied. These ratings are based on a complicated schedule containing detailed anatomical and other analyses of a variety of medical problems. The next step is a Notification of Decision (ND), usually a brief denial. To challenge an adverse regional office decision, the claimant must file a 'Notice of Disagreement' (NOD) within one year of the mailing of the ND. If no NOD is filed, the decision is deemed final.

Upon receipt of the NOD, the VA may reverse its decision or, far more likely, proceed to prepare a "Statement of the Case" (SOC) in which the agency frames the issue for appeal. This document contains a summary of the evidence, a citation to pertinent laws and regulations, the decision reached by the rating board, and the reasons for the decision. If the veteran disagrees with anything in the SOC, he or she must file a "Substantive Appeal." Unless exception is taken to the contents of the SOC, the "appellant is presumed to be in agreement" with statements of fact or law and thus the appeal must "set out specific allegations of error of fact or law." Thereafter, an administrative Board of Veterans Appeals (BVA) in Washington, D.C., hears the appeal and usually disposes of the matter on the records alone. Veterans have no right to appeal to the civil courts from the decision of the BVA. A veteran's failure to comply with the VA's procedures often results in the denial of claims.

"The interrelation between these various rules is so complex," Judge Patel concluded, "that one VA adjudication officer…developed his own personal cross-index on file cards in an attempt to master the complexity."

Judge Patel concluded that the plaintiff's claim had a high probability of success under both the Fifth and First Amendment claims. The judge's unexpected decision to issue a countrywide injunction against the fee cap struck the VA like a bolt of lightning. However, the VA had just begun to fight.

The VA convinced the U.S. Supreme Court to review Judge Patel's decision, and the high court heard oral argument on March 27, 1985. The VA argued that Congress had the right to cap lawyers' fees involving veterans' claims because such proceedings are non-adversarial and because veterans do not have a property interest in the benefits to which they may be entitled. Moreover, the agency claimed that the injunction was improper because the plaintiffs could not demonstrate a high probability of success.

On June 28, 1985, a divided Supreme Court found for the VA. Then Associate Justice William Rehnquist, in a somewhat scathing rebuttal of Judge Patel's reasoning, asserted that the "great majority of claims [to the VA] involve simple questions of fact, or medical questions relating to degree of a claimant's disability." Moreover, a statistical comparison of success rates for all claimants who used attorneys and those who did not revealed that claimants represented by attorneys only had "slightly better success rates than claimants who were not represented at all." In reaching this conclusion, Rehnquist relied on statistics involving *all* VA claims — including the most simple and mundane — not only those involving atomic veterans and other complicated cases, such as "Agent Orange" claims filed by Vietnam veterans who suffered injury as a result of exposure to that toxic defoliant.

More damaging to the plaintiffs, the Court disagreed that the $10 fee cap necessarily violated the First and Fifth Amendments. The primary reason had to do with the nature of veterans' benefits versus welfare. "We think that the benefits at stake in VA proceedings," the Court ruled, "are more akin to Social Security benefits...than they are to welfare payments upon which the recipients...depend for their daily subsistence." Since the Court had previously ruled that recipients of Social Security are not entitled to a hearing before benefits are cut off, then veterans were not entitled to representation by counsel, especially considering that Congress had established a non-adversarial approach to determining the validity of claims. Thus the Court vacated the injunction, ruling that the evidence produced by the plaintiff fell "far short of the kind which would warrant upsetting Congress' judgment that this is the manner in which it wishes claims for veterans' benefits adjudicated."

The setback in the Supreme Court, discouraging as it was, did not dismiss the case; it merely vacated Judge Patel's injunction. Nor did the Supreme Court's chilly rebuff discourage Erspamer's commitment to the cause. It did, however, force the attorney and those with whom he worked to reconsider their approach to the case. Erspamer decided to limit the case while, at the same time, expanding its scope. In order to better manage the case and control its costs, Erspamer transformed the case into a class action limited to atomic veterans, whereas previously, the case had included the concerns of other veterans groups, such as those involved with Agent Orange, post traumatic stress syndrome, and prisoner of war claims. He succeeded in achieving class certification.

"I expected a vigorous opposition, but I never really expected that it would rise to the level it did," Erspamer recalls. "In the end, they had 10 lawyers from the Department of Justice working on it, three or four people from the U.S. Attorney's Office, and a small army of support staff." Litigation can be a socially Darwinistic enterprise in which those with the most resources often are able to obtain the "most" justice. That is a fact of life and law for which Erspamer, backed by the formidable resources of his firm, was prepared. What he didn't expect, however, was for the government to mount an unethical defense involving lying and the destruction of documents. Unfortunately, that is precisely what he got.

On November 26, 1986, Gordon Erspamer received an anonymous letter informing him that the Compensation and Pension Service of the Veterans Administration had engaged in blatant and massive "spoliation," or document destruction. Erspamer successfully sought a temporary restraining order mandating that the VA cease and desist its document purge. Soon thereafter, he asked Judge Patel to order sanctions against the VA for violating Rule 11 of the Federal Rules of Civil Procedure, which empowers courts to punish litigants who fail to comply with ethical and legal duties to the court.

Judge Patel, after considering the evidence, lowered the boom on the VA. Yes, she ruled, it was undisputed that the VA had destroyed "relevant and discoverable material." Indeed, the government had "explicitly conceded" its culpability.

More abuses soon came to light. Throughout the litigation, Erspamer had asked the VA to identify individual veteran claimants who had sought benefits for injuries received due to radiation exposure. The VA had repeatedly and emphatically denied that the names of such claimants had been segregated from those of other claimants for benefits and stated that identifying such claimants would require "a manual review of the virtually millions of individual claim files in the various regional offices of the Veterans Administration." In actuality, there were two computer databases that contained the requested information in an easily retrievable manner. The government was forced to officially retract its false claim.

Judge Patel imposed humiliating sanctions against the VA for blatant discovery abuse. She ordered the VA to reimburse the plaintiffs for "all fees and costs incurred in depositions, discovery, preparation, the hearing, and other matters related to the bringing" of the motion for sanctions and the earlier requests for protective orders. The amount of such reimbursement was deemed by stipulation to be $105,000. The VA was ordered to pay an additional $15,000 to the clerk of the court to compensate for "the unnecessary consumption of the court's time and resources." The VA was ordered to "designate an attorney within the VA" to be responsible at all times for receiving discovery requests, coordinating and preparing their responses, and signing the responses. The judge also ordered that all discovery responses be signed by the General Counsel of the Veterans Administration as well as the designated lawyer within the VA. The attorneys were further ordered to present the Court with a proposed plan to insure the proper circulation within the VA of all future discovery requests. Finally, the judge appointed a special magistrate to supervise all further discovery, an act required because "the Veterans Administration has demonstrated that it is either incapable or unwilling to provide discovery in accordance with the federal rules governing discovery."

Erspamer's victory in the discovery wars was partially attributable to the selflessness and patriotism of an anonymous whistleblower whom the attorney nicknamed "Deep Throat" after the famous *Washington Post* confidential source who helped bring down President Richard M. Nixon during the Watergate scandal. Erspamer's "Deep Throat" wrote him:

> The VA does not systematically provide veterans with adequate due
> process, especially for those claims disallowed for failure to submit
> requested evidence. Instead, those who manage adjudicative actions
> encourage premature denial of claims without notice in order
> to enhance statistically the data that measures the timeliness of
> claims processing.

In other words, VA managers appeared to be more interested in meeting their quotas for processing claims than in dealing justly with veterans. Thanks to the informant, Erspamer learned that managers received credit for the numbers of cases processed — hardly the user-friendly, non-adversarial system pictured by the VA spin machine. Perhaps most important for the lawsuit, the informant provided the key to unlocking the evidence that Erspamer used to prove the cover-up by telling the lawyer precisely how to ask questions in discovery so that the VA was left with no wiggle room to justify its obstructionism.

The precision of Erspamer's discovery caused the VA to switch tactics. Instead of failing to produce documents, the agency now performed one of the great document dumps in history. The tactic was to bury the trial lawyer in a blizzard of paper.

"They ended up producing every single paper at the Veterans Administration," Erspamer recalls with only slight hyperbole. "They produced documents that went back to the Civil War. They produced hernia claims from the Spanish American War. They produced travel vouchers and expense reports for all the people in the VA who had ever done any traveling, back for decades and decades. We had to send a team of 20 legal assistants to Washington, D.C., who spent probably four to six weeks there. I spent a couple of weeks there myself just sorting through the documents. They ended up sanctioned again, because they didn't sort through the responses before turning the documents over to us."

When the smoke cleared, the picture of VA practices came clearly into focus. "We came up with some astonishing results," says Erspamer. "The service officers did nothing to develop the facts in atomic cases. Nor did individual veterans. Lay people simply were unable to mount the factual basis for the claims, nor understand the medical issues. It was only when the veteran had a lawyer that there was ever a realistic chance of obtaining benefits."

The case went to trial in front of Judge Patel in 1987. In 1992, she issued her amended decision granting complete victory to the plaintiffs:

> Based on evidence presented at trial, the court finds unequivocally that attorneys would perform far better than volunteer service representatives in…areas that are key to a proper presentation of an IR [ionizing radiation] claim. Attorneys would conduct more detailed and thorough factual development. Attorneys would respond to VA requests for information, rather than leaving the lay-claimant to his or her own devices to respond to complex questions. Attorneys are more likely to detect and respond to procedural violations by the VA and to ensure that the claimant effectively takes advantage of procedural protections such as the right to a hearing. Attorneys are better able to track down the relevant regulations, manual provisions, and internal documents of the VA in order to muster support for their clients' IR claims and to interpret the myriad of complex regulations and rules relating to IR cases. Moreover, attorneys, because of their training, can more competently prepare briefs and appellate papers, conduct legal research, apply the law to the facts, and bring legal challenges to mistaken agency interpretations of regulations and statutes.

Based on these and other findings, Judge Patel ruled that "the $10 fee limitation violates the due process rights of ionizing radiation claimants and is thus unconstitutional" based on the due process clause. The Court also invalidated the law on First Amendment grounds. "This court...concludes," the order stated, "that the First Amendment guarantees an individual meaningful access to the adjudicatory process and protects efforts to obtain legal representation to effectuate this access."

Gordon Erspamer had spent a decade fighting an unethical defense backed by the resources of the federal government. His victory was a clear demonstration of the power of a dedicated trial lawyer and Morrison & Foerster's commitment to *pro bono* representation.

Erspamer's victory in the trial court, alas, was short-lived. The U.S. Court of Appeals for the Ninth Circuit reversed the decision, following the U.S. Supreme Court's reasoning when it vacated the initial preliminary injunction. Still, much good was achieved on behalf of all veterans in the NARS case. The intense publicity surrounding the case resulted in Congressional hearings, which disclosed to shocked lawmakers the substantive injustices the NARS case had uncovered. Congress rescinded the $10 fee cap. A new law prohibits any fee for initial VA proceedings — still an unjust limitation in complicated cases, since developing facts early in a case can be crucial in obtaining a favorable outcome. Of perhaps greater importance was the creation of the Court of Veterans' Appeals. The first case heard in the new court was that of Gordon Erspamer's mother. The Court awarded her widow's benefits for the service-related death of Earnest Erspamer from ionizing radiation exposure.

Other attorneys deserving of recognition for their important contributions to the atomic veterans' class action include Michael F. Ram, Thomas C. Vinje, Michael L. Zigler, and Richard E. Romaniw of Morrison & Foerster; Matthew L. Larrabee and Christopher Patti of Heller, Ehrman, White & McAuliffe; William C. Morrison-Knox of Sonnenschein, Nath & Rosenthal; and Karen W. Riley.

The reported decisions in this case and its subsequent case history can be found at *National Ass'n of Radiation Survivors (NARS) v. Walters,* 589 F. Supp. 1302 (N.D. Cal. 1984) (preliminary injunction), *probable jurisdiction noted,* 469

U.S. 1085 (1984), *decision reversed*, 473 U.S. 305 (1985) (overturning injunction), *after remand*, 111 F.R.D. 595 (N.D. Cal. 1986) (class certified); *NARS v. Derwinski*, 782 F. Supp. 1392 (N.D. Cal 1991) (entering permanent injunction), *rev'd*, 994 F.2d 583 (9th Cir. 1992), *cert. denied*, 510 U.S. 1023 (1993).

Gordon P. Erspamer

1992 Trial Lawyer of the Year Award Co-Winner
Richard C. Witzel
The Case That SLAPPed Decom Back

University of Denver professors George Pring and Penelope Canan coined the term "SLAPP" (an acronym for Strategic Lawsuits Against Public Participation) to describe legally questionable or meritless lawsuits — usually brought for libel or interference with contract — prosecuted by powerful parties to silence their critics. The actual purpose of a SLAPP is not to win monetary or other damages, but to muzzle the defendants by forcing them to counter expensive and emotionally draining protracted litigation. Thus, SLAPPs abuse legal processes in an effort to punish civic activists for exercising their right, guaranteed by the First Amendment to the U.S. Constitution, to participate actively in public discourse.

SLAPPs are powerful weapons of legal hegemony, but there are ways to thwart the tactic. The best remedy comes in two parts — first, successfully defending the case and then, if facts warrant, bringing a "SLAPP-back" suit for malicious prosecution, intentional infliction of emotional distress, or some similar tort against the original plaintiff.

St. Louis attorney Richard C. Witzel of Witzel, Kearns & Kenney shared the 1992 Trial Lawyer of the Year Award for bringing a landmark SLAPP-back suit. When the Canadian conglomerate Decom wanted to open a medical waste incinerator in Bunker, Missouri, it promoted the idea as a boon to the local economy. Community activists, including Linda Tanner, objected. Decom owned and operated several medical waste incinerators in Canada and the U.S.; those sites were well known among environmental activists and regulators for their gross violations of state and local environmental and health regulations. Therefore, the Missouri activists retained Witzel to help them work through appropriate public channels to prevent the construction.

> *What is public justice? The court system cannot be used by the rich and powerful to silence their critics.*

The trouble for Tanner, a resident of nearby Black, Missouri, began when she wrote to a South Carolina newspaper asking if it had done any stories or research on a similar incinerator Decom operated in that state. Decom officials found out about the letter and decided to punish Tanner with a SLAPP, filing a $1 million libel suit against her.

Tanner asked Witzel to help her. At the outset, the lawyer thought this was a simple case — a nuisance suit that could be easily defeated. As the trial date approached, as often happens in a SLAPP, Decom made several settlement offers that would have left Tanner free and clear, but would have required her to aver that her fears about the company's intentions were baseless.

Tanner knew that to give in to SLAPP pressure would be to expose other opponents of the incinerator to the same tactic. The answer, she and Witzel decided, was to SLAPP-back. When Decom voluntarily dismissed its suit, Tanner sued Decom and its president, Ray Adams, for malicious prosecution.

That's when things really got rough. Dan Patterson, a former mayor of Bunker and a principal in Decom's local subsidiary, accused Tanner of bringing microscope slides containing the AIDS virus to the local hospital where she worked. Patterson, who served on the county's ambulance district board, sought Tanner's dismissal from her job as a medical technician, claiming that patients arriving at the hospital in ambulances requested to go to another hospital nearby since they feared being exposed to the AIDS virus Tanner was allegedly bringing to work. Although she expressly and repeatedly denied the charges and the hospital's administrators found the charges preposterous, the hospital's board of directors — which included two ambulance drivers who worked under Patterson's supervision — terminated Tanner's hospital privileges, resulting in her loss of employment.

Decom also sent a letter to Missouri's governor, the state attorney general, and state legislators, suggesting that Tanner was a mentally unstable fanatic who was unfairly assaulting the Canadian firm and maligning its reputation. The letter, written by Ray Adams and sent under the signature of the president of Decom's U.S. subsidiaries, even went so far as to request that a grand jury be convened to investigate Tanner's activities. These allegations were repeated to a reporter for the *St. Louis Post Dispatch*, which published the remarks in a story about the controversy. Then Decom countered Tanner's SLAPP-back suit by refiling its original SLAPP suit.

Infuriated by Decom's conduct, Witzel quickly took the offensive. He expanded the malicious prosecution suit to include libel, abuse of process, tortious interference with contractual relations, and intentional infliction of emotional distress. The charges and counter charges had become the litigation equivalent of a blood feud.

Witzel was now faced with a daunting discovery task — probing the entire history and extensive operations of Decom. This was especially important since part of proving the case for malicious prosecution would be to prove that Tanner's motives in investigating the company had been warranted. Witzel also conducted an extensive investigation of the company's myriad subsidiaries around the world, which Decom resisted but ultimately to no avail.

At the trial, Witzel successfully challenged Decom's environmental record. He also used as especially damning witnesses the attorneys who handled the original SLAPP suit against Tanner for Decom. In particular, Wetzel was able to get admitted into evidence a notation from one of the lawyers working on the original suit: "GOAL: SHUT PEOPLE UP." Clearly, Tanner had been the victim of a SLAPP.

The outraged jury awarded Tanner $6.5 million in compensatory damages and, in a separate decision requiring only 30 minutes of deliberation, $80 million in punitive damages. The case was subsequently settled for an undisclosed sum.

Witzel's impressive victory against Decom not only prevented further legal attacks by the conglomerate against concerned citizens, but the amount of the verdict served as a warning to others who would resort to SLAPPs to win public controversies.

While the amount of the settlement is confidential, it is public knowledge Decom transferred its Missouri facilities, including 30 acres with a new three-story building and all incineration equipment, to Linda Tanner. Linda and her husband are now semi-retired and, according to attorney Witzel, are "active and generous supporters for a variety of civic, conservation, and environmental activities." Witzel continues to be active in SLAPP-back litigation.

There is no reported decision on the merits in *Tanner*.

Richard C. Witzel

CHAPTER ELEVEN

1993: The Case of the Contaminated Community
The Case of the Colorado Damages Cap

Auto Safety *General Motors Corp. v. Moseley*

Workers' Rights *Okeelanta Corp. v. Bygrave*

Workers' Rights *Caro-Galvan v. Curtis Richardson, Inc.*

Freeing the Innocent on Death Row *McMillian v. State*

Civil Rights *Haynes v. Shoney's, Inc.*

Co-Winners
Escamilla v. Asarco, Inc.
The Case of the Contaminated Community

State v. Defoor
The Case of the Colorado Damages Cap

The finalists for the 1993 Trial Lawyer of the Year Award sought justice in a wide range of areas. They promoted auto safety, fought for workers' rights, battled race discrimination, and freed an innocent man from death row. Attorneys from two different Colorado cases shared the Trial Lawyer of the Year Award. One legal team held a mineral smelter accountable for contaminating the town of Globeville, Colorado. The other overcame an unfair Colorado law to obtain redress for the victims of a horrific bus accident on Berthoud Pass. Both cases demonstrated the ability of trial lawyers to obtain public justice in seemingly hopeless circumstances.

Auto Safety
General Motors Corp. v. Moseley
James E. Butler, Jr. and Robert D. Cheeley

Attorneys James E. Butler, Jr., and Robert D. Cheely of Atlanta's Butler, Wooten, Overby & Cheeley took on General Motors (GM) in one of the most famous of the many lawsuits that have been filed against the auto maker due to injuries and deaths caused by their infamous "side saddle" gas tanks. (See Chapter Fifteen for another prominent case.)

GM mounted "side saddle" gas tanks outside of the mainframe of pickup trucks between 1973 and 1987. The company's design decision made the tanks more vulnerable to rupture and fuel leakage, exposing people in side-impact accidents to the danger of death or significant injury due to explosion or fire.

Shannon Mosely, age 17, died in his 1985 GM pickup truck when a drunk driver broadsided him, causing his side saddle gas tank to explode. His death was one of 300 allegedly caused by GM's faulty side saddle tanks. Mosely's parents retained Butler and Cheely to hold GM responsible for their son's untimely death. It took Butler and Cheely three years to get to trial. During the discovery phase, there were more than 50 depositions and many thousands of documents were produced. One document revealed that GM pickups had a crash fire fatality rate four to eight times higher than Ford's.

Butler and Cheeley also made effective use of two special sources who materialized as a result of what Butler called "the rebellion in the engineering ranks at GM." Some of the best information came from anonymous telephone calls telling the attorneys what to look for. Moreover, their star witness was a former GM engineer who delivered the devastating testimony that GM routinely and systematically concealed evidence of the defective fuel tank design. Evidence presented at trial proved that GM had shredded countless incriminating documents in its cover-up of the pickups' hazards, that GM concealed for 10 years at least 24 side-impact test crashes of its pickups done between 1981 and 1983 that showed that the tanks "split like melons," and that top GM officials had concluded by 1981 that the side tanks were "no longer defensible," yet continued to produce them for six more years.

The jury rendered a $4.24 million compensatory verdict at 11:00 a.m. on February 4, 1993. Following the luncheon recess, GM's counsel began the argument on punitive damages by expressing, for the first time, GM's regret for its part in the tragedy, sympathy for the victim's family, and reassurance that the jury's decision "will make us a better company." Lest the jury be misled by such an apparent change of heart, Butler and Cheely argued that, instead of providing only palliatives, GM should have disclosed to the jury the press release it had already issued at lunchtime, in which the auto maker continued to deny wrongdoing and defended the faulty fuel tank design.

The jury adopted the trial lawyers' proposed formula — at least $20 for each of the five million defective GM pickups still on the road — and awarded $101 million in punitive damages. On appeal, the verdict was affirmed in part and reversed in part, leading to a settlement. The case increased the visibility of the side saddle gas tank issue and brought greater oversight efforts by federal regulators.

The later reported decision in this case can be found at *General Motors Corp. v. Moseley*, 447 S.E.2d 302 (Ga. Ct. App. 1994) (affirming jury verdict in part and reversing in part).

James E. Butler, Jr.

Workers' Rights
Okeelanta Corp. v. Bygrave
James K. Green, David L. Gorman, and
Edward J. Tuddenham

The sugar cane industry routinely exploits Caribbean workers brought to the U.S. for seasonal work in Florida's sugar cane fields. In the absence of effective government regulation to protect these workers' rights as they perform dangerous, arduous labor, litigation has provided a successful avenue for securing justice in some cases.

A prime example is the class action suit filed on behalf of 15,000 sugar cane cutters in state court in West Palm Beach, Florida, by James F. Green and David L. Gorman of West and North Palm Beach respectively, and Edward J. Tuddenham of Austin, Texas. The case involved a simple yet ingenious approach. Joining their talents with experienced commercial litigator David Gorman, the lead trial counsel, the attorneys filed a three-page breach-of-contract complaint against the employers, including the Sugar Cane Growers Cooperative of Florida, Inc. Nowhere did the complaint call for federal action or mention the federal minimum wage, the piece rate, the task rate, or the issue of workers' nationality. "History has taught us that the more complicated actions are not always the better way to go," according to Tuddenham.

The suit charged the growers with breaking their promise to pay cane cutters $5.30 per ton. Instead, the companies paid the workers only $4 per ton, an amount set arbitrarily by field bosses. This pay formula cheated workers out of $16 per day, big money for the poor black workers who came mostly from Jamaica. The workers prevailed on August 21, 1992, winning $51 million in back pay since 1987, or about $3,000 per worker in the class.

The victory provided a glimmer of hope for farm workers. *Washington Post* columnist Colman McCarthy offered this inspiring comment on the decision: "Employment contract violations are rampant, with few migrant farm workers aware of their rights and having the emotional energy to stand up for them. When they do stand, the enduring comfort is that some of the most spirited and idealistic lawyers in the country are next to them." The struggle for the cane field workers' rights, however, is far from over. Three years later, a Florida appellate court reversed the judgment.

The later reported decision in this case can be found at *Okeelanta Corp. v. Bygrave*, 660 So. 2d 743 (Fla. Dist. Ct. App. 1995) (reversing trial court judgment).

Workers' Rights
Caro-Galvan v. Curtis Richardson, Inc.
Steven F. Samilow and Ross B. Bricker

Another Florida case resulted in dramatic improvements for seasonal farm workers throughout the nation. The case involved the 1983 Migrant and Seasonal Agricultural Worker Protection Act (AWPA), the primary federal statute protecting migrant workers. The law, while inadequately protecting exploitable workers, at least provided a minimal safety net. Yet before Miami attorneys Steven F. Samilow and Ross B. Bricker litigated the case of *Caro-Galvan v. Curtis Richardson, Inc.*, the AWPA did not serve to protect farm workers employed to harvest crops year round; it was being limited to migrant and seasonal workers.

At the trial level, nine plaintiffs asserted that their employer had violated AWPA and the Fair Labor Standards Act by, among other things, housing them in seriously substandard facilities, keeping incomplete records detailing the work they performed, and paying them less than the federal minimum wage. Such conditions existed in Florida's $100 million fern industry because the workers were seen as exempt from the protection of the AWPA. Off-season take-home pay for some workers dropped to near zero after the company deducted $150 from their monthly pay as rent for living in company trailers.

Losing the case in the trial court, Samilow and Bricker appealed to the U.S. Court of Appeals for the Eleventh Circuit, urging that the work of "seasonal or other temporary nature" applied to the fern workers. The Court of Appeals concluded that all field work is "seasonal" and thus expanded the coverage of the AWPA not only to the 7,000 fern workers in Florida, but also to one million nursery and farm workers not previously covered by the law. By representing these exploited workers *pro bono*, attorneys Samilow and Bricker of the Miami branch of Chicago's Jenner & Block exemplified the highest ideals of the legal profession.

After the plaintiff's victory in the Eleventh Circuit, the case settled. The defendant Richardson paid approximately $50,000. "This was a good settlement, since Richardson was cash poor," attorney Samilow reports. The lead plaintiff and his family received approximately $10,000. They used the money for a down payment on a house. The case has been cited in more than 30 federal appellate and district court opinions.

Greg Schell, head of Florida Rural Legal Services' migrant farm worker

division, also deserves recognition for his important contributions on this case.
The reported decision in this case can be found at *Caro-Galvan v. Curtis Richardson, Inc.*, 993 F.2d 1500 (11th Cir. 1993).

Steven F. Samilow

Ross B. Bricker

Freeing the Innocent on Death Row
McMillian v. State
Bryan Stevenson

Wherever one may stand on the issue of the death penalty, there is agreement that the criminal justice system's worst nightmare is the execution of an innocent man. Thanks to the work of a determined and compassionate trial lawyer, the life of a wrongly condemned black man named Walter McMillian was spared.

Monroeville, Alabama, McMillian's hometown of 7,000, is best known as the setting of Harper Lee's 1961 novel *To Kill a Mockingbird* about a black man falsely accused of raping a white woman and the courageous white attorney, Atticus Finch, who defended him. In McMillian's case, the charge was murder of a white woman and the courageous black attorney who saved his life was Harvard Law School graduate Bryan Stevenson of the Alabama Capital Representation Resource Center (ACRRC) in Montgomery, Alabama.

Alabama police arrested McMillian, an African-American, in June of 1987, seven months after a white teenage girl was shot to death. McMillian, who had never been convicted of a felony, was a suspect in the killing because he had been dating a white woman. Instead of taking him to a local jail, police took McMillian to a death row cell at nearby Holman State Prison, where he spent 13 months awaiting trial without bail.

"McMillian was given a death row prisoner's orientation and manual, placed in a death row cell, and subjected to all restrictions and treatment received by every death row prisoner in Alabama, although he had never been tried, convicted, or sentenced for any offense," Stevenson later stated in testimony before the U.S. Senate Committee on the Judiciary. McMillian's transfer to death row was the result of a motion by the state prosecutor, granted by Circuit Judge Robert E. Lee Key, Jr.

The State of Alabama presented no credible motive, nor any physical or forensic evidence linking the accused with the murder. However, Ralph Myers, a white career criminal with another murder charge pending against him, identified McMillian as the killer. In exchange for his testimony, Myers was given an opportunity to avoid the death penalty himself. Despite testimony from a dozen defense witnesses that McMillian was at a fish fry when the murder happened, the jury heeded Myers and two other men who split a reward of $7,000 upon McMillian's conviction for their identification of his "low rider" truck at the site of the killing. Even then, the jury recommended life without parole on August 18, 1988. Yet Judge Key disregarded the recommendation and imposed the ultimate sanction of death.

After attorney Stevenson and his two co-counsels, Bernard E. Harcourt of ACRRC and Michael P. O'Connor of the Federal Defenders of San Diego, got involved in the case, Myers admitted that he had been pressured by law enforcement officers to testify falsely against McMillian. In fact, Myers had told several state doctors in a pre-trial evaluation that he was going to frame an innocent man. This opened other avenues of inquiry. Among the new discoveries, Stevenson learned that McMillian had not converted his truck into the "low rider" style supposedly seen by the false witnesses until after the killing. Therefore, if anyone did see a low rider truck at the murder scene, it could not have been McMillian's.

Despite these revelations, Stevenson lost four separate appeals. Then when the two witnesses recanted their testimony, Stevenson filed a motion to dismiss all charges. At last the State conceded its error and joined in Stevenson's motion.

The New York Times summarized the outcome on March 3, 1993, the day McMillian finally walked free: "Whatever the reason, inquiries by Mr. Stevenson and by Alabama Bureau of Investigation agents have since discredited every element of the prosecution's case."

McMillian bitterly told reporters, "I've learned there isn't justice. Just the way they framed me, they could do you, too."

The reported decisions in this case can be found at *McMillian v. State*, 570 So. 2d 1285 (Ala. Crim. App. 1990); *McMillian v. State*, 616 So. 2d 933 (Ala. Crim. App. 1993) (reversing conviction and death sentence).

Bryan Stevenson

Civil Rights

Haynes v. Shoney's, Inc.

Thomas A. Warren, Barry L. Goldstein, and
the NAACP Legal Defense and Education Fund

Henry and Billie Sue Elliott worked for a Captain D's seafood restaurant, a franchise of Shoney's Inc., in Marianna, Florida, where Henry served as manager and Billie Sue supervised the dining room. The restaurant fired the Elliots on the basis of racial discrimination with an unusual twist: both were white. They were fired not because of their race, but because they refused an order from their supervisors to replace their black employees with white substitutes by cutting back the black employees' hours until they quit their jobs.

Attorney Thomas Warren of Tallahassee, Florida, took the case and was soon joined by attorney Barry L. Goldstein of Saperstein, Mayeda, Larkin & Goldstein in Oakland, California, and the NAACP Legal Defense and Education Fund of Washington, D.C. What the lawyers uncovered was a massive pattern of racial discrimination in hiring and promotion that pervaded the entire Shoney's business empire. It soon became clear that black employees were generally limited to the "back of the house" slots, such as cook and dishwasher. "Front of the house" positions, such as server, went mostly to white workers.

The case was soon certified as a class action with four white people and 12 African Americans as the named plaintiffs and Shoney's as a co-defendant with Shoney's founder and long-time chairman and chief executive officer Raymond E. Danner. The litigation team believed that a strategy presenting the claims of both black and white employees would have a greater impact on a Pensacola, Florida, jury. However, because of the class nature of the suit, black employees throughout the chain were represented in the case.

The evidence in the case filled 200 boxes of records and included affidavits and records concerning more than 210 restaurants. The NAACP Legal Defense and Education Fund expended more than 25,000 hours and approximately $1 million in out-of-pocket costs.

Under intense pressure, the defendants buckled and settled before trial. The consent decree required payments of $132.5 million the highest recovery until that time in a race discrimination case. Of the total amount, $105 million comprised damage payments to the named plaintiffs, who received $100,000 each, and the 30,000 class members represented in the case, who received varying amounts. Of greater significance for preventing future discrimination, Shoney's committed to "improve its utilization of blacks."

Specifically, the company agreed to incorporate equal employment opportunity and affirmative action criteria into its regular training, performance, evaluation, and bonus incentive programs for managers. In addition, the company agreed to establish a tuition reimbursement plan for class members and to solicit input annually from every black employee regarding interest in promotion.

Shoney's complied fully with its obligations under the court ruling. In light of its compliance, on February 29, 2000, Judger Roger Vinson terminated the Consent Decree.

The unreported decision in this case can be found at *Haynes v. Shoney's, Inc.*, 1993 WL 19915 (N.D. Fla. Jan. 25, 1993) (approving consent decree).

Thomas A. Warren   *Barry L. Goldstein*

1993 Trial Lawyer of the Year Award Co-Winners

Macon Cowles, Kevin S. Hannon, Mary A. Kane, Kieron F. Quinn, and William A. Rossbach

The Case of the Contaminated Community

The residents of the Denver neighborhood known as Globeville had a major pollution problem. For many years, people in this mostly working class, diverse, metropolitan neighborhood had watched helplessly as heavy metals from industrial smelting invaded their homes, gardens, playgrounds, and yards. Environmental degradation of Globeville became such an acute problem that the State of Colorado passed out flyers in 1989 warning residents to mix home-grown vegetables with store bought varieties to reduce the risk of contracting cancer and other diseases.

A metal processing smelter owned by Asarco primary caused this environmental catastrophe. The smelter, which had been in operation for more than a century, had once processed arsenic. Now cadmium, a metal used in batteries, was the primary metal smelted at the plant. The management and operation of the smelter was a toxic disaster. Asarco brought pulverized ore from Rocky Mountain mines to the facility in uncovered railroad cars and stored it in open piles, where the wind often picked up the ore dust and blew it into Globeville and across Denver. Heated gas made up of processed ore would often escape during the smelting process. So much toxic dust escaped during storage and processing that the company even had a large vacuum cleaner-type machine to sweep the roads outside the plant in order to recover valuable ore that would otherwise be lost.

What is public justice? Corporations do not contaminate the environment and, if they do, they are forced to clean it up.

Environmental attorney Macon Cowles of Boulder, Colorado, who had been the lead counsel representing national and regional environmental groups in the *Exxon Valdez* oil spill case for Trial Lawyers for Public Justice, knew of the disaster from his participation in the steering committee of the Land and Water Fund of the Rockies, a *pro bono* environmental law firm. He was also aware that some Globeville residents — out of sheer desperation — had joined together as activists to pressure all levels of government to clean up their neighborhood. Since the community failed at obtaining meaningful relief from the government, Cowles attempted to help them find good legal representation for a civil suit. When that effort failed, after much research and soul searching, he decided to take on the case himself.

Asarco had the resources to hire the best defense lawyers money could buy in order to put up a protracted — and expensive — fight. Cowles believed that a team of competent lawyers from small firms could defeat Asarco, even with all its money. To assemble a team of trial lawyers, Cowles turned first to trial lawyers who had worked with him on the *Exxon Valdez* case for TLPJ — attorneys Bill Rossbach of Missoula, Montana, and Kieron Quinn of Baltimore. Rossbach was an expert on resisting "risk assessment" defenses, which Cowles calls "the industry's notion of a cancer risk which should be foisted off on the public in order to save money." Cowles chose Quinn because "he has a disciplined and searching way of approaching legal issues, which cuts right to the bone." To "set the hook" in bringing Quinn onto the litigation team, Cowles went fly-fishing with him "one beautiful morning on the Roaring Fork at summer solstice the year we filed the case."

Soon Denver attorney Kevin Hannon joined the team. Cowles describes him as "a serious lawyer who is a fierce competitor." Denver attorneys Mary Kane and her partner Terri Harrington rounded out the team in the fall of 1991. "Kane was a particularly artful examiner of witnesses," Cowles says. "She put her own witnesses at ease, while threading the needle of difficult evidentiary objections, without ever letting the story be broken."

The first job for the legal team was to find the right plaintiffs to represent the community. "I had good relationships with the activists in the community," Cowles recalls. "And I wanted to ensure that these people knew that the lawyers would not take over the case in a way that would disempower the community." Colorado had been litigating a Superfund case against Asarco on account of the Globeville contamination since 1983. Superfund litigation requires many public hearings in parallel with the court proceedings. It was important that the citizen activists be able to represent the community and speak freely at the hearings. It was also important that the statements of the activists not be used against the community — the plaintiffs — in the class action case. So the Globeville legal team chose a small group of people to serve as class representatives who were wholly separate from the activists.

The legal team asked the community activists to distribute intake sheets to

Globeville residents, which when filled out, were returned directly to Cowles. The next step was to find members of the community who had compelling claims, but who were less likely to run afoul of the statute of limitations. "We wanted people with whom the jury would identify," Cowles says. "We found the perfect couple to be lead plaintiffs. Margaret Escamilla, kind and articulate, ran a day care center out of her home. Her husband Bobby, always with a twinkle in his eye, was a mechanic for the Regional Transportation District."

The preliminaries over, the team set to work — legally and from a public education perspective. The media had ignored the situation for years, a silence the legal team believed worked to Asarco's advantage. The lack of coverage helped the company continue with business as usual; it dispirited the residents by making them worry that "the little guys" could never win and it allowed government representatives to shirk their duty to Globeville. So Cowles made a fateful decision. He held a news conference at the gates of Asarco to discuss the litigation, during which he borrowed a quote from Ralph Nader, declaring that the case was "about toilet training of a transnational corporation." This statement became the basis for an ethics charge leveled by Asarco's lawyers against Cowles for violating a Colorado State Bar rule against discussing pending litigation in the press. For the balance of the case, he would not only have to litigate as one of the plaintiffs' lawyers, but would have to defend himself before the Bar.

The press had previously ignored the people of Globeville in their many attempts to get public agencies to make Asarco stop polluting the neighborhood and to require them to cleanup their yards and parks, gardens, schools, and playgrounds. However, when the press learned that Asarco's lawyers had filed an ethics complaint in order to keep a lawyer for the people from speaking publicly about the case, they began to write stories about the plight of Globeville against a powerful mining company, rich lawyers, and unresponsive institutions. For the next 18 months, the press reported closely on every significant action taken in the case — and on every action taken in the ethics proceeding, which eventually was dismissed as being without merit.

As the case progressed, the costs mounted. Cowles and Hannon assumed most of the responsibility for financing the lawsuit. Both took out second mortgages on their houses. Cowles liquidated his and his wife's IRA retirement. During the six week trial, he would slip out periodically to the bank to withdraw $10,000 in cash from one of several gold cards and deposit the money in his operating account to cover experts, exhibits, transcripts and the like. Similarly, Hannon ran his credit cards to their limit, to the point that he went more than $100,000 into debt. All told, the five lawyers would personally finance more than $275,000 in costs as they litigated against a well-heeled, paid-by-the-hour defense firm with no stake in keeping the litigation short or inexpensive.

Four months before trial, with most of the plaintiffs' lawyers fully occupied in six weeks of solid depositions, it became apparent that Asarco would settle its Superfund case with the State of Colorado — which was then pending in federal court — and then use the settlement's inadequate cleanup plan as a shield in the *Escamilla* class action, which was filed in state court. In order to use the federal settlement as a shield, however, Asarco would have to get the federal judge to approve it. "And when that time came, we needed to be parties to the federal court action as intervenors," Cowles recalls. "Kieron Quinn took on the job of writing a motion to intervene, should it become necessary." It did. The legal team filed it the very week before the trial in state court started. "Kieron's brief was very powerful, very well done," Cowles says. "It was just what we needed."

The proposed Superfund settlement would have cleaned up only 50 out of the 475 affected homes. "The intervention allowed us to make sure the federal judge was aware of the context of the settlement," Cowles says. Would this slap-on-the-wrist settlement with Asarco have bound the Globeville residents and barred their private suit? The law was unsettled, but one thing was sure: it would have become the subject of protracted litigation.

Finally, on February 1, 1993, the courtroom doors opened for the residents of Globeville. The case was full of high drama. Kane claimed the courtroom for the plaintiffs with the first witness, plaintiff Robert Escamilla. He spoke of his family, his neighbors, his community, his garden, and the pall of contamination that had settled on Globeville for the past many years as the health and future of the community were discovered to be at risk. With the plaintiffs having to overcome the "risk assessment" that Asarco's experts had done to justify the corporation's refusal to spend money to clean up the community, the Globeville legal team went on the offensive. Rossbach called as an adverse witness Asarco's primary expert on clean up, David Folkes, who had overseen the risk assessment and written the whitewash cleanup plan. Under questioning from Rossbach, Folkes admitted that even though his report had concluded that the poisons in the soil were not dangerous to the community, he required that his staff who went to Globeville to test the soil *wear respirators and safety suits*, as well as take other precautions to avoid exposure to the poisons in the soil.

Kevin Hannon took on Asarco's liability witnesses — the management people who testified that the company had acted properly. One such witness stated with a straight face that it was perfectly acceptable to wait 15 years to carry out a recommendation by an Asarco employee to install technology to trap fugitive cadmium and arsenic emissions from the company's smelter. When Asarco called a historian to blame the contamination of the neighborhood on another smelter that had operated decades previously in the same area, Hannon confronted the witness with a document from the Denver Public Library that proved Asarco had also owned that smelter at the time it was spewing poisons into the area.

The primary issue in the case was the proper standard to apply for damages. The case had failed to obtain certification for a health class action suit, and was thus limited to property damage. Asarco wanted to pay (if at all) only for the loss of property value caused by the pollution, a substantial sum but inadequate, in the legal team's estimation, to redress the losses suffered by their clients. The plaintiffs countered with a full-fledged request for remediation, a remedy that would force Asarco to clean up the neighborhood totally — an expensive proposition.

After a six-week trial, the judge required the jury to come up with two verdicts: one setting the amount of damages for the reduction in value approach desired by Asarco and the other to include remediation, as urged by the Globeville legal team. The Court then made the choice as to which to apply to the case. Happily for Globeville, he chose remediation. The verdict amounted to $28 million, of which $20 million would pay for the cleanup and $8 million would compensate class members for their annoyance and discomfort.

Asarco threatened to appeal, but in a *Wall Street Journal* story published during Asarco's annual meeting, Cowles challenged the company for not taking the case seriously before it went to trial. The company decided to throw in the towel. A defense lawyer called Kieron Quinn and said, "We want to talk settlement. Can you get Cowles to stop talking to the press?" Cowles agreed to keep mum about the negotiations, but not about the case itself or the underlying issues.

Over the next month, Quinn conducted settlement negotiations, which culminated in Asarco settling for more than $35 million. Asarco paid the class members $14 million in two payments and agreed to remove 12-18 inches of topsoil in the entire class area and replace everyone's landscaping at a price tag in excess of $10 million. It was the largest private environmental damages case in Colorado history, and the resulting cleanup transformed the entire community.

As of this writing, the cleaning of Globeville is complete, and the neighborhood now has the look of a small town after a spring rain. The houses are brightly painted and project a feeling of welcome and warmth to the public spaces. After the citizens won their suit, the City of Denver begin to reinvest in Globeville's sidewalks, streets, parks, and street lamps. It is a story of renewal, rebirth, and community vitality. Resident Ray Oletski said, "Our attorneys did a wonderful job. I don't normally like attorneys much, but these attorneys were a Godsend."

The law firms were Macon Cowles & Associates of Boulder, Colorado; the Hannon Law Firm of Denver; Quinn, Ward & Kershaw of Baltimore; Mary Kane and Associates of Denver; and Rossbach & Whiston of Missoula, MT.

There is no reported decision on the merits in this case.

Macon Cowles

Kevin S. Hannon

Mary A. Kane

Kieron F. Quinn

William A. Rossbach

1993 Trial Lawyer of the Year Award Co-Winner
Leland Anderson
The Case of the Colorado Damages Cap

S ometimes, the worst tragedies happen in the most beautiful places. U.S. Highway 40 is one of the nation's most scenic roads, winding through the grandeur of the Rocky Mountains and providing access to Estes Park and Rocky Mountain National Park. Can one imagine anything more pleasurable and seemingly safe than to spend a quiet, lazy August day on a bus tour into these amazing mountains, breathing the clean, crisp high altitude air and snapping pictures of the trees, streams, wildlife, and awe-inspiring craggy vistas?

What thought would you have given to the road maintenance worker clearing rocks and debris from a roadside catch basin with a large orange bulldozer? Perhaps a stray thought of how nice it might be to work in such splendor, out in the open air. Or maybe mild annoyance at a brief whiff of diesel fumes or the engine-roar of the tractor as it maneuvered near the edge of the road. Perhaps you would have noticed the boulder being maneuvered by the bulldozer. "Big rock," you might have thought. But surely, a minute later, when your bus, following the winding road, switched back to a spot hundreds of feet directly beneath the section of Highway 40 where the bulldozer worked, the rock and the highway worker would have already left your conscious awareness.

What is public justice? Citizens can use the courts to hold the government accountable for the injuries caused by the negligence of government workers.

On a fateful date in August 1987, a nearly seven-ton, granite boulder suddenly crashed through a stand of uphill pine trees above a tour bus. The driver had no time to react as the boulder smashed into the right front of the bus at the passenger door, sheered along the vehicle's right side, crushing and tearing, and then rolled out of sight further down the steep mountain slope. Amazingly, the driver kept the bus from going over the side of the road as he brought the vehicle to a stop.

Attorney Leland Anderson of Denver's Sears, Anderson & Swanson would later describe the bus as looking "like a small village ravaged by a bomb." Six passengers were already dead; two more would die within two days. Four were grievously injured; of these, a German tourist named Marcus Lang would die a year later in his homeland.

Rockslides happen in the mountains, of course, but this boulder was not set into motion by nature. Moments after the tour bus passed the Berthoud Pass work site, a State maintenance worker operating a bulldozer maneuvered a 6.7-ton granite boulder to the side of the road. He got out and looked down the hill. Thinking it safe and believing that the boulder would slide to a stop as others had, he pushed the car-sized granite rock off the edge of the road, down the hill.

Unseen by the worker, who could have done nothing at this point to change the future, the rock did not slide. It rolled 725 feet down the 66 percent slope, seemingly taking dead aim at the approaching bus. Thus was set into motion a terrible tragedy that would give rise to a noble legal struggle for which attorney Anderson would share honors as the 1993 Trial Lawyer of the Year Award winner.

In any civil case, two key questions must be asked — whether there is liability and whether there are damages. In this case, liability was easy to prove. If the State worker had not pushed the boulder onto the steep slope, the rolling rock never would have hit the bus. Moreover, later investigation would reveal scarring in several trees from rolling boulders and rocks, proving that this had not been the first such case of a huge rock rolling down the slope instead of sliding. In addition, the work at the site clearly violated the Colorado Department of Highway's work rules that required dump areas to be graded so that rocks would not roll out of dump areas. The steep slope at the accident site was anything but graded. The rules also required a traffic stop whenever there was a "possibility" that a rock pushed over an embankment could cause damage to persons or property below. Not only was there no traffic stop, but the worker in the bulldozer was alone at the time of the accident and only became aware of the collision when told by a passing motorist. Proving liability was not the problem.

What about damages? Unfortunately, with nine deaths and the costs associated with recovering from serious injuries to redress, the State of Colorado had much to answer for — later estimates put the damage total near the $14 million level. Surely, any trial lawyer worthy of the name would be able to obtain a substantial recovery for his or her clients.

As personal injury cases go, then, this one would seem relatively straightforward. However, during the 1980s, Colorado had passed a number of "tort reform" statutes, enacting scores of laws designed to protect wrongdoers from having to fully compensate people injured by their behavior. One of these laws, the 1983 Colorado Government Immunity Act, capped civil damage awards for negligence against the state at $150,000 per person, or $400,000 aggregate per accident. Relying on this cap, the state dropped its liability insurance. This cap would limit damages in the bus accident case to a mere $13,000 per victim. Yet the medical bills incurred by Marcus Lang alone reached $400,000 before he finally died.

In this case, winning public justice would require a public-minded trial lawyer, rallying a team with the battle cry, "Hoka hey!"

"Hoka hey!" was the cry of the great Sioux warrior Crazy Horse before the Battle of the Greasy Grass River, better known as the Battle of Little Big Horn. Translated into English, the exclamation means, "This is a good day to die." The essential meaning of the war cry was not a defeatist expression that the time had come to die, but rather an exhortation to "give it everything you've got," come what may. "Hoka hey!" would become the cry around which Leland Anderson would rally a group of trial lawyers willing to strive *pro bono* against the grievous injustice of the damage cap.

On the date of the accident, it happened that the Colorado State Trial Lawyers Association annual conference was taking place in Snowmass, Colorado, gathering together some of that state's best legal minds and most determined advocates for civil justice. As word spread about the tragedy, the attendees naturally talked among themselves about the legal issues that might arise. Everyone knew that barely a year before, the Colorado Supreme Court had upheld the damage caps of the Government Immunities Act. In short, the bus accident case was a loser; logically, the only legal issue would be how to fashion a "just" division of the paltry $400,000.

The more the lawyers thought about it, the more angry they grew and the more determined to at least attempt to redress this doubly grievous wrong. Some of the lawyers got together to organize an *ad hoc* meeting. The mood was grim. Suddenly, a lawyer stood up. "We have to take this case for free," he asserted. "There was nervous laughter" at the suggestion, Anderson recalls. "Then, a long silence, as eyes drifted to the floor." *Pro bono* work is an ethical imperative for all lawyers. But litigating against the state, with its unlimited resources, for free? That would be like falling on one's own sword.

Then, another lawyer named broke the silence. "We don't have a choice," he declared. "It is the right thing to do."

The first step was to form a committee to organize the representation. Fifteen lawyers agreed to represent the various parties. Anderson represented the family of Marcus Lang and was named lead attorney, upon whose back much of the work would fall. The Public Justice Foundation of Colorado, a non-profit organization dedicated to the pursuit of civil justice, agreed to finance the effort. The group recruited law students to donate work in support of the case. An economist donated his expertise to determine the proper level of damages. A highway department whistleblower revealed the inner workings of the Highway Department. The pleadings and briefs began to mount.

Knowing that a direct attack on the damage cap would fail, Anderson and his legal warriors decided upon a more oblique approach. This would not be a suit for negligence; it would be a constitutional rights case. The lawyers propounded three primary challenges to the damage cap — heightened scrutiny under the due process clause, equal protection of the laws, and almost as an afterthought, a civil rights challenge under U.S. Code section 1983, which prohibits persons acting under color of law from depriving others of their constitutional rights and liberties. Of the three, the 1983 action seemed the most rickety: the U.S. Supreme Court had previously ruled that negligence does not support a 1983-based, federal civil rights case.

Meanwhile, the lawyers applied political pressure on the Colorado State Legislature to permit the State to compensate the victims justly. Unfortunately, the Colorado Constitution forbids special legislation of the sort that would have been required to free the bus accident victims of the fee cap. But what if the legislature retroactively repealed the law or expanded the caps? The legislative attempt generated much media and public support. Edward Conry of the *Denver Post* wrote in his July 30, 1990, column that governments should behave as moral teachers:

> When the Colorado legislature limits its liability, it ignores morality and
> justice. It ignores its role as moral teacher. When governments do that,
> they damage society in about the same way the boulder damaged the
> bus and the lives of those 28 people.

Despite the public pressure, in the face of angry editorials, the legislature refused to act. The damage cap held. Soon the state won summary judgment, dismissing all claims.

The only thing between the bus victims and sheer injustice was the wispy hope that the Colorado Supreme Court would see the caps as a constitutional violation, rather than an exercise of legislative discretion. On February 3, 1992, the Colorado Supreme Court ruled in favor of the plaintiffs, on the basis of their third, and least likely, claim. The Court wrote, "In order to state a claim for relief under section 1983, a plaintiff must allege that a defendant acted under color of state law and that the defendant's action deprived the plaintiff of a right secured by the federal constitution or federal laws...." Noting that the parties "against whom summary judgment is sought [are] entitled to the benefit of all favorable inferences that may be drawn from the facts...we are not convinced that there was no genuine issue of material facts with respect to claimants' section 1983 allegations. We thus reinstate and remand the section 1983 claim for further hearings."

It wasn't much of a favorable ruling, at most a bare toehold upon a sheer granite cliff. The lawyers were discouraged. The ruling permitted the plaintiffs to proceed with litigation, but the chances of actually winning the claim seemed remote.

To rally his colleagues, Anderson wrote what came to be known as the "Hoka hey! Memo," urging the group to fight on — regardless of the time it would take, regardless of the costs, regardless of the seemingly slim chance of prevailing. Their obligations as professionals and simple justice demanded it. Clear-eyed that their options were severely constrained and their odds of prevailing were slim, the lawyers agreed to press on. Indeed, this was a good day to defy the odds in battle.

"We knew we would have to demonstrate that state actors engaged in intentional misconduct, or perhaps reckless conduct that could be construed as reckless indifference to human life," recalls Anderson. "We had put together facts and evidence of practices over decades that might have allowed us to prove our case. They had dumped rocks for two decades at the sight, and we saw evidence of old rock damage to trees and the highway guardrail showing that similar occurrences had occurred in previous years. We concluded that a reasonable argument could be made that rolling rocks at this location directly over a switchback did rise to the level of deliberate indifference to human life."

When the State failed in its attempt to obtain a U.S. Supreme Court review of the section 1983 claim, it opened a window of opportunity to settle the case. Both the plaintiffs and the defendant eagerly took the opportunity, settling the case for $2.5 million — $2.1 million higher than the $400,000 damage cap. It wasn't full redress. The tort reform movement had seen to that. However, adding to the justness of the result was the fact that all of the money would go to the victims. The lawyers, who had each donated thousands hours to the cause — Lee Anderson alone invested about 2,000 hours — would not take a single dime.

Other attorneys deserving recognition for their important roles in this case include the following members of the Colorado Trial Lawyers Association: Bennett Aisenberg, Ricardo Barrera, Roger Castle, Thomas Downey, Greg Greenstein, Neil Hillyard, Paul Himes, Bruce Kaye, Scott Lawrence, Forrest Lewis, Jerome Malman, Mark Martens, Alan Richman, Tom Roberts, John Rossi, Peter Smith, David Struthers, and Vicki Swanson.

The reported decision in this case and its subsequent case history can be found at *State v. Defoor*, 824 P.2d 783 (Col. 1992), *cert. denied,* 506 U.S. 981 (1992).

Leland Anderson

CHAPTER TWELVE

1994: The Case of the Innocent Angler
The Case of the Reassured Witness

Gun Safety *K-Mart Corp. v. Kitchen*

HMO Accountability *Fox v. Health Net*

Civil Rights *Guzman v. Oxnard Lemon Assocs.*

Human Rights *In re Estate of Ferdinand E. Marcos Human Rights Litigation*

Co-Winners
Cooper v. Dupnik
The Case of the Innocent Angler

Wallace v. City of Los Angeles
The Case of the Reassured Witness

The Trial Lawyer of the Year Award finalists for 1994 fought for public justice on a number of fronts — holding a gun retailer responsible for the harm caused by its illegal sale of a deadly weapon, forcing an HMO to fulfill its legal duty, combating sexual discrimination in employment, and holding an infamous international abuser of human rights accountable in civil court. The co-winners of the Trial Lawyer of the Year Award both brought cases centering on misconduct within law enforcement. Their cases illustrate that the civil justice system provides a means of redress against intentional wrong-doing and negligence by law enforcement officers.

Gun Safety
K-Mart Corp. v. Kitchen
Robert F. Garvey

Each year, U.S. consumers purchase more than two million firearms. Criminals use readily available handguns and other firearms in more than one million violent crimes annually, including the nearly 18,000 homicides in 1994. Gun-related deaths are so common that unless the victim is a notable person, the story will barely cause a ripple in the media.

One way to reduce the carnage is to make it more difficult for criminals to obtain guns by passing and enforcing laws that require waiting periods to purchase firearms. Another is to enact bans on certain weapons. A third approach has been attempted through the civil justice system — holding retailers responsible for illegal gun sales. Attorney Robert F. Garvey of Thomas, Garvey & Garvey in St. Clair Shores, Michigan, believes that retailer responsibility offers an effective method of using the civil courts to induce retailers to be careful whenever they sell a firearm.

Deborah Kitchen asked Garvey to represent her after an ex-boyfriend wounded her with a rifle, rendering her a quadriplegic. Kitchen's assailant, Thomas Knapp, had drunk a case of beer and a fifth of whisky before he purchased the shotgun from K-Mart. He was so drunk that could not fill out the required federal firearms form legibly. Instead of abiding by the law, which requires that the purchaser of a gun fill out the top half of the Federal Firearms Transaction Form, the K-Mart clerk filled the form out for him and immediately gave him possession of the shotgun along with ammunition. Knapp tracked down Kitchen and shot her in the neck as she tried to run to her car to escape. Knapp pleaded guilty to the shooting and was sentenced to 40 years in prison.

Garvey proved not only that the clerk who sold Knapp the shotgun violated the law, but that his employer had not properly trained him or its other employees on a retailer's legal obligations when selling firearms. To demonstrate how poorly the store prepared its sales clerks, Garvey subpoenaed K-Mart's training manual. The training materials consisted of three pages of very general information with no mention of K-Mart's store policy of barring firearms sales to intoxicated customers. Even K-Mart's expert toxicologist agreed that an individual whose handwriting becomes illegible as a result of excessive drinking would show other visible signs of intoxication. The jury agreed that the retailer bore some of the responsibility for Deborah's cata-strophic injuries and awarded her over $12,000,000.

"What that jury gave this woman is what she needs so that the taxpayers won't have to support her," said Garvey. "About $10.5 million is for future med-ical costs and $2.5 million for the pain and suffering of being a quadriplegic for 45 years. I don't call that sympathy. She needs 24-hour care."

"While retailer responsibility is not the only solution to the huge problem of gun-related violence in America, it is an answer to a certain percentage of those deaths and injuries caused by easy access of guns and ammunition to those who are unfit," said Garvey.

After Garvey was honored, the Florida Court of Appeals reversed the ver-dict on the ground that a prior Florida Supreme Court ruling barred a finding of liability. However, the Florida Supreme Court reversed the Court of Appeals and sent the matter back for trial on liability only. The case settled soon there-after.

Attorney Gregory Stine of West Palm Beach, Florida, deserves recognition for his work in assisting Garvey at trial.

The later reported decision in this case and its subsequent case history can be found at *K-Mart Corp. v. Kitchen*, 662 So. 2d 977 (Fla. Dist. Ct. App. 1995) (reversing jury verdict), *review granted*, 675 So. 2d 120 (Fla. 1996), *decision quashed*, 697 So. 2d 1200 (Fla. 1997) (holding that defendant may be held liable).

Robert F. Garvey

HMO Accountability
Fox v. Health Net
Mark O. Hiepler and Alan R. Templeman

When Nelene Fox was diagnosed with breast cancer, her insurance company refused to cover a bone marrow transplant recommended by her doctor. Fox turned to two Oxnard, California, attorneys: her brother Mark O. Hiepler of Hiepler & Hiepler and attorney Alan R. Templeman of Lowthrop, Richards, McMillan, Miller, Conway & Templeman. The attorneys' legal crusade on behalf of Hiepler's sister helped expose how managed care plans ration health care to maximize profits.

The excuse of Fox's HMO, Health Net, for not covering the transplant procedure was that it was "experimental," despite the fact that her doctor strongly recommended the procedure as the last, best chance to save her life after other cancer therapy failed to halt the progress of the disease. In response, the attorneys sued Health Net for breach of contract and bad faith, claiming that the HMO denied the procedure only because it was too expensive.

Fox and her family raised the funds for the procedure through a nationwide fundraising campaign. For almost a year, her cancer went into remission, but then returned. Fox died at the age of 40, just months before her suit was scheduled for trial.

After the death of his sister, Hiepler was more determined than ever to proceed with the case. He deposed Health Net's medical expert as part of his extensive discovery into the HMO's operating procedures. In the process, he discovered a system in which Health Net empowered non-practicing physicians with oversight authority over the HMO's network of practicing physicians. Moreover, the HMO rewarded these overseers financially for holding down costs, thus putting them in a direct conflict of interest with patients such as Fox. Hiepler also discovered documents revealing that a medical consultant commissioned by Health Net had determined in 1990 that bone marrow transplants should no longer be considered experimental and, thus, should be a covered procedure.

At trial, Hiepler and Templeton proved that the HMO had approved the identical procedure for two other patients with medical conditions strikingly similar to Fox's. Their bone marrow transplants had been approved months prior to Fox's being denied. In fact, one of the approved procedures had been for one of Health Net's top sales representatives, so it looked like the company provided favored treatment to a key employee and a profit-motivated rejection to Fox.

The jury took only three hours to conclude that Health Net's refusal constituted a bad faith breach of contract imposing "reckless infliction of emotional distress" on Fox and her family. The jury returned a record verdict against the HMO, awarding the plaintiffs $77 million in punitive damages, $12.1 million in compensatory damages, and $212,000 for medical expenses.

Hiepler and his wife, attorney Michelle R. Hiepler, who performed invaluable services in the case, have since become two of the most notable attorneys using the civil justice system to battle unfair and unwarranted denials of medical care by HMOs. Another attorney who deserves recognition for his important work in the case is Glenn J. Campbell of Lowthrop, Richards, McMillan, Miller, Conway & Templeman.

There is no reported decision on the merits in this case.

Mark O. Hiepler

Alan R. Templeman

Civil Rights
Guzman v. Oxnard Lemon Assocs.
Paul Strauss and Lee Pliscou

Oxnard, California, was also the site of a case brought by other Trial Lawyer of the Year Award finalists in 1994. Frances Guzman started working for the Oxnard Lemon Company after dropping out of high school. Although she was a good and steady employee, by the time she was in her early 40s her employer had repeatedly passed her over for higher-paying jobs in favor of less senior male workers. Finally, she had had enough of sex discrimination and filed a complaint with the Equal Employment Opportunity Commission (EEOC).

Despite being promoted, Frances noticed that sex discrimination continued at the plant. She sought help from Chicago attorney Paul Straus of Davis, Miner, Barnhill & Galland, who teamed up with Oxnard attorney Lee Pliscou of California Rural Legal Assistance (CRLA) and filed suit in the U.S. District Court of California, charging the company with segregating men and women into different job classifications, giving less work to women, refusing to promote women and refusing to hire women for jobs that had traditionally gone to men. At the time the suit was filed, for example, there had never been a female supervisor at the company.

After discovery, the evidence of discriminatory hiring was so overwhelming that U.S. District Court Judge David Kenyon awarded partial summary judgment on that aspect of the case. Still to be decided was whether the company engaged in discriminatory practices when deciding on promotions and job assignments. Reading the handwriting on the wall, the company settled the case, paying $575,000 to the class and agreeing to restructure its job assignment procedures, promote based on seniority, and institute grievance procedures. A corner had been turned, leading to greater opportunities for women.

Since the settlement, the company has implemented changes that give women an opportunity to work in what had been considered men's jobs. The suit also served as a catalyst to a union organizing drive that did not succeed.

The company fired Guzman, and CRLA is assisting her in an administrative complaint with the EEOC.

The unreported decision in this case can be found at *Guzman v. Oxnard Lemon Assocs.*, 1992 WL 510094 (C.D. Cal. Aug. 28, 1992) (certifying plaintiff class).

Lee Pliscou

Human Rights

In re Estate of Ferdinand E. Marcos Human Rights Litigation
Robert A. Swift and Sherry P. Broder

The dictatorship of Ferdinand E. Marcos was the subject of litigation brought by attorneys Robert A. Swift of Philadelphia's Kohn, Swift & Graf and Sherry P. Broder, then President of the Hawaii State Bar Association. Their achievements were so extraordinary that they were ultimately named finalists for the Trial Lawyer of the Year Award three times — in 1994, 1996 and 1997. (See Chapters Fourteen and Fifteen.)

Between 1972 and 1986, Ferdinand Marcos had almost unlimited control over the Philippines. As his power came under increasing challenge, Marcos engaged in increasingly repressive behavior, ruthlessly suppressing his political opponents in what turned out to be a fruitless attempt to maintain power. When he was forced to flee the country in the face of a popular uprising, he left behind a legacy of over 10,000 acts of human rights abuses.

When Marcos and his wife Immelda moved to Hawaii, they subjected themselves to U.S. laws. Here was a rare chance for human rights victims to use the rule of law to seek proper redress for being tortured, oppressed, and abused for their political beliefs. Swift and Broder filed *In re Estate of Ferdinand Marcos* — the nation's first human rights class action ever brought — under the Alien Tort Claims Act, a 200-year-old federal statute adopted by Congress, which provided that claims for tortious violations of international law could be brought in federal court. Swift and Broder received assistance from Jon Van Dyke, a professor of international law at the University of Hawaii.

Over the next eight years, Swift made 15 trips to the Philippines preparing his case. Aided by Philippine human rights groups, he met with countless victims of the Marcos regime. It took time and great effort, but Swift was able to overcome stiff Army opposition and obtain Marcos' presidential papers and other records of abuse, including arrest orders personally signed by Marcos. During this time, the lawyers overcame an original dismissal of the case in the trial court by having the suit reinstated by the U.S. Court of Appeals for the Ninth Circuit.

The case was eventually certified as a class action and trifurcated. The first issue tried was whether Marcos could be held liable for the years of torture and abuse he instigated. To prove their case, Swift and Broder brought in experts on the Philippine military, intelligence agencies, and human rights. These witnesses painted a vivid picture of a dictator who ordered the arrest of those he perceived as political opponents. These unfortunates were then held incommunicado, subjected to torture, and forced to betray their colleagues. Some victims died, after which the government covered up their deaths.

Winning the first phase of the trial, the lawyers obtained a verdict that Marcos was liable and successfully argued that their clients were entitled to punitive damages. The attorneys proved that Marcos personally profited from the abuses he directed. After a two-day trial in this second phase, the jury awarded a huge — but entirely appropriate — punitive damage verdict of $1.2 billion. For this accomplishment, Swift and Broder were named finalists for the 1994 Trial Lawyer of the Year Award.

An early reported decision in this case can be found at *In re Estate of Ferdinand E. Marcos Human Rights Litigation*, 25 F.3d 1467 (9th Cir. 1994) (denying immunity, recognizing actionability of claims).

Robert A. Swift

Sherry P. Broder

1994 Trial Lawyer of the Year Award Co-Winners
Michael J. Bloom and Stephen M. Weiss
The Case of the Innocent Angler

E arly one morning, Michael J. Cooper drove to a local Tucson, Arizona, park to go fishing in the lake. As he got out of his car, a woman jogged by. She was a lab technician for the Tucson Police Department. She noticed that Cooper was wearing army camouflage fatigues and that he had an unusual license plate: ANGLR. This chance encounter would set events into motion that would destroy Cooper's life and lead to a years of bitter litigation by him against the City of Tucson, the Tucson Police Department, the Pima County Sheriff and several individually named law enforcement officers.

Starting in 1984 and through the time Cooper decided to go fishing at the park, a notorious serial rapist/robber known in the press as the "Prime Time Rapist" attacked women in the Tucson area. The rapist had escaped apprehension for more than two years, and the sheriff and police department had created a task force to solve the crime.

Michael Cooper looked nothing like the composite drawing or physical description of the "Prime Time Rapist" that had been published in local papers. In these depictions, the unknown subject was described as a white male between the ages of 27 and 34, about five feet-seven to five-feet-ten-inches tall, weighing 140-160 pounds with an athletic build, having brown wavy hair and a brown mustache, and speaking with a Southern accent. In contrast, Cooper was in his 40s, had very dark close cropped hair, did not have an athletic build, and did not have a Southern accent.

What is public justice? Law enforcement officers are held personally liable when they intentionally deprive individuals of their Fifth Amendment protection against compelled self-incrimination or their constitutional guarantee of due process.

With the city in a near panic over the ongoing crime spree of the "Prime Time Rapist," it may be understandable that the lab tech overreacted to seeing Cooper wearing army fatigues in the park at such an early hour. Deciding to act on her suspicions, she had a colleague run Cooper's license plates. The police learned his identity and discovered that he had recently been convicted for receiving unemployment benefits to which he was not entitled. That meant his fingerprints were available. The technician took Cooper's prints to a colleague who 10 years earlier had been a fingerprint identification technician. He compared Cooper's prints to prints lifted at two of the rape scenes and concluded there was a match. He was wrong. However, the police would not acknowledge the misidentification until the damage to Mr. Cooper was already done.

The lab technicians excitedly contacted the task force to tell them they had broken the crime. Two task force detectives, Weaver Barkman and Karen Wright, learned that Cooper would be meeting with the probation department in connection with his recent guilty plea and conviction in the unemployment benefits case. The detectives, dressed in plain clothes, waylaid Cooper at the meeting.

"I was escorted into a back office where I met a man and women in civilian clothes," Cooper recalls. "I thought they were part of the probation process. Then they introduced themselves as police officers and asked if I was aware of the program that permitted citizens to report crimes and receive a reward."

Cooper said that he was. Barkman then said he was with the Prime Time Rapist Task Force and they wanted to talk with him about the crime. Cooper told them he knew nothing about the crimes and that he resented the implication that he could do such awful acts. The officers then placed Cooper in handcuffs and told him they were arresting him for rape.

Barkman "read" Cooper his rights to an attorney and to remain silent, but he did so in a joking fashion, using his driver's license instead of the usual "Miranda rights card." He later admitted this was part of the previously arranged plan to make the Prime Time Rapist suspect feel that these rights were not important in the hope that the suspect would waive his constitutional rights. A very alarmed Cooper did not fall for the trap. Instead, he asked to call his lawyer. The officers ignored his right to counsel and continued to question him. This, too, was according to plan. The detectives drove Cooper to the police station, questioning him en route. By then he was distraught.

"I was crying and telling them I didn't do it," Cooper says. "I was volunteering all kinds of information. I told them they could search my house, take blood tests, give me a lie detector test. They ignored my protestations and they were telling me that I did all of these terrible things that I did not do. Then I heard one of the officers tell a third officer that I faced the death penalty. Now, I was really freaked out."

At the police station, the police brought Cooper into an interrogation room where Detectives Barkman and Wright continued to question him.

"Barkman told me that he was going to be my friend and that if I would only talk, I could find peace with myself," says Cooper. "He told me I needed to admit I was a sick man. Knowing I was Jewish, he even said that Jewish people had a built-in sense of guilt, by virtue of our having a persecution complex."

Next the investigating officers brought in a fingerprint expert, who told Cooper that his prints matched the prints of the rapist. Cooper was astounded and horrified. How could this be? He hadn't raped anyone. What he did not know was that the fingerprint tech was lying. For hours Cooper continued to maintain his innocence and asked to speak to his attorney, but the police refused to let him call a lawyer.

"Wright told me that I had chased these women over beds and done terrible, horrible things to women," says Cooper. "I was starting to break. I was cracking up. I felt like I was suffocating. I was ready to vomit. I finally said, 'I am telling the truth! You are going to have to apologize to me because I did not do these things.'"

To further pressure Cooper, the officers then conducted what is known as a "perp walk," taking the alleged perpetrator to the jail in front of the press. News photographers and television cameras captured Cooper's every move. As a result, Cooper's wife and parents learned of his arrest via the television news report. So did Cooper's wife's parents, who lived in Mexico. Finally, one empathic officer, Detective Bruce Clark, put a coat over the arrestee's head.

Even as the police were publicly humiliating Cooper, their case against him was turning to dust. A second look at the prints by a more experienced fingerprint expert revealed that Cooper's and the rapist's prints did not match. Despite the clear truth that they had made a terrible mistake, worried detectives, hoping against hope that their case could be resurrected, sent Cooper's prints to the FBI.

That night, as Cooper lay awake all night in his cell, the police turned his apartment upside down looking for evidence that simply was not there. Finally, the officers admitted to the County Attorney that the fingerprints did not match. Nevertheless, Tom Taylor, the head of the Prime Time Rapist Task Force, still wanted to prosecute Cooper. Instead, Cooper was finally released.

That should have been the end of it. Unfortunately for all concerned, the Tucson police would not admit publicly their mistake. The police chief held a press conference and, despite the fact that not one scintilla of evidence existed against Cooper, the chief maintained that the arrest was proper and asserted that Cooper was still a suspect. The next day, Cooper's picture was on page one of the local papers, identifying him as the Prime Time Rapist suspect. The press frenzy continued unabated. Media haunted the street outside his door. Cooper's landlord/employer quickly evicted him from his apartment and fired him from his job.

Things only began to look up when the public defender referred Cooper to Tucson, Arizona, attorneys Michael J. Bloom of the Law Offices of Michael J. Bloom, P.C., and Stephen M. Weiss of Karp & Weiss.

Two months later, the police finally admitted that Cooper was definitely the wrong man. Weiss and Bloom filed a civil suit in the Federal District Court for the District of Arizona on behalf of Cooper and his wife seeking damages for denial of Cooper's right to counsel, false arrest, false imprisonment, improper training and procedures, injury to reputation and property interests, invasion of privacy, illegal search and seizure, and conspiracy. Defendants included the individual members of the Prime Time Rapist Task Force, the Tucson Police Chief, Pima County Sheriff Clarence Dupnik, the City of Tucson, and Pima County.

The defendants immediately sought a dismissal via summary judgment. Instead, the Court permitted Weiss and Bloom to conduct discovery, during which they obtained shocking admissions about the existence of the Prime Time Rapist Task Force's plan to intentionally violate an arrestee's civil rights. Prior to Cooper's arrest, another innocent suspect had been questioned and his request for an attorney had also been ignored. Concerning this issue, Barkman testified in deposition, "The point of flouting the requirements...was to ensure such a suspect would not rely on his right to remain silent."

The conspirators knew that any confession so illegally obtained would not be admissible in court during the prosecution's case in chief, but that wasn't their concern. By obtaining an unconstitutional confession, they hoped either to prevent a defendant from taking the stand in his own defense because the coerced confession could be used to rebut his testimony or to help defeat a plea of insanity. The conspirators based their illegal strategy on a case decided by the U.S. Supreme Court that *inadvertent* violations by police of the rights of constitutional suspects did not prevent evidence thereby obtained to be used in rebuttal. The violation of Cooper's rights was anything but inadvertent.

When the District Court refused to grant defendants summary judgment on their claim of qualified immunity, the defendants appealed to the U.S. Court of Appeals for the Ninth Circuit, where a divided three-judge panel ruled that the violations of Cooper's rights were merely violations of the procedures set forth in the famous *Miranda v. Arizona* decision. Disappointed but undaunted, Weiss and Bloom requested an *en banc* hearing. The Court granted their motion and an 11-judge panel affirmed the trial court by a 9-2 vote. In a long and detailed decision, the Court ruled that Cooper had made statements which "could and probably would have been used against him had he gone to trial," and that law enforcement officials had "engaged in the premeditated elimination" of Cooper's Fifth Amendment and Fourteenth Amendment rights. The Court also called the Task Force's conduct "iniquitous," finding that "the Task Force's conduct unquestionably shocks the conscience, and thus violates substantive due process."

Considering the sorry history of Arizona law enforcement in violating constitutional rights of criminal suspects, the Court concluded with a clear and unequivocal message to the State's police agencies:

> One would have thought it unnecessary to spend so much time
> reiterating the settled law in an appellate opinion. Yet the facts of this
> case indicate that these law-enforcement officers resist that message.
> It is this stubborn resistance that has generated this lawsuit, not any
> lack of clarity in the law.

> This case is an example of officials who deliberately choose to ignore the
> law and Constitution in favor of their own methods. For victims caught
> in their snare, the Constitution of the United States becomes a useless
> piece of paper. When law-enforcement officials act this way, they invite
> redress under section 1983.

The case settled more than seven years after Cooper's arrest for an undisclosed sum. None of the police officials involved in the case were ever disciplined or suffered any sanction.

The reported decision in this case and its subsequent case history can be found at *Cooper v. Dupnik*, 963 F.2d 1220 (9th Cir. 1992), *cert. denied*, 506 U.S. 953 (1992).

Michael J. Bloom

Stephen M. Weiss

1994 Trial Lawyer of the Year Award Co-Winner
Raymond P. Boucher
The Case of the Reassured Witness

emetria Wallace was a good citizen. The young high school honors graduate, who was attending Los Angeles City College as part of her preparation to become a member of the California Highway Patrol, decided to do the right thing when she became a crucial witness in the robbery and murder of a cab driver. Instead of feigning ignorance or refusing to discuss the shooting, she identified the prime suspect in the case, whom she knew from her high school days, and agreed to testify at the murder trial. Her decision to live out her principles would cost Wallace her life.

What made Wallace's death especially tragic — and maddening — is that the Los Angeles Police Department (LAPD) knew that her life was in danger. The accused killer, Grant Christon, was a known hoodlum and gang member. Worse, as the murder case approached the date of trial, Wallace's mother, Lula Wallace, received an anonymous death threat: "Listen, your daughter has no business opening up her goddamn mouth and if she shows up down

What is public justice? The police warn witnesses of the dangers they face and act appropriately to protect them.

here [at court], I'm going to blow her goddamn head off. I know where she goes, when she goes, and I also know where you go."

Alarmed and fearful, the family reported the threat to Donald Richards, the LAPD homicide detective in charge of the investigation. He came to Wallace's home and assured her that she had nothing to worry about, that she was only one of a dozen eyewitnesses, and that in his opinion as an experienced detective, he did not believe that Christon was an actual threat. Richards went so far as to tell her that she did not have to vary her daily routine and that if he ever came to believe she was in danger, he would be sure to let her know.

Lulled into a false sense of security, Wallace did not leave town to visit relatives in Arizona as she had considered. Instead, she went about her business until one morning, following her usual routine, she walked to the bus stop near her home, where someone killed her in a drive-by shooting. Her mother heard the fatal shots as she washed the breakfast dishes.

The truth about the known danger posed to Wallace because of her willingness to testify was a far different story from the soothing assurances given the family by Detective Richards. Years later, after a protracted discovery battle, Los Angles attorney Raymond P. Boucher of Nordstrom, Steele, Nicolette & Jefferson in Los Angeles got Richards to admit that he had not told Wallace that Christon was a suspect in two other murders, that the detective felt Christon was a danger to the community, or that Christon had threatened witnesses in other murder investigations.

In his own handwritten police reports before Wallace's murder, Richards wrote, "Detectives have received information that since the defendant [Christon] has bailed out of jail, he is allegedly approaching unknown citizens and stating he is going to get the people who are witnesses against him." Richards also wrote that he had received credible information that "Grant Christon is carrying a .45 auto, looking for informants who snitched on him."

When Lula Wallace wanted to sue the City of Los Angeles for her daughter's death, she found it difficult to find quality representation. The first lawyer she went to refused to take the case because she could not afford to pay the $98 filing fee. She went to another lawyer who felt the case was not right for him. One lawyer filed the case but could not find a way to get past the City's demurrer. Another lawyer filed an amended complaint, and sometime later, Lula faced the demise of her case due to a motion to dismiss for lack of prosecution.

Finally, Wallace approached Boucher, who had a reputation among his colleagues as something of a crusader. Boucher met with her and was appalled at what had happened to Wallace. He recalls, "I thought that if there is such a thing as justice in the State of California, there had to be a remedy for this woman."

Boucher opposed the demurrer and the motion to dismiss and pleaded around the government immunity defenses thrown up by the City in an amended complaint. The City finally answered the complaint and, in Boucher's words, "we went off to the races."

The City's defense attorneys tried to obstruct the discovery of documents, forcing Boucher to file several motions to compel discovery responses. Each motion succeeded and he was even awarded thousands of dollars in sanctions against the City. By the time the matter was set for trial, he had pried 15 boxes of documents out of the reluctant defendant.

The trial judge, who had formerly represented the City of Los Angeles and had a reputation as protective of the city's interests, prevented much evidence from reaching the jury and granted the City's motion for nonsuit at the end of the City's presentation. The dismissal devastated both Boucher and his client. Boucher appealed the dismissal and prevailed. The Court of Appeals ruled:

> As a general rule, one owes no duty to control the conduct of another, or to warn those endangered by such conduct. Such a duty may arise, however, if (a) a special relationship exists between the actor and the third person which imposes a duty upon the actor to control the third person's conduct, or (b) a special relationship exists between the actor and the other which gives the other a right to protection. ... When the government's actions create a foreseeable peril to a specific foreseeable victim, a duty to warn arises when the danger is not readily discoverable by the endangered person.

The Court, applying the awful facts surrounding the death of Wallace to the law, found that the trial judge had wrongly taken the case away from the jury and that the government immunity that applies to "discretionary" acts by public workers did not apply:

> Detective Richards did not engage in discretionary acts when he (1) minimized the importance of the threatening phone call which plaintiff received, (2) determined at various points in his investigation of the Foley murder [a different killing than the cab driver's] that he would not inform Demetria or her mother about Grant Christon's possible involvement in other murders nor inform them about Christon's other threats against witnesses, (3) determined that he would not inform them he considered Christon to be a threat to the community at large and especially to persons who might testify against Christon, and (4) determined that he would not offer protection to Demetria despite what he knew about the phone call and about Christon.

The Court also stated clearly the public policy reasoning behind its decision:

> If we were to hold that an officer can, with impunity, fail to disclose important information to a witness regarding his or her safety, or induce a witness to detrimentally rely on the officer regarding such safety, the number of persons who would henceforth be willing to testify on behalf of the prosecution would most likely fall dramatically. Consequently, so

would the number of criminals convicted for their crimes....Criminal prosecution would screech to a grinding halt....Society reaps enormous benefits when a witness's testimony succeeds in getting a criminal off the streets and placed behind bars. Society must be willing to pay for that benefit by affording necessary protection to both the witness and family...To the extent that government fails to meet this essential responsibility, it cedes control of our cities to the criminals.

Two days before the new trial was to begin, the case settled for a substantial amount. Lula Wallace used the money to move her family out of her crime-ridden neighborhood in Los Angeles to be near family in Phoenix. Boucher presented Lula Wallace and her family members each with a copy of the 16th volume of the *California Reporter 2nd* "so they would always have a copy of the decision available to them and they could see that Demetria's death would be used by many others in the future as a means of protecting themselves against government indifference."

After The TLPJ Foundation named Boucher as a co-winner of the 1994 Trial Lawyer of the Year Award, Lula Wallace and her family sent him a plaque. It says:

Raymond P. Boucher, Esq.

A remarkable Attorney, Advisor, and Friend.
You have stood by our side from beginning to end,
devoting your time unselfishly. Reassuring our hopes
when things seemed hopeless, rendering
your loyal and moral support.

Ray, we would like to thank you for your outstanding
dedication and for making a difference "in the law."
Thank you for your compassion, efforts and time.
May God continue to Bless you in all of
your endeavors.

Always Love,
the Wallace Family, Lula, Yolanda, Andrea,
Demetria (in loving memory), Stephanie, O'Neisha, and Na'toya.

The reported decision in this case can be found at *Wallace v. City of Los Angeles*, 16 Cal. Rptr. 2d 113 (Cal. Ct. App. 1993).

Raymond P. Boucher

CHAPTER THIRTEEN

1995: The Case of the *Exxon Valdez* Oil Spill
The Cases of the Foreign Generals Brought to Justice

Medical Safety *Snyder v. American Ass'n of Blood Banks*

Insurer Accountability *Adams v. California State Automobile Ass'n*

Drug Safety *Oxendine v. Merrell Dow Pharmaceuticals, Inc.*

Co-Winners
In re Exxon Valdez
The Case of the *Exxon Valdez* Oil Spill

Xuncax v. Gramajo, Ortiz v. Gramajo,
Todd v. Panjaitan, and *Paul v. Avril*
The Cases of the Foreign Generals Brought to Justice

The finalists for the 1995 Trial Lawyer of the Year Award pursued public justice for a man infected by HIV during a blood transfusion, victims of insurance fraud and defective products, and a child born with birth defects. Two teams of attorneys shared the award for Trial Lawyer of the Year in 1995. In one case, a team of lawyers forced Exxon to pay for the environmental destruction caused by the *Exxon Valdez* oil spill in Alaska. In another set of four cases, trial lawyers held international human rights abusers accountable in U.S. courts.

Medical Safety
Snyder v. American Ass'n of Blood Banks
George T. Baxter

Attorney George T. Baxter of Ridgewood, New Jersey, won a precedent-setting verdict against the American Association of Blood Banks (AABB), the blood industry trade association, for failing to establish donor-screening practices that would have reduced the risk of recipients being exposed to the human immuno-deficiency virus (HIV). Baxter represented a man who contracted HIV from a blood transfusion after heart surgery in 1984.

Baxter alleged that the AABB knew as early as 1983 of a "surrogate test" that could have screened out blood donated by HIV carriers. In fact, the Centers for Disease Control had recommended in January 1983 that the blood banking industry use surrogate testing to reduce the risk of exposure to HIV. The AABB nevertheless recommended against its member blood banks adopting the test. Baxter demonstrated that, since the AABB traditionally published blood-bank-ing standards for donor screening and conducted annual inspections, it exer-cised sufficient control over member blood banks to hold it responsible for fail-ing to recommend the surrogate test. Baxter also compiled evidence demon-strating that the scientific research and cost/benefit analysis used by the AABB as the basis for rejecting the surrogate testing was flawed.

After a six-year battle through the trial court, the New Jersey appellate court, the New Jersey Supreme Court, and back to the trial court, Baxter obtained a $570,000 verdict against AABB for its unreasonable and imprudent conduct. It was the first such award in the U.S., and the New Jersey Supreme Court ulti-mately affirmed the groundbreaking verdict.

The later reported decision in this case and its subsequent case history can be found at *Snyder v. American Ass'n of Blood Banks*, 659 A.2d 482 (N.J. Super. Ct., App. Div. 1995) (affirming jury verdict for plaintiffs), *aff'd*, 676 A.2d 1036 (N.J. 1996).

George T. Baxter

Insurer Accountability
Adams v. California State Automobile Ass'n
Gary Gwilliam

Attorney Gary Gwilliam of Oakland, California's Gwilliam, Ivary, Cavalli & Brewer reached a landmark settlement with the California State Automobile Association (CSAA) in one of the largest insurance bad faith lawsuits in California history. The case involved the arbitrary and wrongful denial of medical coverage for 80 auto accident victims. CSAA cut off payment of their medical bills by forcing them to submit to "independent" medical examinations (IMEs) by insurance company-selected doctors who claimed that no further medical treatments were "reasonable or necessary." Over the years, the company had become notorious for denying coverage for soft tissue injuries — particularly those involving chiropractic treatment.

Gwilliam and his firm took over 350 depositions to prepare for trial. Discovery proved particularly difficult because the insurance company contested virtually every document request. After an intensive investigation, Gwilliam identified a number of former adjusters for CSAA who testified that the company had a strong bias against chiropractors and policyholders with soft tissue injuries. They said that the IMEs were known at the insurance company as "cut off exams" and were used to control costs. This testimony directly contradicted that of many of CSAA's then-current claims managers. Gwilliam also retained experts who testified that the IMEs were biased and that their use was unreasonable and arbitrary.

After five years of litigation, the case settled on the eve of trial for a significant sum. CSAA was forced to change the way it deals with claims. The case also helped discourage other insurance companies from wrongfully denying coverage for routine treatment. Gwilliam received invaluable assistance from co-counsel A. Lee Sanders and David S. Hobler, as well as a large number of associate attorneys.

There is no reported decision on the merits in *Adams v. California State Automobile Ass'n.*

Gary Gwilliam

Drug Safety
Oxendine v. Merrell Dow Pharmaceuticals, Inc.
Barry J. Nace

For many years, attorney Barry Nace of Paulson, Nace & Norwind in Washington, D.C., has worked tirelessly to obtain justice for people injured by major
corporations. Since the early 1980s, Nace has represented women born with
birth defects allegedly caused by their mother's use of Bendectin, an anti-nausea
drug, during pregnancy. One of these women is Mary Oxendine, who claimed
that her shortened forearm and three fingers on one of her hands were caused
by her mother's use of Bendectin.

At the original trial in 1983, Nace presented an expert witness who testified
that, based on his review of the available studies and data, Oxendine's birth
defects were caused by Bendectin. Nace skillfully cross-examined Merrell
Dow's expert witnesses, discrediting the studies that the company had sponsored. He also demonstrated that Merrell Dow had marketed Bendectin, knowing for years that it had been linked with damage to cells in developing fetal
vertebrae.

After a month-long trial, a jury awarded Oxendine $750,000 in compensa-
tory damages — the first such successful trial and the only Bendectin verdict to
be upheld on appeal. Due in part to this verdict and other suits filed in its wake,
Merrell Dow removed the drug from the U.S. market. Nace was named a finalist for the Trial Lawyer of the Year Award in 1984 for winning the verdict and
in 1986 for winning the appeal. (See Chapters Two and Four.)

Merrell Dow, however, continued to insist that it should not pay for
Oxendine's injuries and filed appeal after appeal. When the case was sent back
to the trial court, the company moved to vacate the verdict and obtain a new
trial on the basis of perceived failings in plaintiffs' expert witness. The trial
court granted the motion. The appeals court, however, again reversed, ordering the trial court to reinstate the jury verdict and proceed to a hearing on
punitive damages. The trial court reinstated the verdict, but it postponed the
punitive damages hearing, and Merrell Dow again appealed. The appellate court
dismissed the appeal because there was no verdict yet on punitive damages.

In the meantime, Merrell had filed a motion before the trial court to dismiss the punitive damages claim, vacate the verdict on federal preemption
grounds, and obtain a new trial or judgment in its favor on the basis of newly-
developed scientific evidence about Bendectin. After extensive briefing, the
trial court dismissed the punitive damages claim, rejected Merrell's preemption

defense, and refused to consider the newly-developed scientific evidence. In 1994, Merrell Dow filed its fourth appeal of the 1983 verdict and, this time, the appeals court upheld the federal preemption ruling but ordered the trial court to consider the new scientific evidence. The case was then remanded again for further proceedings.

In 1995, in recognition of his ongoing battle for his client Mary Oxendine, Barry Nace was again honored as a finalist for the Trial Lawyer of the Year Award. Against a company trying every legal tactic at its disposal, Nace refused to be cowed. His indomitable dedication to his client's cause was truly remarkable.

Nace received assistance from co-counsel Thomas H. Bleakley, Thomas Kline, and Edward Lee Norwind on this important case. It ultimately ended with a ruling in Merrell Dow's favor.

The later decision in this case can be found at *Oxendine v. Merrell Dow Pharmaceuticals, Inc.,* 1996 WL 680992 (D.C. Super. Ct. Oct. 24, 1996) (vacating jury verdict and entering judgment for defendant).

Barry J. Nace

1995 Trial Lawyer of the Year Award Co-Winners
Brian O'Neill and Matt Jamin
The Case of the *Exxon Valdez* Oil Spill

A t 9:00 p.m. on the evening of March 23, 1989 — Good Friday — the *Exxon Valdez* oil supertanker lay low in her berth at Valdez, Alaska. The ship, longer than three football fields, carried 50 million barrels of crude oil to be transported from Alaska's North Slope down the western coasts of Alaska, Canada, Washington, Oregon, and California to its ultimate destination of Long Beach, California.

Captain Joe Hazelwood, who was responsible for overseeing the ship's mandatory precheck, had spent the day in town drinking. Hazelwood had gone through alcohol rehabilitation, but had often relapsed, as his employer, the Exxon Corporation, knew. Exxon nevertheless allowed Hazelwood to continue bearing responsibility for guiding the *Valdez* on its circular route between Alaska and California, 60 days on and 60 days off.

A little before 10:00 p.m. on March 23, the massive tanker slipped slowly out of her berth as the port's pilot guided her down the Valdez Narrows toward Prince William Sound and the open sea. At 11:30 p.m., the pilot left the supertanker and Hazelwood took control of the ship, which was traveling at about 12 knots. Navigation to the Prince William Sound required the captain's full attention. The Narrows held many hazards for shipping, including reefs, islands, and floating ice. To prevent ship-to-ship collisions, buoys divided the Narrows into two navigation channels: one for inbound vessels and one for outbound vessels.

What is public justice? Companies are held accountable and punished when their reckless conduct causes an environmental disaster.

Ice reports indicated that ice floes lay ahead, so Hazelwood decided to steer the *Exxon Valdez* into the inbound channel. The U.S. Coast Guard advised that there were no inbound ships close enough to pose a hazard, so Hazelwood ordered the helmsman to negotiate the maneuver.

As the *Valdez* approached Busby Island, Hazelwood decided to navigate the ship back into the outbound channel. The maneuver would begin when the ship reached a light on the island, about three minutes away. Three miles beyond the island, directly in the supertanker's path, lay Bligh Reef. It was vitally important that the ship be navigated properly back into the outbound channel to ensure safe passage.

This was no time for Captain Hazelwood to quit the bridge. Indeed, Exxon's manual specifically stated that the captain was to remain on the bridge "whenever conditions presented a potential threat to the vessel, such as passing in the vicinity of shoals, rocks, or other hazards presenting any threat to navigation." Nevertheless, Hazelwood departed the bridge, ordering the third mate to begin the maneuver when the ship reached the light — in three minutes' time. Hazelwood then went below, he said, to do some paperwork.

Three minutes passed, but the third mate made no maneuver. In fact, no one was even on the bridge to order the turn. The third mate, nervous over being given such a heavy responsibility, had stepped into the chart room to plot the coming turn on sea charts. Neither he nor Hazelwood noticed the passage of time. Four minutes passed, then five, six, seven, and eight.

Suddenly, the lookout burst into the bridge with the urgent message that the red buoy light marking Bligh Reef laid to the immediate starboard side of the ship. It should have been on the port side! The third mate ordered a 10-degree turn and called to the captain that there might be ice in the ship's path. Hazelwood said he would be up immediately.

A ship the size of the *Exxon Valdez* does not turn on a dime. The third mate's order served only to place the ship on a collision course with the reef. "Hard right rudder!" he ordered. Aghast, he saw that it was already too late. The ship would run into Bligh Reef.

Then a terrible shudder and a series of sharp jolts shook the entire ship, as the *Exxon Valdez* ran aground. Hazelwood raced to the bridge and saw that the damage to the ship was severe. Even worse, he saw a geyser of oil flowing into the sea. Hazelwood turned to the bridge bathroom and threw up.

The grounding of the *Exxon Valdez* caused utter devastation, as 11 million gallons of oil escaped, polluting 1,200 miles of Alaska coastline. The resulting ecological catastrophe killed untold birds and other wildlife, destroyed pristine beaches, and ruined the local fishing industry. The accident also led to one of the most monumental lawsuits in U.S. history.

On the night the infamous supertanker ran aground, Minneapolis attorney Brian B. O'Neill of Faegre & Benson, LLP, the future hero of *In re Exxon Valdez*, was a corporate litigator, immersed in a patent dispute trial over goose decoys. But O'Neill was not a stereotypical gray-suited corporate attorney. He was a committed environmentalist who enjoyed representing environmental groups *pro bono*.

"I was sort of in a Robin Hood kind of practice," O'Neill says. "I'd make money doing the sort of litigation where two big companies move money back and forth across the table. That would fund the environmental litigation which was both fun and where I thought I would make a contribution, where I thought the world needs a little help."

O'Neill first heard about the Alaskan oil spill in a news report on his car radio the day after it happened. He had an immediate epiphany — he was going to try this case. In *Cleaning Up: The Story Behind the Biggest Legal Bonanza of Our Time*, author and attorney David Lebedoff recounts the path that led O'Neill to become lead counsel in the mammoth environmental suit. O'Neill and several volunteers from his firm moved from their Minnesota homes to Alaska to begin years of litigation, a decision that would not only test their mettle as lawyers, but would literally change the course of many of their lives.

However, the legal team could not just fly to Alaska and hand out their business cards. They had to earn a reputation as environmental lawyers. They did this by salvaging a floundering lawsuit involving an earlier oil spill in Cook Inlet caused by a tanker called the *Glacier Bay*. As a result of their success in that case, they became widely known in the Alaska fishing community as lawyers who got results. Soon, they were hip deep in clients devastated by the *Exxon Valdez* disaster. That led O'Neill and his legal team into an alliance with the many plaintiffs' lawyers from more than 60 firms representing other victims of the oil spill. O'Neill's work so impressed his colleagues that, eventually, they named him the plaintiffs' lead trial counsel. His co-lead counsel was Matt Jamin of Jamin, Ebell, Bolger & Gentry in Kodiak, Alaska, who represented several municipalities.

There were 40,000 parties in the case. To prepare for eventual trial, the plaintiffs' lawyers had to fight 275 discovery disputes, retain 500 experts, take 2,000 depositions, and review over 10 million documents. The plaintiffs' lawyers also invested more than $30 million in the case, plus untold hours of their labor.

There were more than 700 defense attorneys involved in the case, including some of the best in the country: James Neal, a Watergate prosecutor; the late Charles Ruff, who later represented President Clinton during the impeachment hearing; former Attorney General Griffin Bell; and former federal judge Shirley M. Hufstedler.

Early on in the case, O'Neill and one of his Minnesota colleagues, attorney Lori Wagner, began the mind-numbing but essential task of creating an approach to calculate damages that was both understandable and comprehensive. This approach was memorialized in a document known as the Damage Matrix. In *Cleaning Up*, Lebedoff explained how the Matrix worked to apportion damages among 40,000 claimants:

> The Damage Matrix divides all the claimants into groups, for example, Kodiak fishermen, and within each group determines each year's loss by subjecting its components to a uniform formula: price times the number of [fishing] permit holders times the number of pounds of fish caught....The Damage Matrix is to most other damage claims what the census is to headcounts.

The trial opened with jury selection on May 9, 1994, more than five years after Captain Hazelwood ran the *Exxon Valdez* aground on Bligh Reef. The case was divided into three phases: Phase One involved determining whether Exxon was liable for the oil spill. If the jury found liability, then Phase Two would determine the compensatory damages to be awarded to fishermen and others injured by the spill. Finally, Phase Three would determine the amount of punitive damages, if any, to be paid by Exxon.

The keys to proving Exxon's liability lay in demonstrating Hazelwood's alcoholism, his continued drinking while on duty, and Exxon's knowledge of its captain's dangerous conduct. O'Neill made the case comprehensible by describing it as the world's biggest "drunk driving case," a matter no different at its core than a trucking company permitting a known alcoholic to continue driving after executives learn that he is still drinking.

One of the obstacles to proving this theory was that, in all of Exxon's files, there were only two documents that addressed Hazelwood's drinking. The absence of documents was, however, somewhat damning in itself. After a drunk driving conviction, Hazelwood had gone through alcohol rehabilitation and the company had decided to monitor his sobriety. Proving Hazelwood's drinking on the date of the accident was easy. The former captain admitted it, although he may have downplayed its extent significantly. Moreover, he had a .06 blood-alcohol level 12 hours after the ship ran aground and his voice sounded slurred on the tape recordings of his calls for help to the Coast Guard after the accident. O'Neill also proved that Hazelwood had consumed alcohol regularly with many Exxon employees before the accident. Under these circumstances, the absence of Exxon's documentation on Hazelwood's drinking wasn't so much proof of the company's ignorance, but rather evidence that the monitoring was wholly inadequate — at least that was the idea O'Neill hoped the jury would accept.

O'Neill also pioneered "video cross examination" in the liability phase of the case, a tactic that relies on compact disks and bar codes to permit smooth presentation. This is now common in trials, but was quite innovative then. "It was the first time this tactic was used, as far as I know," O'Neill recalls.

"We had a video of Larry Rawl, the former Chairman of the Board of Exxon, testifying that Hazelwood was not drunk when the accident occurred," O'Neill recounts. "And then we'd hit the bar code and suddenly there he was testifying before Congress that Hazelwood was drunk. It was devastating."

On June 6, the judge sent the Phase One liability questions to the jury. The verdict in this phase of the trial was crucial. Without a finding of recklessness, the case would be limited to compensatory damages. One week later, on June 14, the jury found that Hazelwood was negligent, which was no surprise. More important, the jury found that Hazelwood was reckless and that his reckless conduct caused the *Valdez* to run aground. Most important, the jury unanimously found that Exxon was reckless and that its recklessness caused the oil spill.

The claimants who filled the courtroom burst into cheers. Phases Two and Three of the trial would go forward.

Before the punitive damages phase could begin, the jury would have to determine how much money the claimants had lost as a result of the spill. Most of the compensatory damages phase of the trial was devoted to expert testimony on the number of fish not caught because of the spill, the effect of the spill on prices, the long-term impact of the spill, and other such matters. It took a month for the jury to deliberate and the news was not good for the plaintiffs. Although the jury awarded three times what Exxon had offered, its $286.7 million verdict was less than a third of what O'Neill had requested.

Swallowing his disappointment, O'Neill plunged ahead into Phase Three of the trial. Oddly, presenting the request for punitive damages was the shortest and easiest part of the case. Exxon defended against punitive damages by pointing out that it had spent more than $1 billion to settle claims with federal and state governments and had invested $2 billion in cleanup costs. In short, the company argued that it had been punished enough.

The jury saw the situation differently. After 50 ballots, the jury came in with a sizeable verdict — $5 billion, approximately one year's after-tax, net income for Exxon. The jury also hit Hazelwood with punitive damages in the amount of $5,000.

Everything seemed to be over except the appeals and working out a just disbursement formula — a daunting task that took O'Neill years to complete after the trial. But then a secret settlement was uncovered between Exxon and the "Seattle Seven," a group of major seafood processors who had sued Exxon for the diminution in the number of fish that the companies could process. The terms of the secret settlement exposed Exxon's hypocrisy. In return for a $70 million settlement, the Seattle Seven had agreed to apply for a share of the punitive damages award and then secretly return to Exxon any share it received. This could have amounted to 15 percent of the entire punitive damages award!

Judge Russell Holland was furious. Expressing "shock and disappointment," the judge stated, "What is really pernicious about the Seattle Seven issue is that Exxon sought to reduce its exposure to punitive damages twice: once by informing the jury of its voluntary payments to the seafood processors, and a second time through its secret agreement with the Seattle Seven. The Court will not countenance Exxon's astonishing ruse and allow it to manipulate the jury and negate its verdict." The judge then ruled that the Seattle Seven would not participate in the punitive damages award.

The many appeals generated by the verdict in *In re Exxon Valdez* are still ongoing. The U.S. Court of Appeals for the Ninth Circuit reversed Judge Holland on the Seattle Seven issue, and has not yet ruled on whether the award is too large.

O'Neill has moved back to Minnesota and is settling back into his former law practice. "I was 42 when the case started," O'Neill says wistfully. "Now I am 53, and these were years when you're old enough to know what you are doing and still young enough to have some energy about doing it. I have essentially taken my most meaningful years and put them all into this case."

What was it like to return home after living in Alaska for five years? "It was a little like Ulysses returning," says O'Neill. "Nobody remembers who you are. Your partners don't remember who you are and your clients are all gone. Everything had changed. And I just finished full-time work on the case a few months ago. That has left something of an empty place in my psyche. You go through mourning."

Still, O'Neill has no regrets. He was privileged, he says, to try one of the most difficult and important environmental cases in history. It was an odyssey that changed his life. "I had the chance to make the world a better place," he says. "In a sense, it was a calling, and I was able to respond. How many people get that opportunity in life?"

Other attorneys who deserve recognition for their work on this important case include co-lead counsel for the plaintiffs Jerry Cohen; courtroom trial team members David Oesting, Lori Wagner, Richard Gerry, Gerard Nolting, Laddie Montague, and Steven Schroer; trial team members Sarah Armstrong, Steve Crandall, Peter Erhardt, Suzanne Etpison, Karen Hansen, Bill Hirsch, Trudy Johnson, Barry Klinckhardt, Melanie Muckle, Bill Rossbach, Lynn Sarko, Brian Toder, and Mike Woerner; and federal law team members Ellen Chapnick, Dave Copley, Peter Kahana, Cassi Kinkead, Pam Parker, Bill Saupe, and Dave Tarshes.

There is no reported decision on the merits in *In re Exxon Valdez*. The Ninth Circuit's decision upholding the company's secret settlement with the Seattle Seven can be found at *In re Exxon Valdez*, 293 F.2d 985 (9th Cir. 2001).

Brian O'Neill

Matt Jamin

1995 Trial Lawyer of the Year Award Co-Winners

Michael Ratner and Beth Stephens
The Cases of the Foreign Generals
Brought to Justice

For Hector Gramajo, the former Minister of Defense of Guatemala, it was a proud day. He had been in the U.S. for nearly a year, pursuing post-graduate studies at Harvard's Kennedy School of Government, trying to improve his chances of being elected as his country's President. His education complete, Gramajo walked with other members of his class toward the site of the graduation ceremony.

A man approached. He smiled warmly and asked, "Señor Gramajo?"

"Sí," the former general smiled back.

The man handed Gramajo some papers, smiled again, and walked away.

Gramajo took the papers, perhaps assuming that they were from admirers, and walked to his graduation unaware that he had just been served in a lawsuit involving claims for millions of dollars by several victims of egregious human rights abuses perpetrated in Guatemala years earlier by military personnel under Gramajo's command.

With the help of attorneys Michael Ratner and Beth Stephens of the Center for Constitutional Rights (CCR) in New York, Gramajo's victims sued him under the Alien Tort Claims Act (ATCA). This federal statute was passed in 1789 as an anti-piracy law and permits non-citizens to sue in U.S. courts for tortious conduct that violates "the laws of the nations." CCR also filed a similar suit against Gramajo on behalf of a nun who was a U.S. citizen. That suit included a claim under the 1992 Torture Victim Protection Act (TVPA), which permits individuals to sue in U.S. courts for acts of torture and other crimes against humanity.

What is public justice? Those who commit international human rights abuses cannot evade responsibility by coming to America; if they come here, their victims can hold them accountable.

CCR was founded in the 1960s to litigate civil rights cases. Over the years, it has used the law and the courts to pursue a progressive agenda that has included anti-war efforts and the protection of the rights of aliens living in the United States. CCR maintains a "human rights docket," bringing suits under American civil law to punish international human rights abusers.

In 1995, attorneys Ratner and Stephens were named as co-winners of the Trial Lawyer of the Year Award for four cases successfully brought in U.S. courts to redress horrific human rights abuses. Their victories in these cases have helped to lay the foundation for an international common law, pursuant to which civil courts throughout the world enforce universally accepted standards of human rights. Each of the four cases is summarized below.

Xuncax v. Gramajo and *Ortiz v. Gramajo*: In these two consolidated cases, General Hector Gramajo was held civilly responsible for the infliction of terrible human rights abuses by the Guatemalan military during the 1980s. The plaintiffs in the *Xuncax* case were 11 Guatemalan nationals who had been victimized in various ways by the Guatemalan military. A brief recitation of just a few of the plaintiffs' grievances — each one more horrific than the next — illustrates the brutality experienced by the people of Guatemala during this period.

■ On July 18, 1982, soldiers broke into Xuncax's house. They stripped, bound, and masked her husband, and then beat him, kicked him, dragged him outside, and walked him naked through the village. His crime: he had worked for a period of time in the U.S. That evening he was summarily executed. Fearing for her and her children's lives, Xuncax fled and lived in refugee camps in Mexico. She eventually found sanctuary in the U.S. and filed for political asylum.

■ Juan Diego-Francisco faced a similar fate after working in America. On July 6, 1982, 300 soldiers entered his village, broke into his house, grabbed him, tied him, and began a vicious interrogation, during which they beat him with their hands and guns and also beat his wife. For 14 hours, the soldiers took turns torturing him, putting him inside thick plastic bags, and holding a knife to his head. When he was finally released, Diego-Francisco fled with his wife. He later learned that three of his cousins had been executed and his house had been burned down. He made his way to the U.S. and sought political asylum.

- In July 1982, members of the Guatemalan military shot Elizabet Pedro-Pascual's older sister to death and beheaded her, while she was visiting a neighboring village. When Pedro-Pascual learned that these same soldiers were headed for her home village, she and her family ran for their lives. After spending time in Mexico, she arrived in the U.S. and sought political asylum.

- In November 1988, Guatemalan soldiers tortured, mutilated, and killed 21 civilians in Jose Alfredo Callejas' village. Among the victims were Callejas' brother and cousins, whose abused bodies he saw. After the massacre, the army pressured survivors to blame "guerillas" for the murders. Later, Callejas began to receive threatening letters and heard that his name was on an army "death list." His father then "disappeared" and is presumed dead. Soon thereafter, soldiers threw a grenade at Callejas, wounding him. After meeting with human rights workers in September 1990, Callejas was fired upon by a machine gun in a drive-by shooting. He eventually found sanctuary at the Canadian Embassy and became a resident of Canada.

The plaintiff in the *Ortiz* case was U.S. citizen Dianna Ortiz, a member of the order of Ursuline Sisters of Maple Mount, Kentucky. Ortiz had traveled to Guatemala as a missionary and an educator. Through 1988, she worked in San Miguel with other Ursuline Sisters, teaching Bible studies and reading to children. In September 1988, the local Bishop told the Sisters that he had received a warning that the nuns were planning to meet with leftist guerrillas. Assuring their Bishop that the charge was not true, the nuns thought little about it.

Then in 1989, Sister Ortiz's self-described "nightmare" began. First, she received letters threatening that she would be killed if she did not leave the country. But her commitment to the people she served was stronger than her fear. Sister Ortiz steadfastly continued her work with the poor people of Guatemala. She was eventually accosted on the street. Fearing for her life, she left Guatemala briefly, but after much prayer and reflection, she returned to the people whom she felt called to serve. Soon after she returned, Sister Ortiz was kidnapped. She was locked in a room, blindfolded, partially stripped, and then tortured by her abductors. In a court affidavit, Ortiz described her torture as follows:

He told me that they were going to explain the rules of a game. He said they were going to ask me some questions. If I gave an answer they liked, he said that they would let me smoke; if they didn't like the answer, they would burn me with a cigarette. When I said the rules were unjust, they burned me with a cigarette.

They began to ask me questions. They asked me my name, age, where I lived....Every time I answered, they burned me with a cigarette. It didn't matter what answer I gave; they burned me....I was crying and screaming with pain.

Sister Ortiz's abductors removed her blindfold and asked her questions about people depicted in photographs. Then, the abuse continued:

One of the men blindfolded me again. Then one of them hit me in the face so hard that I fell to the floor. My face was scraped and bleed-ing....Two of them pulled me into a sitting positing. They took off the rest of my clothes and began to abuse me sexually in horrible ways. Wine was poured on me and they used and abused my body in ways that are too disgusting and too humiliating for me to describe in detail. They told me they would stop if I gave them the names of the people in the photographs.

Sister Ortiz blacked out. When she awakened, she found herself again the subject of interrogation. She was raped repeatedly. Then, she could hear peo-ple moving some sort of heavy block that was on the ground. Her affidavit con-tinues:

There was a horrible smell and I was lowered into a pit. It seemed to be filled with bodies; I remember trying not to walk on them. There were rats falling on me. I passed out again. I remember waking up somewhere on the ground. The men were again amusing themselves with my body.

The abuse continued for some time. Finally, someone who sounded like an American told her torturers that she was a North American and they should let her go. The man removed her blindfold and helped her back into her clothes. He brought her to his car and began to drive her, he said, to the U.S. Embassy. But Sister Ortiz did not trust him. At a traffic light, she bolted from the car and escaped.

When Sister Ortiz came forward with her experiences, Hector Gramajo denied that they ever happened. Indeed, he accused her of fabricating the story to cover up a "sadomasochistic lesbian affair." As a result, Ortiz was more than willing to help sue the former general.

Gramajo sought to dismiss both cases. In holding that Gramajo could, upon proper proof, be held liable for the atrocities alleged under the ATCA and the TVPA, U.S. District Court Judge Douglas P. Woodlock ruled that there was no doubt that the human rights abuses alleged in the complaints "are recognized in international law as violations of the law of war." Even if Gramajo did not direct or personally participate in the individual acts of torture, the court ruled that such an excuse "overlooks the fact that the gist of the charge is an unlawful breach of duty by petitioner as an army commander to control the operations of the members of his command by permitting them to commit the extensive and widespread atrocities specified."

After the court permitted the cases to proceed, Gramajo defaulted rather than participate in discovery. The court ordered Gramajo to pay damages in the amount of $47.5 million to the plaintiffs in *Xuncax* and *Ortiz.*

Todd v. Panjaitan: Kamal Ahmed Bamadhaj, a New Zealand citizen, was a 20-year-old student at the University of New South Wales in Australia on the day he died in East Timor. A pro-democracy activist, Bamadhaj had traveled to that Indonesian-occupied country to offer his services as a translator on a United Nations (UN) fact-finding mission and to interact with East Timor pro-democracy activists. Unexpectedly, the UN cancelled the mission, disheartening the East Timorese and emboldening the Indonesian military occupying forces.

On November 12, 1991, Bamadhaj participated in a peaceful demonstration and funeral for an activist. As a few thousand mourners walked toward the cemetery, they periodically shouted independence slogans. They also carried banners. When the crowd arrived at the cemetery, troops appeared and moved forward, raising their rifles and opening fire on the defenseless people. More than 250 people died.

Bamadhaj was injured in the gunfire, but did not die immediately. He staggered down a street and a military vehicle approached. Shots rang out and Bamadhaj fell to the pavement. The soldiers stole his camera and roared off, leaving the young man to bleed to death.

Bamadhaj's mother, Helen Todd, sued on behalf of herself and the estate of her son under the ATCA and the TVPA. The defendant was Sintong Panjaitan, the commander of the Indonesian military at the time of the slaughter. Panjaitan had been in direct control of the soldiers who massacred the East Timorese mourners. Panjaitan was in the U.S. attending Harvard's Business School when the suit was filed and served.

Not surprisingly, Panjaitan fled the U.S. and never answered the suit. A default judgment of $4 million in compensatory damages and $14 million in punitive damages was entered in favor of Todd and her son's estate.

Paul v. Avril: Prosper Avril was the Lieutenant General of the Haitian military and a supporter of General Henri Namphy, who took control of Haiti after the overthrow of the dictator Jean-Claude "Baby Doc" Duvalier. After succeeding Namphy, Avril ruthlessly oppressed all political opposition, including opposition voiced by the six plaintiffs in this case.

On November 1, 1989, the Presidential Guard invited plaintiffs Evans Paul, Jean-Auguste Mesyeux, and Marino Etienne to a conference about human rights abuses. Rather than enter into a discussion with these democracy advocates, about 40 soldiers, all members of Avril's personal security detail, surrounded them and viciously beat them, hitting them with truncheons and the butts of their rifles, and repeatedly kicking them with their heavy combat boots.

The soldiers stripped their prisoners of all of their identification papers, jewelry, money, and keys, and hauled them outside, where the beatings continued. They were then transported to the Port-Au-Prince police headquarters and the beatings resumed. Soldiers set the activists' hair ablaze and put lit cigarette lighters in their nostrils.

By the end of one of these sessions, Etienne had been beaten so badly that both his eyes were swollen shut, blood was dripping from his skull, and his clothes were entirely caked in his own blood. Meanwhile, Paul had suffered six broken ribs, a herniated disc, a perforated lung, a crushed hip, a swollen scrotum, and severe psychological trauma. The other plaintiffs suffered similar injuries.

On November 2, 1989, the government publicly displayed the plaintiffs on state-controlled television. Government agents falsely accused the plaintiffs of planning to assassinate Avril. They jailed the plaintiffs and never brought them to trial. Eventually, the Haitian government released the plaintiffs. They fled to the U.S. and later filed suit.

Three other Haitian political activists — Gerald Emile Brun, Serge Gilles, and Fernand Laforest — also sued Avril due to events that occurred on January 20, 1990, after Avril had declared a state of siege. These plaintiffs were beaten and tortured, held without counsel, and forcibly deported. During their ordeal, they were also denied medical care and representation of counsel.

The six plaintiffs were ultimately awarded $41 million in a default judgment. None of the plaintiffs in the four cases described above has been able to collect on the judgments, although collection efforts continue. This does not mean that these suits have been mere *pro forma* exercises. "Our ultimate point is to stop these abuses from happening," says Stephens, "and we passionately believe that one way to stop these activities is to make people pay a price."

The CCR's Jennifer Green, Matthew Chachere, Mahlon Perkins, Jose Luis Morin, and David Cole also served as co-counsel in all four cases. Serving as co-counsel in *Gramajo* were Professor James F. Smith, Paul Soreff, Frank LaRue, Mark Simonoff, Susan Shawn Roberts, Wally Mason, Anna Gallagher, Todd Howland, and Robert Bertsche. Ira Kurzban served as co-counsel in *Avril*. Harvery Kaplan, Maureen O'Sullivan and Jeremiah Friedman served as co-counsel in both *Gramajo* and *Panjaitan*. All of these attorneys deserve recognition for their work in these important cases.

The decisions in these cases can be found at *Xuncax v. Gramajo* and *Ortiz v. Gramajo*, 886 F. Supp. 162 (D. Mass. 1995) (consolidated cases); *Todd v. Panjaitan*, 1994 WL 827111 (D. Mass. Oct. 26, 1994); and *Paul v. Avril*, 901 F. Supp. 330 (S.D. Fla. 1994).

Michael Ratner

Beth Stephens

CHAPTER FOURTEEN

1996: The Case of the Secret Skunkworks

Product Safety *Horowitz v. Raybestos-Manhattan, Inc.*

Government Accountability *City of Fremont v. Adams*

Government Accountability *Dole/Talamaivao v. County of Los Angeles*

Environmental Protection *Marbled Murrelet v. Pacific Lumber Co.*

Toxic Injury Prevention *White v. City of Newark*

Human Rights *In re Estate of Ferdinand Marcos Human Rights Litigation*

Winner
Lockheed Toxic Torts Litigation
The Case of the Secret Skunkworks

The finalists for the 1996 Trial Lawyer of the Year Award took on Big Tobacco, combated improper police practices, protected an endangered bird species and the environment, prevented lead poisoning of children, and continued the pursuit of justice for the victims of former Philippine dictator Ferdinand Marcos. The winner fought for compensation for 625 workers whose employer, Lockheed Corporation, failed to warn them about toxic chemicals that they were using in the construction of the Stealth Bomber.

Product Safety
Horowitz v. Raybestos-Manhattan, Inc.
Madelyn Chaber

Attorney Madelyn Chaber of San Francisco's Wartnick, Chaber, Harowitz, Smith & Tigerman scored a huge victory against Big Tobacco. In an unusual asbestos and tobacco case, she won the largest jury verdict to that date against the cigarette industry.

The *Horowitz* case presented a tragic twist to the usual dangers associated with cigarette smoking. From 1952 to 1956, P. Lorillard Cigarette Company manufactured its Kent Micronite Filters cigarette brand with blue crocidolite asbestos — the most carcinogenic form of commercially used asbestos fibers. Milton Horowitz smoked Kents during that time, as a result of which he later contracted a terminal asbestos-related lung tumor. The jury learned that, during the years in question, Lorillard advertised Kent filters as being "completely harmless," and claimed that Kent "offered the greatest health protection of any cigarette." The obvious falsity of the claims — and Chaber's exceptional advocacy — led the jury to award $1.3 million to Horowitz in compensatory damages and $700,000 in punitive damages.

The case took an important step toward holding tobacco companies liable for the harm that their products cause. As the tobacco industry's winning streak against plaintiffs injured by smoking started to wane, many state legislatures began to pass legislation protective of tobacco company interests. By focusing on the harm caused by the filter rather than the risks associated with tobacco, *Horowitz* pioneered an innovative strategy against Big Tobacco.

There is no reported decision on the merits in this case.

Madelyn Chaber

Government Accountability
City of Fremont v. Adams
Gary Gwilliam and James Chiosso

Attorneys Gary Gwilliam and James Chiosso of Oakland, California's Gwilliam Ivary, Chiosso, Cavalli & Brewer held the City of Fremont's police department liable for the wrongful death of Patrick Adams. When Adams threatened suicide, police surrounded him in his own backyard. As officers attempted to disarm him, Adams shot himself in the chest. Police officers responded by firing 35 rounds; 18 of their bullets struck Adams in the back. The shooting sparked intense controversy about the training received by Fremont police officers in crisis intervention involving potential suicides.

On the face of the case, it may be difficult to understand why the jury held the police liable for conduct brought on by the decedent's irrational behavior. However, all was not as it seemed on the surface. Gwilliam and Chiosso discovered an audio tape recording made by a police officer in the yard adjacent to Adams' home. The contents of the tape directly contradicted police testimony about the shooting, exposing misconduct by officers that led to the tragic denouement of Adams' self-destructive confrontation with police.

In one of the largest police misconduct verdicts in California history, the jury awarded Adams' widow $2.5 million for emotional distress and $1.2 million for wrongful death, and $1.5 million to the couple's daughter for emotional distress. The verdict served as a warning to police departments to provide proper training to officers and to forthrightly recount controversial law enforcement actions for the record.

After the attorneys were honored, however, the verdict's impact was greatly limited. First, the trial court reduced the verdict. Then the appellate court reversed it.

The later reported decision in this case can be found at *City of Fremont v. Adams*, 80 Cal. Rptr. 2d 196 (1998) (reversing jury verdict).

Gary Gwilliam

James Chiosso

Government Accountability

Dole/Talamaivao v. County of Los Angeles

Garo Mardirossian, Hugh Manes, and Thomas Beck

Los Angeles attorneys Garo Mardirossian of Mardirossian & Associates, Hugh Manes of Manes & Watson, and Thomas Beck of Thomas E. Beck & Associates won justice for a group of 36 Samoan-Americans attending a bridal shower in 1989, who were beaten, arrested, and jailed without justification by members of the Los Angeles County Sheriff's Department. The attorneys first represented — and won acquittals for — three bridal shower attendees subjected to criminal charges for allegedly assaulting the deputies with rocks and bottles. After winning acquittals on all charges, the attorneys then filed a civil suit to hold the County of Los Angeles responsible for the wrongdoing of its deputies.

The trial consumed seven months and featured a videotape of deputies beating the family members and friends of the bride-to-be on the front lawn and driveway of her house. The video, along with testimony by neighbors, effectively refuted the false testimony by some deputies that guests had thrown rocks and bottles at them. The jury returned a $15.9 million damage award and found the

County liable for maintaining and applying a policy of deliberate indifference to the civil rights of plaintiffs.

There is no reported decision on the merits in this case.

Garo Mardirossian

Hugh Manes

Thomas Beck

Environmental Protection
Marbled Murrelet v. Pacific Lumber Co.
Mark Harris and Macon Cowles

Attorneys Mark Harris of Arcata, California, and Macon Cowles of Boulder, Colorado, won a groundbreaking victory enforcing the Endangered Species Act (ESA). They spearheaded a suit on behalf of the Environmental Protection Information Center (EPIC) and a rare seabird against the Pacific Lumber Company.

The timber company had planned to cut down the murrelet's last critical breeding ground in Owl Creek Grove, an old-growth forest. After bitterly contested discovery and an eight-day trial, a U.S. District Court judge concluded that the lumber company's plan would violate the ESA, in that felling trees would both harass the rare bird and cause irreparable harm by destroying crucial habitat.

Preservation of the bird's nesting grounds was essential to the species' survival because, although the birds can live up to 25 years, they reproduce at a very low rate, laying only one egg a year. The bird's population is declining at a rate of about five to seven percent each year.

The lawyers obtained a restraining order preventing the company from logging Old Creek Grove. The victory, which the U.S. Court of Appeals for the Ninth Circuit subsequently upheld, significantly aided the cause of protecting the bird from potential extinction.

This was the second time Cowles was named a finalist for the Trial Lawyer of the Year Award. In 1993, he and his co-counsel were co-winners of the Trial Lawyer of the Year Award for their landmark toxic contamination case against Asarco. (See Chapter Eleven.)

The reported decision in this case and its subsequent case history can be found at *Marbled Murrelet v. Pacific Lumber Co.*, 880 F. Supp. 1343 (N.D. Cal. 1995), *aff'd sub nom. Marbled Murrelet v. Babbitt*, 83 F.3d 1060 (9th Cir. 1996), *cert. denied*, 519 U.S. 1108 (1997).

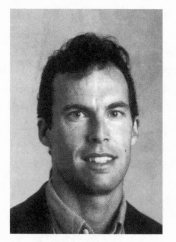

Mark Harris

Macon Cowles

Toxic Injury Prevention
White v. City of Newark
Christopher M. Placitella and Barry R. Sugarman

Woodbridge, New Jersey, attorneys Christopher M. Placitella and Barry R. Sugarman represented 28,000 children in a *pro bono* lawsuit to protect children in Newark, New Jersey, from lead-based paint poisoning. The class action lawsuit forced Newark to take appropriate actions to safeguard its youngest citizens from toxic poisoning.

While representing lead poisoning victims, the trial lawyers discovered that children poisoned by lead-based paint often returned to toxic environments after their release from treatment because Newark failed to insure that lead-poisoned apartments were properly abated. Vowing to remedy this outrage, the lawyers filed a class action seeking to correct the problem.

After years of discovery, the trial began on January 16, 1996. The plaintiffs' counsel outlined the severe environmental threats to the children and the trial was then suspended so settlement talks could proceed. These discussions led to a landmark agreement and consent decree under which the City must follow strict guidelines to insure proper inspection, abatement, medical follow-up, and record keeping to protect children at risk of lead poisoning. In spite of the intensity of the effort and the time required to obtain this result, the lawyers, on behalf of their firm of Willentz, Goldman & Spitzer, waived all fees and costs. This settlement, the first of its kind, set a high standard for similar cases, compelling agencies to perform statutory and regulatory responsibilities.

There is no reported decision on the merits in this case.

Christopher M. Placitella

Barry R. Sugarman

Human Rights
In re Estate of Ferdinand Marcos Human Rights Litigation
Robert A. Swift and Sherry P. Broder

Attorneys Robert A. Swift of Philadelphia's Kohn, Swift & Graf and Sherry P. Broder of The Law Offices of Sherry P. Broder in Honolulu performed outstanding work on behalf of almost 10,000 Filipinos who were tortured, summarily executed, or "disappeared" during the martial law rule of dictator Ferdinand E. Marcos. Finalists for the 1994 Trial Lawyer of the Year Award for their work in successfully completing the liability and punitive damage portions of the case, Swift and Broder were 1996 finalists for their litigation in the compensatory damages phase. In a fight that lasted more than a decade, Swift and Broder achieved an almost $2 billion judgment.

In the compensatory damages phase, Swift and Broder convinced the trial judge to use an aggregate method of damages, entailing the random selection of 137 claims to be tried before the jury. These efforts culminated in a compensatory award to the victims of Marcos' brutality in the amount of $766 million. Of special note — and directly to the benefit of the late dictator's victims — the lawyers doggedly pursued ownership of a house in Hawaii where Marcos lived his last years, obtaining in the process a $1 million settlement. This was the first known collection of a civil judgment for violation of international human rights, an important breakthrough in the effort by trial lawyers to construct a civil common law to combat human rights abuses around the world.

A reported decision in this case can be found at *In re Estate of Ferdinand Marcos Human Rights Litigation*, 94 F.3d 539 (9th Cir. 1996) (denying injunction against Republic of Philippines and recognizing Republic's immunity claim).

Robert A. Swift

Sherry P. Broder

1996 Trial Lawyer of the Year Award Winner
Thomas V. Girardi
The Case of the Secret Skunkworks

The "Skunkworks," a factory owned by the defense contractor Lockheed Corporation, helped develop the U.S. Air Force's Stealth Bomber and other top-secret military aircraft that through design and material selection are virtually undetectable by radar. Due to national security interests, the buildings used to develop these aircraft remained completely sealed. Even the windows were painted black to prevent satellite detection.

Over the years, 625 Lockheed employees and former employees who had worked at the Skunkworks facilities developed serious health maladies. These ranged from relatively modest symptoms, such as rashes and bronchial congestion, to life threatening illnesses, including organic brain damage, liver disease, peripheral nerve damage, kidney malfunction, and cancer. Toxic chemicals found in the solvents, sealants, paints, adhesives, and bonding agents used by Skunkworks laborers to manufacture stealth aircraft caused these illnesses. The lack of proper ventilation and the failure of the company to introduce safety precautions exacerbated the hazards posed by these chemicals to the workers. Lockheed failed to take necessary precautions or to warn its workers of the known risks arising from daily exposure to the toxic chemicals.

What is public justice? Employers and product manufacturers warn workers of the health dangers posed by toxic chemicals in the work place.

The Lockheed toxic torts cases began in the 1980s as a workers' compensation matter pursued by a sole practitioner. However, it soon became clear that more was involved in these injuries and that the workers were the victims of tortious conduct by Lockheed and the chemical suppliers, including Shell Oil Corporation, Exxon Corporation, Dupont Corporation, Unocal Corpora-tion, 3M, and General Electric, among the 25 companies eventually named as defendants.

After the case dramatically transformed from a large workers' compensation case into a huge civil action against the world's most powerful and tenacious corporations, reinforcements arrived in the person of attorney Thomas V. Girardi of Girardi & Keese in Los Angeles. Unsurprisingly, Girardi and his co-counsel developed proof that Lockheed had lied to its workers. As a result, Lockheed was barred from raising the workers' compensation defense, based on the fraud exception to the general rule that an injured worker may not sue his or her employer for injuries arising out of employment.

Girardi and his colleagues faced the most bitter and protracted litigation tactics, having to force disclosure of the evidence essential to proving the case. They also faced a significant legal defense from most of the defendants: the chemical manufacturers sought to shirk all blame for the plaintiffs' injuries by claiming that their warnings to Lockheed of the dangers associated with the chemicals were sufficient and that they had no duty to the workers themselves. Moreover, many of the actions were brought by family members of the plaintiffs who had died, or by those who were aged or infirm, or whose memories were impaired due to chronic toxic exposure. Some of the plaintiffs were so badly injured that they could no longer find their way to their local supermarkets.

Lockheed settled for $33 million during the trial in 1992. However, the chemical companies still had to be held to account for their failure to warn the workers of the health hazards of constant exposure to the toxic chemicals. In 1993, Girardi brought the case against the chemical companies to trial. Fifteen plaintiffs were selected out of the more than 600, representing a sample group to demonstrate the range of injury. After hearing 10 months of testimony and deliberating for 12 weeks — the longest jury deliberation in U.S. history — the jury deadlocked 8-4 in favor of the workers. So the judge declared a mistrial. Girardi's litigation team pressed on to a second trial in 1994.

To make the case easier for the jury to digest, the second trial was bifurcated into two phases. First, Girardi would litigate issues of exposure and causation of injuries. Next would come the hearings on damages. This time, the jury reached a verdict, finding eight of 18 defendant chemical companies liable to four selected plaintiffs for $2.1 million. It was the first time that a jury had held the chemical company defendants liable for failure to warn in a mass toxic exposure workplace setting.

Before a third trial could begin that would permit 14 additional defendants to present their cases, the trial lawyers discovered a Lockheed inventory list containing all of the chemicals that the defendants supplied to the Skunkworks.

Lockheed had never divulged the list in discovery. The defendants strove to keep this new information from being used against them at trial by insisting that the plaintiffs were collaterally estopped from pursuing any additional claims the new information raised against the defendants. However, their struggles were to no avail. Girardi used this information as devastating proof against many of the defendants in the third trial.

This trial commenced on March 6, 1995. Once again, the trial was bifurcated for ease of presentation and jury comprehension. Most of the trial dealt with adequacy of warnings with regard to the newly discovered chemicals. The plaintiffs triumphed. The jury found that 51 hazardous chemicals contained inadequate warnings. This finding held 15 of the 18 remaining defendants liable, and the finding would be binding on all of the future trials to be held by the remaining plaintiffs. Of greater significance was a jury finding that the actions amounted to "despicable conduct," the key to opening the door to potential punitive damages. This third trial culminated in a verdict of $10.6 million in favor of seven of 14 plaintiffs.

The success of the third trial broke the back of the resistance of most of the chemical company defendants. After eight years of litigation, many of the defendants settled — a tremendous achievement for the injured workers. In October 1998, Girardi won a $785 million verdict against the remaining defendants on behalf of 29 plaintiffs. The award included $25 million in compensatory damages and substantial punitive damages: $252 million against Exxon; $236 million against Shell; $145 million against Ashland; $81 million against Unocal; and $45 million against Dupont. Los Angeles Superior Court Judge Richard C. Hubbell, who presided over the trial, reduced the total punitive damages by half, to $380 million, in November 1998, and the defendants all appealed. The three-judge panel of the 2nd District Court of Appeal ruled on June 6, 2000, in *Aguilar vs. Ashland Chemical Co.* that there was no evidence of "despicable conduct" by Exxon, Unocal, Shell, Ashland and DuPont. The court threw out the $380 million in punitive damages and $25 million in actual damages, but sent the case back to the trial court to reconsider compensatory damages.

There is no reported decision on the merits in this case. Unreported opinions in two related cases can be found at *Patterson v. E.I. DuPont de Nemours & Co., Inc.*, 1999 WL 117693 (Cal. Ct. App. Feb. 25, 1999) (affirming compensatory damages award for most plaintiffs), and *Arnold v. Ashland Chem. Co.*,

2000 WL 1094103 (Cal. Ct. App. Feb. 18, 2000) (reversing compensatory damages award and remanding for new trial, reversing punitive damages award and ordering judgment for defendants on all punitive damages claims).

Thomas V. Girardi

CHAPTER FIFTEEN

1997: The Case That Couldn't Be Brought

Human Rights *Roxas v. Marcos*

Workers' Rights *United States v. Irving*

Toxic Injury Prevention *E.I. DuPont de Nemours & Co. v. Castillo*

Civil Rights *Roberts v. Texaco, Inc.*

Toxic Injury Prevention *Anderson v. Pacific Gas & Elec. Co.*

Workers' Rights *Rosario v. Diamond Shamrock Corp.*

Human Rights *In re Estate of Ferdinand Marcos Human Rights Litigation*

Civil Rights *In re Louisiana Energy Services, L.P.*

Environmental Protection *Sierra Club v. Tri-State Generation and Transmission Ass'n*

Winner
Kirkwood v. General Motors
The Case That Couldn't Be Brought

The finalists for the 1997 Trial Lawyer of the Year Award fought for human rights, civil rights, workers' rights, social justice, and victims of toxic torts and environmental degradation. The winner took on a case that could not be brought, persuaded the state legislature to change the law so it could be pursued, and then used it to hold General Motors accountable for valuing profits over lives.

Human Rights
Roxas v. Marcos
Daniel C. Cathcart

Attorney Daniel C. Cathcart of Los Angeles' Magaña, Cathcart & McCarthy successfully pursued former Philippine dictator Ferdinand Marcos and his wife Imelda for torturing and stealing from an amateur treasure hunter.

In 1971, Filipino locksmith Roger Roxas discovered an old tunnel beneath Baguio City, which is about 150 miles north of Manila, filled with gold bars and boxes of gold bullion that apparently had been looted by Japanese troops in World War II. It is believed that Lt. Gen. Tomoyuki Yamashita buried the treasure in secret tunnels under his headquarters when he commanded the Japanese forces occupying the Philippines. A tip from a former Japanese army interpreter led Roxas to the tunnels.

Roxas took home 17 gold bars and a 22-carat gold Buddha statuette that stood almost three feet tall, weighed about a metric ton, and was supposedly filled with diamonds. Then he made the mistake of reporting his discovery to a local judge, Pio Marcos, a relative of Ferdinand Marcos. When Marcos learned of the astonishing discovery, he stole the Golden Buddha and the gold bars and threw Roxas into prison. Roxas was then beaten and tortured for two years, until he revealed where the rest of the treasure lay buried. Marcos ordered his troops to dig out the remaining gold in the tunnel. Fearing for his life, Roxas assigned to Marcos all of his interest in "The Golden Buddha Corporation" and fled the country.

Marcos ruled the Philippines for 21 years before being overthrown in 1986. Marcos and his wife then moved to Hawaii to live in exile and, in 1988, Roxas sued them. Marcos died in September 1989, facing charges in the U.S. for human rights violations involving torture, murder, and false imprisonment, as well as charges in the Philippines for looting and theft.

Cathcart worked on Roxas' case for 10 years, tracking down the few people who could testify that the Golden Buddha even existed. He endured phone taps, office break-ins, and advanced more than $1 million in costs to litigate the case. Making matters even more difficult, Cathcart had to rely almost exclusively on videotaped depositions because witnesses were afraid to appear in person. Their fears were warranted — on May 23, 1993, the day Roxas was scheduled to fly to Hawaii to plead his case in court, he mysteriously died. According to attorney Cathcart, Roxas was poisoned in Manila.

Cathcart argued the case with his son, Peter T. Cathcart. Although a Honolulu jury cleared Imelda Marcos, it held Ferdinand Marcos' estate accountable, awarding $6 million to Roxas' estate for the pain and suffering caused while Roxas was held in captivity, $1.4 million to The Golden Buddha Corporation for the stolen Buddha and gold bars, and over $22 billion to The Golden Buddha Corporation for additional stolen treasures. Cathcart then began collecting the judgment, obtaining a $450 million attachment on a Marcos bank account in Switzerland.

In November 1998, however, after Cathcart was honored, the Hawaii Supreme Court held that the plaintiffs' evidence on the quality and quantity of the gold in the tunnels was too speculative and reversed the $22 billion award. The Court also set aside the $1.4 million judgment, which the Roxas estate claimed was too low. The Court remanded the case for retrial on both issues. The parties waived a jury trial and stipulated that the judge make a finding based on the evidence in the record. The judge determined the value of the gold to be $13 million. That decision is now on appeal to the Hawaii Supreme Court. According to Cathcart, the decision may permit the Marcos estate to "make an enormous profit as a result of the theft."

The later decision in this case can be found at *Roxas v. Marcos*, 969 P.2d 1209 (Haw. 1998) (affirming jury verdict in part and reversing in part).

Daniel C. Cathcart

Workers' Rights
United States v. Irving
Paul R. Cox

On October 10, 1979, Gail Merchant Irving, a 21-year-old employee of the Somersworth Shoe manufacturing plant in Somersworth, New Hampshire, bent down to retrieve a dropped glove from the floor. As she leaned over, an unguarded, rotating drive shaft of a "marker" machine, which is used to stamp the inner soles of shoes, caught her hair. The drive shaft's rotation created a vacuum that sucked her hair into the machine and tore her scalp from her skull. Irving suffered cardiac and respiratory arrest, and a fractured cervical vertebra that left her with permanent nerve damage. The accident paralyzed her from the neck down and she could not speak for some time. Although Irving's condition has improved over time, her reflexes and sensations throughout her body remain impaired and she still experiences loss of balance.

The U.S. Occupational Safety and Health Administration (OSHA) had inspected the plant and failed to notice the blatantly dangerous unguarded drive shaft in both 1975 and 1978. After the accident, OSHA inspected again and determined that the machine's unguarded drive shaft violated OSHA standards. The agency assigned the violation a severity value of eight, the highest value used at the time.

Attorney Paul R. Cox of Burns, Bryant, Hinchey, Cox & Rockefeller in Dover, New Hampshire, fought for more than 15 years on Irving's behalf to hold OSHA liable for its negligence under the Federal Tort Claims Act (FTCA). The district court twice dismissed the claim, ruling that OSHA was immune from suit under the FTCA's "discretionary function" exception. After Cox obtained reversals of both of those dismissals, the same judge finally tried the case on the merits and still ruled in favor of the government. The appeals court reversed the decision yet again and granted Cox's request to have the case retried before a different judge. This time Cox prevailed, winning a $1 million judgment for his client. He was then honored as a Trial Lawyer of the Year Award finalist for his tenacity and achievement.

According to Cox, the subsequent history of *Irving* is "a sad one." The government appealed the case to the U.S. Court of Appeals for the First Circuit. The Court affirmed the decision. However, as the verdict was about to be paid, the Court acted *sua sponte* to order an *en banc* hearing. The full Court, although sharply divided, dismissed the case, holding the "discretionary function" exception barred recovery. The U.S. Supreme Court then denied *certiorari.*

The later decision in this case and its subsequent case history can be found at *United States v. Irving*, 162 F.3d 154 (1st Cir. 1998) (*en banc*) (reversing judgment against government), *cert. denied*, 528 U.S. 812 (1999).

Paul R. Cox

Toxic Injury Prevention
E.I. DuPont de Nemours & Co. v. Castillo
James L. Ferraro

As Donna Castillo was taking one of her daily walks in November 1989 near Miami, Florida's Pine Island Farms tomato fields, farm workers sprayed her with the fungicide Benlate. She was about seven weeks pregnant. Normally, a baby's eyes develop during the first trimester of pregnancy, but when Castillo gave birth to her son John in June 1990, he had no eyes. The newborn had sockets with small cysts where his eyes should have been.

Attorney James L. Ferraro of Ferraro & Associates in Miami, Florida, filed suit against DuPont, the manufacturer of Benlate, and Pine Island Farms. He set an important precedent by convincing a jury that the pregnant woman's exposure to Benlate caused John Castillo to be born without eyes. This is an extremely rare birth defect known as bilateral anopthalmia. It is the first case ever successfully prosecuted against a chemical company for causing a birth defect.

Ferraro endured three years of discovery, which included taking 63 depositions in four countries, reviewing tens of thousands of documents, and battling more than 60 pretrial motions. Ferraro also had the onerous task of ruling out all other potential causes of the birth defect. In addition, the trial included complex hearings on highly technical scientific issues that involved studies on rats and humans to determine the potential effects of Benlate exposure.

After a six-week trial, the Miami-Dade jury returned a $4 million verdict against DuPont and Pine Island Farms with half the amount for pain and suffering and the other half for future medical expenses. The jury found that DuPont was 99.5 percent responsible and co-defendant Pine Island Farms was 0.5 percent responsible. This meant that DuPont's share of the damages was $3.98 million.

So far, this is the only successful verdict on a claim that Benlate, often associated with widespread crop damage, can cause children to be born blind. The plaintiff's victory opened the courthouse doors to many children born without eyes due to DuPont's wrongful conduct. Ferraro has since filed 12 suits on behalf of other children in similar situations.

DuPont appealed the verdict to the Florida Supreme Court, which heard oral arguments on February 6, 2001, but has not yet ruled. On April 19, 2001, DuPont announced that it would stop selling Benlate. Attorney Ferraro states,

"It is anticipated that this decision will govern science in the courtroom in Florida for the next 20 to 30 years."

The later reported decision in this case and its subsequent case history can be found at *E.I. Dupont de Nemours & Co. v. Castillo*, 748 So. 2d 1108 (Fla. Dist. Ct. App. 2000) (reversing jury verdict), *review granted* (August 31, 2000).

James L. Ferraro

Civil Rights

Roberts v. Texaco, Inc.

Michael D. Hausfeld, Cyrus Mehri, Max W. Berger, Daniel L. Berger, and Steven B. Singer

Michael D. Hausfeld and Cyrus Mehri of Cohen, Milstein, Hausfeld & Toll in Washington, D.C., and Max W. Berger, Daniel L. Berger, and Steven B. Singer of Bernstein, Litowitz, Berger & Grossman in New York, won what was then the largest settlement in the history of employment race discrimination in the widely publicized case, *Roberts v. Texaco, Inc.* The team filed this class action on behalf of approximately 1,400 African Americans employed by Texaco, alleging race discrimination in violation of federal and state laws. It focused on breaking through Texaco's "glass ceiling," which had long thwarted the career development of African-American employees.

The oil company experienced a public relations debacle when former Texaco personnel executive Richard Lundwall, of Danbury, Connecticut, turned over tapes that he had secretly made of Texaco executives making racist comments. On the tapes, executives were heard belittling African-American employees and their class action lawsuit. The tapes also revealed that Texaco executives plotted to hide or destroy documents that the six named plaintiffs needed to prove their case. After three years of litigation, the case settled following 10 days of negotiations that began on November 12, 1996 — the day after the disclosure of the infamous tapes.

The attorneys won monetary and programmatic relief worth more than $172 million for the class. The settlement included a payment of $115 million to class members, a special salary increase of 11.34 percent for each class member, and the creation of an Independent Equality and Tolerance Task Force to alter Texaco's human resources programs and monitor its progress toward racial equality. The settlement sent a "wake-up call" to Corporate America, demonstrating that institutional racism will not be tolerated.

"The era of the 'good ol' boy network' at Texaco is coming to an end," attorney Mehri told *The Los Angeles Times,* adding, "It's going to be a new Texaco."

"Since the settlement was approved by the court in 1997," said attorney Singer, "Texaco has made significant strides in expanding understanding of diversity for all its employees and has created managerial incentives that are directly tied to the company's achievement of diversity goals. The end result: in recent years, the overall percentage of women and minorities in Texaco's workplace has increased significantly."

Barri-Ellen Roberts and Jack E. White told the full story of the case in *Roberts v. Texaco: A true story of race & corporate America.*

There is no reported decision on the merits in this case.

Cyrus Mehri   *Max W. Berger*   *Daniel L. Berger*   *Steven B. Singer*

Toxic Injury Prevention

Anderson v. Pacific Gas & Elec. Co.

Walter J. Lack, Gary A. Praglin, Jill P. McDonnell,
Thomas V. Girardi, Robert W. Finnerty, Carrie J. Rognlien,
and Edward L. Masry

In 1991, Erin Brockovich hired the law firm of Masry & Vititoe in Toluca Lake, California, to represent her in a car accident case. The case settled for $17,000, but Brockovich still had debts, so she begged the firm to hire her as a file clerk. Not long after she started working at Masry & Vititoe, Brockovich reviewed a *pro bono* real estate case file containing some medical records that piqued her curiosity. After getting permission from attorney Edward L. Masry, she began to probe.

Brockovich's investigation showed that hundreds of residents in and around the high desert town of Hinkley, California, had suffered devastating health effects from exposure to Chromium 6. Chromium 6, a carcinogen, had leaked into the groundwater from a nearby compressor station operated by Pacific Gas and Electric Company (PG&E). The town's residents unwittingly had been drinking, bathing in, and inhaling Chromium 6 for decades. Their injuries ranged from serious digestive disorders to various cancers and respiratory disorders. Thus began the landmark toxic tort case against the world's largest publicly-owned utility.

Attorneys Walter J. Lack, Gary A. Praglin, and Jill P. McDonnell of Engstrom, Lipscomb & Lack in Los Angeles; Thomas V. Girardi, Robert W. Finnerty, and Carrie J. Rognlien of Girardi & Keese in Los Angeles; and Masry sued PG&E on behalf of 648 injured residents of Hinkley and ultimately succeeded in holding PG&E accountable for poisoning the rural town's groundwater since 1956.

These dedicated attorneys had to review over 1 million documents, take several hundred depositions, overcome egregious discovery abuses, prove medical causation in a toxic tort setting, reconstruct a complex hydro-geological water system, and endure a nearly two-year trial before forcing PG&E into an historic global settlement. Retired state appeals court Judge John K. Trotter presided over the settlement, which required PG&E to compensate its victims with $333 million, conduct an extensive environmental cleanup, and stop using chromium. The case has prompted other utilities to take similar actions and has resulted in environmental remediation at other contaminated sights.

The story of Brockovich's investigation, personal issues, and legal triumph became the basis for the 2000 hit movie *Erin Brockovich*, which earned Julia Roberts a Golden Globe and an Academy Award for best actress in the title role. Brockovich now serves as Director of Environmental Research at Masry & Vititoe, where she is involved in researching and helping prosecute other major toxic tort lawsuits. For example, another 1,000 current and former residents of Hinkley, Topock, and Kettleman Hills, California, sued PG&E in 1995, claiming that the utility poisoned their groundwater with chromium. That suit, *Aguayo v. Pacific Gas & Elec. Co.*, had been slated for trial in 2001. But those pollution victims may die before seeing a penny, say plaintiffs' lawyers; PG&E filed for Chapter 11 bankruptcy in April 2001.

On the other hand, attorney Masry says that the bankruptcy filing could backfire on the utility. "It won't affect the litigation at all," Masry told the Associated Press on April 11, 2001. "It will give us an opportunity to get into the financial information and the books of PG&E, which will make us happy. We don't see this as a setback at all. We think they're cooking their own goose." There is no reported decision on the merits in this case.

Walter J. Lack

Gary A. Praglin

Jill P. McDonnell

Thomas V. Girardi

Robert W. Finnerty

Edward L. Masry

Workers' Rights
Rosario v. Diamond Shamrock Corp.
Aaron Simon

Attorney Aaron Simon of Kazan, McClain, Edises, Simon & Abrams in Oakland, California, fought for 14 years to overcome a California workers' compensation provision that bars employees from suing their employers in a civil suit, and finally won justice for 10 personal injury and wrongful death victims.

Simon represented 10 employees of an oil and chemical conglomerate, Diamond Shamrock Corporation, who contracted lung cancer from workplace exposure to chloromethyl ether (CME) and bis-chloromethyl ether (BCME), both deadly carcinogens. After 10 years of discovery, a 16-week trial of the first personal injury case, and an outlay of almost $1 million in case costs, the plaintiffs prevailed due in large part to Simon's innovative theories of liability. Simon creatively and successfully argued that the plaintiffs' claims satisfied two exceptions to the workers' compensation bar — one for aggravating an employee's injury and one for negligently managing a separate operating unit of the company.

When plaintiff Samuel Rosario's case went to trial, Simon showed that Diamond Shamrock had evidence that CME and BCME were highly carcinogenic and had caused lung and nasal passage cancers in laboratory rats. Even more damaging, Simon proved that company doctors had examined the workers semi-annually, but had told workers like Rosario, who exhibited abnormal cell readings but no apparent tumors, that they were fine. Rosario eventually developed a tumor in his neck. The jury returned a $4.6 million verdict in this first personal injury case, but the company appealed. The appellate court eventually ordered a new trial on the damages issue.

On the eve of the second personal injury trial, Diamond Shamrock settled all 10 cases for a confidential, multi-million dollar amount. These cases send a strong message to companies that they must prevent injury to their workers, particularly when the potential injuries are clearly known and life-threatening.

There is no reported decision on the merits in these cases.

Aaron Simon

Human Rights

In re Estate of Ferdinand Marcos Human Rights Litigation
Robert A. Swift and Sherry P. Broder

Attorneys Robert A. Swift of Philadelphia's Kohn, Swift & Graf, and Sherry P. Broder of Honolulu, won a nearly $2 billion judgment on behalf of 9,541 Filipinos who were tortured, were summarily executed, or "disappeared" during the years when dictator Ferdinand Marcos held his country in the grip of martial law. *In re Estate of Ferdinand Marcos Human Rights Litigation* was the first class action on human rights issues and the first human rights case in the U.S. successfully litigated on the merits.

Swift and Broder were honored as finalists for the Trial Lawyer of the Year Award in 1994 for their work on the liability and punitive damages portions of this case, and in 1996 for the compensatory damages phase. They were honored a third time in 1997 for their continuing success in this extraordinary lawsuit.

The third nomination for the pair honored victories in which the court upheld the nearly $2 billion judgment, as well as a contempt citation against Marcos' heirs for failing to appear for depositions and for violating an injunction prohibiting disposition of estate assets. Once the judgment was final, Swift and Broder vigorously pursued collection. Money that the late dictator had stashed in Swiss banks finally found its way into the hands of the victims and their families under a $150 million settlement announced on February 24, 1999.

"This result holds a dictator accountable and finally fulfills the goal we sought in 1986 when Ferdinand Marcos fled to Honolulu from the Philippines," said attorney Broder.

"Never before have human rights victims in any country recovered on a judgment against the perpetrator," said attorney Swift. "It is no longer satisfactory to just demonstrate vile abuses in a court of law. Victims must be compensated. The average victim, or the heir of a deceased victim, will receive enough to buy land, start a business, educate children, or just improve his or her quality of life. Because the money will be spent in the Philippines, the economy as a whole will benefit."

The reported decision in this case can be found at *In re Estate of Ferdinand Marcos Human Rights Litigation*, 94 F.3d 539 (9th Cir. 1996) (denying injunction against Republic of Philippines and recognizing Republic's immunity claim).

Robert A. Swift

Sherry P. Broder

Civil Rights
In re Louisiana Energy Services, L.P.
Nathalie M. Walker and Diane Curran

Racism comes in many forms. Sometimes it reveals itself over time, such as when African Americans or other racial minorities find their careers stymied based on discriminatory employment practices. Sometimes it is less blatant, but nevertheless reprehensible. Such was the case when Louisiana Energy Services, L.P. (LES) decided to put a new uranium enrichment plant in African-American communities.

The company chose a locale between Forest Grove and Center Springs, two rural towns in northern Louisiana with predominantly African-American populations. The proposed plant would have turned the communities into a de facto toxic waste dump — jeopardizing the residents' subsistence fishing, hunting, and gardening — by producing and storing more than 100,000 tons of radioactive waste on the site.

Attorneys Nathalie M. Walker of the Sierra Club Legal Defense Fund (now Earthjustice Legal Defense Fund) in New Orleans, and Diane Curran of Harmon, Curran & Spielberg in Washington, D.C., convinced the licensing board of the Nuclear Regulatory Commission (NRC) that race played a determining role in the site selection process. The trial lawyers also showed that the plant was not needed, that the financing for the entire project was questionable, and that the ability of the company to clean up the site once the plant ceased operations was dubious. The project died after the NRC, for the first time in history, refused to license a proposed uranium enrichment plant. This was the first decision by any U.S. governmental agency or court turning on the issue of "environmental racism."

On appeal, the NRC commissioners affirmed the original finding that LES's Environmental Impact Statement (EIS) had not adequately addressed the disparate impact of the proposed plant on the adjacent African-American communities, but they reversed the finding of racial discrimination. Because the ruling required a new EIS, however, LES withdrew its application.

There is no reported decision on the merits in this case.

Nathalie M. Walker

Diane Curran

Environmental Protection
Sierra Club v. Tri-State Generation & Transmission Ass'n
Reed Zars

Attorney Reed Zars, a solo practioner from Laramie, Wyoming, working *pro bono* with a mere $5,000 allocated for costs, obtained a precedent-setting decision under the Clean Air Act and a stunning settlement against three of the West's largest utility companies. Zars filed a citizen suit against a coal-fired power plant for polluting nearby air and lakes, and convinced the court to consider as evidence the records from the utilities' own emission monitors in the plants' smoke stacks. Prior to the case, only evidence obtained by individual inspectors was accepted by the courts to prove pollution standard violations. Issuing the first ruling to permit citizens to use this valuable monitor evidence, the court found more than 17,000 violations of the Clean Air Act.

After three years of litigation and six months of negotiation, Zars achieved a comprehensive settlement in which the companies agreed to install $130 million in pollution control equipment and pay $2 million in civil penalties, $2 million for conservation easement purchases, and $250,000 for wood and coal stove conversions. The new pollution controls are preventing the emission of 20,000 tons of air pollution each year.

The reported decision in this case can be found at *Sierra Club v. Tri-State Generation & Transmission Ass'n*, 173 F.R.D. 275 (D. Colo. 1997).

Reed Zars

1997 Trial Lawyer of the Year Award Winner
Lawrence Baron
The Case That Couldn't Be Brought

Attorney Lawrence Baron of Portland, Oregon, took on a case that could not be brought, persuaded the Oregon state legislature to change the law so he could pursue it, and then fought off over 150 motions by defendant General Motors to win justice for his client.

Hundreds of people have suffered severe burns in fiery crashes involving pickup trucks that General Motors (GM) manufactured between 1973 and 1987. Some survived the collisions, but were terribly burned when the trucks' gas tanks exploded. The problem is an unsafe design — GM put the "side-saddle" gas tanks outside the trucks' steel frame rails, rather than in a more protected area. The truck is, therefore, susceptible to explosion in a side impact or an angled front impact because sheet metal, bolts, or other objects can easily puncture the tank and cause a fire.

What is public justice? The law ensures that corporations can be held accountable for wrongful conduct that causes injury and, if it doesn't, it is changed.

Anne Kirkwood of Bend, Oregon, was horribly burned and disfigured when, through no fault of her own, her car collided with a 1976 GM pickup truck with side-saddle gas tanks that exploded upon impact. Kirkwood's granddaughter burned to death and her grandson suffered serious burns in the crash. Kirkwood was hospitalized for five months in a burn unit, where she endured nearly 30 surgeries. She lost the sight in her left eye and doctors had to amputate her right leg. Her medical bills are projected to be approximately $3 million.

When Kirkwood approached Baron for help, she had no chance of prevailing because Oregon had a "statute of repose" that banned any lawsuit against a manufacturer whose product was more than eight years old. GM had manufactured the pickup truck involved in Kirkwood's accident 18 years earlier.

"When Mrs. Kirkwood's son visited me, I had to tell him the unhappy news about the statute of repose," Baron recalls. Nevertheless, when Baron met Kirkwood, he was so moved by the extent of her injuries and so outraged by the unjust law that he took the case.

Ever the optimist, Baron planned to persuade the state legislature to create an exception to the law that would allow lawsuits involving side-saddle gas tanks. "I knew there had to be an answer for her," Baron recalls. "She was the victim of a well-known product defect. She had been utterly brutalized by it. I knew we had a meritorious case — if we could only figure out how to help her get past the statute of repose."

A legislative subcommittee was considering a new, corporate-sponsored "tort reform" bill designed to further limit Oregonians' access to the courts by, for example, instituting a "loser pays" system and abolishing joint and several liability. The lawmakers had even created a Joint Senate-House Committee on Tort Reform to facilitate the passage of the tort reform legislation. Baron hired lobbyist Brad Higbee to advance Kirkwood's cause.

Kirkwood's state senator, Republican Neil Bryant, chaired the committee. Her state representative, Republican Bev Clarno, served as Speaker of the House. Both were dedicated to tort reform, but they were so moved by Kirkwood's case that they agreed to cooperate in crafting a narrow, statutory exception. Oregon Senate Bill 447 provided:

1. A civil action against a manufacturer of pickup trucks for injury or
   damage resulting from a fire caused by rupture of a sidesaddle gas
   tank in a vehicle collision, including any product liability action...
   based on negligence, must be commenced not later than two years
   after the injury or damage occurs. A civil action against a manufacturer
   of pickup trucks for death resulting from a fire caused by rupture of
   a sidesaddle gas tank in a vehicle collision, including any product
   liability action... and any action based on negligence, must be
   commenced not later than three years after the death.

2. A civil action against a manufacturer of pickup trucks for death,
   injury or damage resulting from a fire caused by rupture of a sidesaddle
   gas tank in a vehicle collision is not subject to...any statute of repose
   in Oregon Revised Statutes.

The first step was to get the proposed legislation through the joint committee — no small task, given that the legislative body was committed to protecting corporations and insurance companies, often at the expense of consumers. However, because GM's lobbyists were not expecting a consumer-friendly proposal to be introduced and because General Motors' name did not appear in the statute, they apparently failed to notice the proposed exception. As a result, GM's advocates did not act to defeat the bill and the committee unanimously approved it.

GM may have been asleep at the wheel during the committee deliberations, but the bill caught its attention once it was approved by the joint committee. GM hired eight lobbyists to personally contact every legislator and bemoan the "unfairness" of singling out one defective product. No doubt, GM failed to point out that its advertisements hyped the trucks as likely to last 18 years — 10 years longer than the statute of repose. Still, SB 447 passed the Senate by a comfortable 20-8 margin.

Then the action shifted to Oregon's House of Representatives and it became clear that, if the legislation were to pass, Kirkwood would need expert advocacy to champion her cause and counter GM's lobbyists. This would not come cheaply. Baron's firm wasn't able to fully fund the lobbying campaign.

So Kirkwood's daughter stood up in church, spoke of her mother's plight, and asked her congregation for financial support in the lobbying effort. She said she was forming a "Justice for Anne Kirkwood Committee" and asked for volunteers and financial contributions. The church and other community members embraced the cause. The committee sponsored a series of fundraising events, including bake sales, a karaoke contest, and an auction. In one weekend alone, Madras, Oregon, raised $20,000 to pay for the services of Higbee, who became known as the "bake sale lobbyist."

On March 30, 1995, SB 447 faced its final vote in the House. On the morning of the vote, the GM lobbyists had become so shrill in their advocacy that some Representatives denounced them from the House floor. Even so, no one doubted GM's power to sway votes. Speaker Clarno made two tactical moves that would carry the day. First, she drafted House Joint Memorial 8, a resolution declaring certain farm workers who saved Kirkwood's life to be heroes of the State of Oregon. She then scheduled that resolution for a vote immediately before the vote on SB 447. To seal the deal, she positioned Kirkwood in the visitors' gallery, so that legislators would have to vote down her right to seek compensation to her face. The legislation passed by 53-6 — an astonishing example of the power of citizen advocacy in a good cause. Oregon's Governor quickly signed the bill.

As the passage of SB 447 opened one door, it closed another. Baron's differences with his partners over the *Kirkwood* case had grown so deep that they had become irreconcilable.

"I was very disappointed with my firm," Baron recalls. "When I originally proposed our taking the case, I got lukewarm support from some partners, but others were just flat-out opposed. As the case progressed, we had many, many meetings about the case and I managed to keep it going because I kept persevering with them…. Many were leery of tackling GM — we had lost a case against GM previously — and wanted to bring in another firm to share that burden. So I told them if the statute passed, I would leave; after that, they never did anything that would have allowed me to stay."

Baron approached attorney Paul Whelan of Seattle's Stritmatter Kessler Whelan Withey Coluccio, whose paralegal he had met at a convention in Atlanta. "Paul told me that I could have anything I wanted from him," Baron says gratefully. "And he didn't even ask for a share of the case. In that second, he hooked me. I owe Paul and his firm a lot for what happened in this case."

Before Baron could get to the merits of Kirkwood's case, he would have to defend the new law that created the exception to the statute of repose. "GM brought in one of Kenneth Starr's partners and we had Professor David Schumann, a recognized constitutional scholar from the University of Oregon School of Law. We were able to prevail and the Oregon Supreme Court refused to hear the case."

Having finally won the right to fully litigate the case, Baron still faced stiff opposition. GM tried to bury Baron, who was now a sole practitioner, with time delays, litigation and discovery intransigence, and the high costs of pursuing the case.

But Baron refused to buckle. He pursued an innovative offense involving confidential settlements that GM had entered into with other litigants claiming to have been injured in side-saddle gas tank explosions. Baron knew that GM had secretly settled hundreds of other side-saddle cases and that he could not obtain the details of those settlements in discovery. But he had a brainstorm. He asked for the total number of such settlements and the aggregate amount paid out of GM's coffers as a result. Such information, he argued, would be relevant under Oregon's punitive damages statute, which permits juries to consider a litigant's attempts to hide misconduct — surely, a primary purpose of confidential settlements!

GM howled in outrage, arguing that evidence of prior settlements is not admissible to prove liability. But Baron convinced Circuit Judge Stephen N. Tiktin that his purpose was not to prove liability, but to establish other issues, including the amount of punitive damages. On September 12, 1996, Judge Tiktin ruled:

Defendant shall disclose:

1. The aggregate dollar amount of all settlements of all claims relating in any way to burn injuries or deaths allegedly relating to 1973-1987 CK series pickup trucks.

2. The time period which these settlements were entered into and paid.

3. The total number of these settlements.

4. How many were confidential.

5. How many required the return of discovery documents or imposed limitations on the dissemination of those documents.

6. Whether GM has ever paid punitive damages as a result of any claim made relating in any way to burn injuries or deaths allegedly relating to 1973-1987 C/K series pickup trucks and, if so, the aggregate amount.

Judge Tiktin protected the results of such discovery from disclosure, but by this innovative line of inquiry, Baron moved his case forward.

Baron had to contend with continuous stonewalling by GM that required further court orders. First, the judge fashioned an order requiring GM to conduct thorough searches for records and to explain the reasons that relevant records might have been destroyed. He also required GM to explain the reasons for any redaction and to provide a factual justification for claims of privilege.

Moreover, apparently believing that GM was not litigating the case in good faith, the judge required GM's representatives and lawyers to sign all discovery responses, personally attesting to a good faith response to discovery. Yet another order required GM to ensure that representatives with proper knowledge appeared at depositions, rather than employees with little or no ability to respond to deposition questions.

After years of struggle, trial was about to begin. GM's lawyers did not want to face a jury with Kirkwood sitting in court, a living illustration of the catastrophic injuries caused by GM's exploding gas tanks. Before the trial started, GM filed 56 motions *in limine*, all of which took five days to litigate. The court denied the vast majority of those motions. Then, in a desperate attempt to stop the inevitable, GM's chief trial counsel sought to delay the trial claiming that he was otherwise engaged.

Baron smelled a rat. He obtained transcripts from other GM cases that were set for trial. Not once did GM's lawyer advise the judges in those cases that he was already scheduled for trial in the *Kirkwood* case. As Baron told *Trial Lawyer* Magazine, "When [GM's lawyer] tried to use the conflicts to delay our case, he was met by both transcripts [of the other trial settings] and scathing argument by Mike Withey about General Motors' complete disregard for the judicial system." Instead of a lengthy continuation, GM's tactics merely delayed the case for three weeks.

GM was finally ready to surrender. The company asked for mediation and, after three sessions, the case settled on January 10, 1997, for a confidential amount.

"I feel very much elated, very happy," Kirkwood told the *Detroit Free Press*. "I do feel with the grace of God, we had a good victory. I hope we taught GM a lesson." The settlement was also a personal and moral victory for Baron and the attorneys who helped him take on one of the toughest adversaries a trial attorney can face.

In addition to attorneys Baron, Whelan, and Withey, David Schumann and Dan Keppler also deserve recognition for their contribution to this important case.

There is no reported decision on the merits in this case.

Lawrence Baron

CHAPTER SIXTEEN

1998: The Case That Made Big Tobacco Pay

Access to Justice *Best v. Taylor Machine Works, Inc.* and *Isbell v. Union Pac. R.R. Co.*

Insurer Accountability *Taylor v. State Farm Ins. & Cas. Co.*

Consumer Protection *Flores v. Phillips College*

Auto Safety *Toyota Motor Corp. v. McCathern*

Workers' Rights *In re Columbia Falls Profit Sharing Litigation*

Civil Rights *Hispanics United v. Village of Addison*

Winner
State of Minnesota v. Philip Morris, Inc.
The Case That Made Big Tobacco Pay

The finalists for the 1998 Trial Lawyer of the Year Award challenged the constitutionality of "tort reform" legislation that arbitrarily capped damages, prevented insurance company abuses, won important victories for the victims of unsafe products, exposed consumer fraud, vindicated employees' rights, and protected the victims of racism. The Trial Lawyer of the Year Award winners produced a decisive turning point in the decades-long struggle between consumers and the tobacco industry. Thanks in part to these attorneys, the tobacco industry was forced to disgorge billions of dollars in damages and settlements nationwide — a breakthrough in advancing public justice and public health.

Access to Justice

Best v. Taylor Machine Works, Inc.
and *Isbell v. Union Pac. R.R. Co.*

Jon G. Carlson, Eric J. Carlson, Todd A. Smith,
Devon C. Bruce, Bruce M. Kohen, Curt Rodin,
Kevin J. Conway, Geoffrey L. Gifford, Gary Laatsch,
Jeffrey M. Goldberg, William J. Harte, Keith A. Hebeisen,
Bruce R. Pfaff, Howard Schaffner, Kenneth Chesebro,
Jonathan Massey, Ned Miltenberg, and Laurence Tribe

The Illinois Trial Lawyers Association (ITLA) Constitutional Challenge Committee won a major victory for Illinois citizens and created an important precedent for injury victims nationwide by getting Illinois' Tort Reform Act struck down as unconstitutional. Corporate interests had successfully pressed legislation through the Illinois Legislature that arbitrarily capped non-economic damages such as pain and suffering at $500,000 regardless of the actual damages a jury might determine should be justly awarded. The new law also abolished joint and several liability, and compelled plaintiffs to disclose all of their medical records from the time of birth when suing for personal injury — even records with no relevancy to the lawsuit.

The ITLA Committee brought an action on behalf of several accident victims for declaratory relief to strike down the entire statute as unconstitutional. The committee prevailed at the trial court. Defendants then appealed directly to the Illinois Supreme Court, and the state's attorney general intervened on their behalf. Professor Laurence Tribe of Harvard Law School argued the case before the Illinois Supreme Court. The Court issued a landmark ruling throwing out the entire statute as unconstitutional. The Court found that the law interfered with the prerogatives of the judiciary and discriminated against litigants who had suffered the greatest harm.

As a consequence, the plaintiffs' attorneys — who represented one person who was killed at a dangerous railroad crossing and another who was severely burned after becoming engulfed in a fireball while operating a defective forklift — were able to litigate their cases without having their clients' rights to recovery impinged by laws designed to protect corporate tortfeasors.

After the "tort reform" legislation was overturned, the *Best* case settled for $2.3 million. Jon and Eric Carlson tried *Isbell* in May 1999 and won a verdict of $2.5 million, which was reduced to $1.25 million based on the jury's finding that the deceased plaintiff was 50 percent at fault. The Union Pacific Railroad Company appealed, but the appellate court affirmed the verdict. As of this writing, the railroad is seeking a hearing from the Illinois Supreme Court.

The constitutional victory striking down the Illinois law was a true team effort, capped by Professor Tribe. Members of the Constitutional Challenge Committee that coordinated the litigation included Jon G. Carlson and Eric J. Carlson of Carlson Wendler & Associates in Edwardsville, Illinois; Chicago attorneys Todd A. Smith and Devon C. Bruce of Power, Rogers & Smith; Bruce M. Cohen and Curt Rodin of Anesi, Ozman & Rodin; Kevin J. Conway of Cooney & Conway; Geoffrey L. Gifford and Gary Laatsch of Pavalon, Gifford, Laatsch & Marino; Jeffrey M. Goldberg of Jeffrey M. Goldberg & Associates; William J. Harte of William J. Harte, Ltd.; Keith A. Hebeisen of Clifford Law Offices; Bruce R. Pfaff of Bruce R. Pfaff & Associates, Ltd.; and Howard Schaffner of Hofeld & Schaffner; Kenneth Chesebro of Cambridge, Massachusetts; and Washington, D.C., attorneys Jonathan Massey and Ned Miltenberg, Associate General Counsel of the Association of Trial Lawyers of America.

Other attorneys deserving recognition for their important work in this case include James M. Collins, Executive Director of ITLA in Springfield, Illinois; David A. Decker of Decker & Linn in Waukegan, Illinois; Theodore R. Diaz and David W. Dugan of Pitts, Dugan & Diaz in Wood River, Illinois; and Chicago attorneys Terrence J. Lavin of Terrence J. Lavin & Associates, and Gary D. McAllister of Gary D. McAllister & Associates, Ltd.

The reported decisions in these cases can be found at *Best v. Taylor Machine Works, Inc.*, 689 N.E.2d 1057 (Ill. 1997); and *Isbell v. Union Pac. R.R. Co.*, 745 N.E.2d 53 (Ill. App. Ct. 2001).

Jon G. Carlson

Eric J. Carlson

Todd A. Smith

Devon C. Bruce

Bruce M. Kohen

Curt Rodin

Kevin J. Conway

Geoffrey L. Gifford

Gary Laatsch

Jeffrey M. Goldberg

Keith A. Hebeisen

Bruce R. Pfaff

Laurence Tribe

Insurer Accountability
Taylor v. State Farm Insurance & Cas. Co.
Bernie Bernheim

Attorney Bernie Bernheim of the Law Offices of Bernie Bernheim in Los Angeles exposed corporate crime and scored a victory for consumers when he uncovered a widespread scam at the State Farm Insurance & Casualty Company. Bernheim filed suit on behalf of Rod and Krista Taylor after State Farm denied that their policy covered the destruction of their home by an earthquake.

State Farm stonewalled discovery efforts, repeatedly requesting extensions to respond and then producing evasive witnesses who claimed not to recognize their own handwriting or voices. State Farm then moved for summary judgment on the basis of Rod Taylor's application for insurance, which did not include a request for earthquake coverage. Bernheim tried to convince the judge that Taylor's signature had been forged, but the judge granted State Farm's motion.

The judge later reversed his ruling based on information Bernheim uncovered. A few weeks after the summary judgment ruling, a former claims manager in State Farm's litigation unit called Bernheim with information that revealed a company-wide scheme of fraud, forgery, and perjury. Based on this information, the judge reversed his prior ruling and allowed the case to proceed. The case settled confidentially in an amount rumored to exceed $7 million.

The later decision in this case and the subsequent case history can be found at *State Farm Insurance & Cas. Co. v. Superior Court,* 62 Cal. Rptr. 2d 834 (Cal. Ct. App. 1997), *review denied* (July 9, 1997).

Bernie Bernheim

Consumer Protection

Flores v. Phillips College

Mark Allen Kleiman and BethAnne Yeager

Insurance policyholders were not the only Los Angeles consumers whom trial lawyers had to defend from fraud. Attorneys Mark Allen Kleiman of the Law Offices of Mark Allen Kleiman and BethAnne Yeager, both of Santa Monica, California, won justice for the victims of a vocational school's scheme to make profits by preying on the disadvantaged with false promises of quality education and career advancement.

Lured to the paralegal program at Phillips College of Los Angeles by promises of high-paying jobs and the ability to transfer credits to public colleges, the nine plaintiffs in this case found that the school had defrauded them. Behind the marketing promises lay a scheme by the college, part of a national chain, to induce poor and intellectually challenged students to take out student loans to pay for their tuition, thereby enabling the corporation to pocket federally insured funds. After committing to repay the government, the students found to their dismay that they could not transfer credits or, indeed, obtain jobs based on their training.

Kleiman filed suit under common law, contract, fraud theories, the California Consumer Legal Remedies Act, and the Maxine Waters Act. The defendant obstructed discovery and impeded the progress of the litigation in every conceivable way, including the filing of nine summary judgment motions. The discovery obstructionism required 30 motions by Kleiman and Yeager to overcome. The pair took 50 depositions in nine states, reviewed 60 feet of files, and overcame spoliation — destruction by the defendant of corporate files. Kleiman and Yeager labored through discovery for four years before the four-month trial in front of a judge who issued numerous, unfavorable evidentiary rulings. Despite these obstacles, the jury awarded the plaintiffs $4.2 million, including $3.3 million in punitive damages.

There is no reported decision on the merits in this case.

Mark Allen Kleiman

BethAnne Yeager

Auto Safety
Toyota Motor Co. v. McCathern
Jeffrey P. Foote and Jana Toran

On Sunday of the 1995 Memorial Day Weekend, Linda McCathern was returning from an Idaho family reunion, riding as a passenger in a 1994 Toyota 4-Runner. She was anticipating another family reunion, one for which she had fought for seven years, ever since her ex-husband had kidnapped her two daughters from the U.S. and absconded with them to Libya. It was difficult to arrange to see her daughters because the U.S. had no diplomatic relations with that country. However, the previous Thursday, the Libyan mission at the U.N. gave her permission to go visit her daughters. So McCathern was riding the crest of a small victory when the Toyota's driver suddenly swerved to avoid a collision with an oncoming car. The 4-Runner rolled over and its roof collapsed, paralyzing McCathern.

First, doctors thought McCathern would not likely survive and that, in any case, she would never breathe independently of a respirator. Despite the fact that she is now a quadriplegic who had been through severe physical and emotional trauma, McCathern defied doctors' expectations in both respects.

Attorneys Jeffrey P. Foote and Jana Toran, of Portland, Oregon, represented McCathern in her suit against Toyota for personal injuries that resulted from the 4-Runner's faulty design. Arguing that the popular sport utility vehicle rolled over because a defective design made it unstable as a whole, Foote and Toran obtained a $7.65 million verdict, the first verdict in the nation against the 4-Runner.

During trial, Foote and Toran presented evidence of numerous similar rollover accidents and Toyota's own testing of the 4-Runner. A sole practitioner, Foote worked on the case nearly full-time for a year and a half, battling against a defendant that boasted of having spent hundreds of thousands of dollars on the case. As a result of this verdict, Toyota began to settle other 4-Runner cases, making it easier for consumers to receive just compensation for the injuries they suffered as a result of the auto company's defective design. Toyota appealed, but the verdict was affirmed by both the intermediate appellate court and the Oregon Supreme Court.

In the meantime, although U.S. sanctions against Libya remained in force, Foote worked with U.S. Representative Elizabeth Furse (D-Oregon), Libyan diplomats and the U.S. State Department to obtain permission from Libyan head of state Moammar Gadhafi for McCathern and her caregivers to travel to

Libya to have a reunion with her children in 1997. Libya received her like a state guest. She returned in 2000 to visit her daughters again in Tripoli and she reports that she has been able to bond with them.

In January 1998, the Oregon Trial Lawyers Association magazine asked Foote what was the highlight of his representation of McCathern. "Talking to her daughters on the phone," Foote replied. "They called up and this little girl says, 'This is Sarra,' speaking very broken English. And she says, 'Thank you for making my mother happy.' And her sister Jamelah got on and said essentially the same thing. It was a pretty remarkable experience, something that I didn't really bargain for in law school. This was not part of our training, I guess."

The later decisions in this case and the subsequent case history can be found at *Toyota Motor Corp. v. McCathern*, 985 P.2d 804 (Or. Ct. App. 1999) (upholding jury verdict), *aff'd*, 2001 WL 492464 (Or. May 10, 2001).

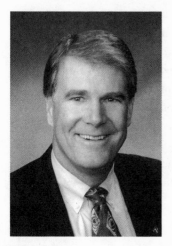

Jeffrey P. Foote

Jana Toran

Workers' Rights
In re Columbia Falls Profit Sharing Litigation
Allan M. McGarvey and Roger M. Sullivan

What does it take to win a multi-million dollar settlement on behalf of 1,000 employees denied proper profit-sharing participation through wrongful business machinations? For Montana attorneys Allan M. McGarvey and Roger M. Sullivan, it took protracted litigation against the Columbia Falls Aluminum Company after its parent company, Atlantic Richfield, sold the company to one of its executives. The purchase price? All of one dollar.

In order to make the company profitable, the executive, Drack Duker, and the company's employees entered into an unusual agreement: in return for the employees accepting a cut in pay and benefits, the plants owners agreed to share half the company's profits with its workers. This worked well during tough times. But when aluminum prices and profitability soared, suddenly the agreement ceased to be a two-way street. When an accountant for the company came to McGarvey and Sullivan with evidence that it was shortchanging employees, the battle over just compensation was on.

Justice rarely comes easily and it certainly did not for the employees of Columbia Falls or their attorneys, whose dedication to their clients' cause reached the extraordinary level of going nearly $1 million in debt to finance the case. The law firm that stood behind the workers was McGarvey, Heberling, Sullivan & McGarvey of Kalispell, Montana, which backed six years of litigation, while the attorneys racked up 10,000 hours on the case. During the course of the legal struggle, McGarvey and Sullivan fought against the company's attempts to hide documents, extracted key admissions from Duker, and prevented assets from being transferred offshore by obtaining injunctions in U.S. and foreign courts. Finally, the attorneys and the workers whose loyalty the company had betrayed won justice when the defendants settled for $97 million.

McGarvey and Sullivan worked with Jon L. Heberling and Dale L. McGarvey of McGarvey, Heberling, Sullivan & McGarvey; R. Michael LaBelle and Thomas P. Powers of Powers & Lewis in Washington, D.C.; and Joan Jonkel of Jonkel Law Offices in Missoula, Montana, all of whom deserve recognition for their important work in the case.

There is no reported decision on the merits in this case.

Allan M. McGarvey

Roger M. Sullivan

Civil Rights
Hispanics United v. Village of Addison
Matthew J. Piers and Jonathan A. Rothstein

Attorneys Matthew J. Piers and Jonathan A. Rothstein of Chicago's Gessler, Hughes & Socol saved more than 800 Hispanic families from losing their homes in the predominantly white Village of Addison, Illinois. Piers and Rothstein achieved this victory for racial equality by successfully advocating a novel application of federal anti-discriminatory laws.

The Village of Addison began the chain of events by designating an area in which Hispanics resided in modest apartments as "neighborhoods in need of redevelopment." Under this designation, the Village created tax increment financing districts with the power to acquire and condemn the apartment buildings under the guise of implementing a redevelopment plan. By the time of the lawsuit filing, the Village had already acquired and demolished 11 of 145 buildings, and had evicted 44 families.

Over a three-year period, Piers and Rothstein developed the case, reviewing 100,000 pages of documents, taking 200 depositions, and interviewing more than 100 witnesses. Their doggedness eventually convinced the Village to settle. Piers and Rothstein obtained the largest recovery ever achieved under the Federal Fair Housing Act. In a consent decree, the Village agreed to be enjoined from further acts of discrimination and to develop parks, a community resource center, and new affordable housing in the two neighborhoods. In addition, Addison paid $2 million in damages, making the total value of the settlement approximately $20-30 million.

After the attorneys were honored, further litigation was required to enforce the consent decree. These efforts resulted in a supplemental order from the district court requiring the Village not to remove any additional housing until binding plans are submitted for court approval. That order has been appealed to the U.S. Court of Appeals for the Seventh Circuit. As of this writing, a decision is pending.

Other attorneys who deserve recognition for their important work in the case include Dana H. Sukenik, Jennifer L. Fischer, and Charles J. Holley of Gessler, Hughes & Socol; Jennifer Soule and James Bradtke of Chicago's Soule & Bradtke; Theresa Amato of Citizen Advocacy Center in Elmhurst, Illinois; Edward Voci of Chicago's Leadership Council, one of the plaintiffs; Robert Graham of Chicago's Jenner and Block; and U.S. government attorneys Joan Laser, Elizabeth Singer, Robert Berman, Isabel Thabault, and Jeff Senger.

The reported decision in this case can be found at *Hispanics United v. Village of Addison*, 988 F. Supp. 1130 (N.D. Ill. 1997) (approving class action settlement).

Matthew J. Piers

Jonathan A. Rothstein

1998 Trial Lawyer of the Year Award Winners

Michael V. Ciresi, Roberta B. Walburn, Hubert H. "Skip" Humphrey III

The Case That Made Big Tobacco Pay

I n the past few years, the tobacco industry has been in full-scale retreat and retrenchment, reeling from court decisions and huge settlements. So much has changed recently that it may seem odd that believers in public justice ever despaired at successfully bringing Big Tobacco to account for its decades of wrongdoing, obstructionism, and harm to the health of millions of smokers.

One reason for this tremendous transformation in the legal balance of power was the visionary lawsuit brought by State of Minnesota and Blue Cross and Blue Shield of Minnesota, which joined together to sue Philip Morris, R.J. Reynolds Tobacco Company and others in the tobacco industry. The suit succeeded in large part because it employed a new strategy crafted by two exceptional lawyers.

In 1989, attorneys Michael V. Ciresi and Roberta B. Walburn of Robins, Kaplan, Miller & Ciresi in Minneapolis began contemplating tobacco litigation.

"We knew that the industry had a decades-long history of winning every case," Walburn recalls, "and not just winning but trampling their opponents. So we knew it would be a great challenge. But this is an industry that kills people, and we were convinced that something had to be done."

Over time, Ciresi and Walburn became convinced that the traditional approach to litigation that had been tried against Big Tobacco since the early 1950s — individual lawsuits filed by smokers with cancer or wrongful death lawsuits — would no longer do. A case against Big Tobacco could be expected to cost in the millions of dollars and take more than a decade. Considering the limited

> *What is public justice? Companies that sell deadly and addictive products while lying to the public about their dangers are held accountable for the injuries and social costs those products cause.*

potential for recovery in individual cases, the financial risk and time commitment of litigating against the tobacco companies was all but untenable. For example, since *Cipollone v. Liggett Group, Inc.* had been reversed on appeal, the attorneys who brought that case lacked resources to pursue a second trial (see Chapter Six), so the industry had remained 100 percent successful in defending suits brought by individual smokers.

Ciresi and Walburn did not rush in where angels feared to tread. They read cases and researched the law, and studied tobacco documents elicited in the *Cipollone* case. They became convinced that Big Tobacco was beatable. But which case and what approach? The answer, the lawyers decided, was to sue for the health care costs associated with treating the illnesses caused by smoking, rather than by seeking compensation for personal injury to individual smokers.

Hubert H. "Skip" Humphrey III, then the Attorney General of Minnesota, agreed that the State of Minnesota would be a party to the planned litigation, seeking damages for the costs the State incurred paying for the health needs of ill smokers. Humphrey negotiated a good deal for the citizens of Minnesota: the state would participate in the case as a party plaintiff, but would not be responsible for costs of suit, which would be borne primarily by Ciresi and Walburn's firm.

"I viewed the suit as a law enforcement action," Humphrey says. "In Minnesota, we have strong consumer protection and anti-trust statutes. Moreover, by working with a private firm, which I usually did not do, I saw this as an opportunity for the State to enforce its laws without taking State lawyers away from their other important duties on behalf of the citizenry."

Blue Cross and Blue Shield of Minnesota was also interested in being a plaintiff, to recover the losses it incurred from having to pay the medical expenses for its policyholders' smoking-related illnesses. After meeting with Ciresi, the company committed to the case and agreed to bear some of its cost.

When the case was filed, the industry took notice. Tobacco defense lawyers recognized that this lawsuit was different from anything they had faced before.

"It was clear that they were worried about the novel approach we were taking," Walburn recalls. Corporate attorneys filed motions to redefine the case as one in subrogation, that is, as representing individual smokers suffering from smoking-related illnesses. But Walburn and Ciresi were adamant: they would litigate their own case under their own theories. The Minnesota Supreme Court eventually decided the matter on an interlocutory appeal.

Then the litigation really got nasty.

The key to the success of tobacco company lawyers had always been their ability to prevent plaintiffs' lawyers from obtaining key internal documents during discovery. The tobacco lawyers' approach may have been underhanded and bordering on the unethical — but it was rational. Without the evidence, it was difficult to prove the case.

The situation was reminiscent of the saying, "Where there is smoke, there is fire." Metaphorically, smoke had hung like a pall around the tobacco companies for decades. Lawyers and consumer advocates just *knew* that tobacco companies had hidden the dangers of smoking and its addictive nature for years. But lawyers in previous cases, with the exception of the *Cipollone* trial lawyers, had never been able to show juries the fire.

Ciresi and Walburn determined to cut through the smoke screen and force Big Tobacco to disgorge its secrets. Walburn became the case's documents czar, leading a team of 10 attorneys and three legal assistants assigned the responsibility of prying the tobacco companies' documents out of their tightly-clenched fists. Defense lawyers used every trick in the book to obstruct discovery. They would play word games, for example, claiming that they did not know the meaning of terms such as "smoking and health" or "the properties and effects of nicotine" or words such as "addictive."

The heaviest early combat concerned Ciresi and Walburn's attempt to obtain tobacco industry indices that indexed tobacco documents in the wake of the *Cipollone* litigation during the 1980s. The litigation over these indices alone took 16 months, eight orders from the trial court, and unsuccessful appeals by tobacco lawyers to the Minnesota Supreme Court and the U.S. Supreme Court. In the end, the trial court ordered the tobacco industry to produce from its data bases only the most basic data, including document dates, numbers, dates, titles, types, and so forth.

Among the real finds in the document war was a memo revealing that Philip Morris had shipped crucial documents to Cologne, Germany, to avoid disclosing them. The memo plainly revealed the author's intent: "If important letters or documents have to be sent, please send to home — I will act on them and destroy." Here was clear evidence of the near panic boiling within Big Tobacco's executive suites about the nefarious truth that their own records would reveal to the world.

Walburn and her team moved forcefully to demonstrate that the documents they sought were not properly protected by the many privilege claims asserted by the tobacco lawyers. The plaintiffs argued that the "crime-fraud" exception should be applied to the defendants' privacy privileges, making the documents discoverable. One reason the privilege did not, in the end, apply, was that the documents in question were really related to scientific research conducted by the tobacco companies on the safety of smoking. If the tests were deemed helpful to tobacco interests, they were readily disclosed as research. But if the lawyers deemed the results or data harmful, they were placed in attorney files and labeled "confidential and privileged."

Proof that the privilege should not apply came from the tobacco companies' own documents. In its findings of fact, the trial court noted that the tobacco industry had issued a pledge in 1954 entitled "A Frank Statement to Cigarette Smokers," specifically promising to provide "aid and assistance to the research efforts into all phases of tobacco use and health;" establish "the Tobacco Industry Research Committee;" name as head of the Committee a scientist "of unimpeachable integrity and national repute," and create an "Advisory Board of scientists disinterested in the cigarette industry" to "advise the Committee on its research activities."

This pledge was disingenuous. Rather than being an independent source of information about smoking and health, the Research Committee became instead an advocacy tool to promote smoking. This despite the fact that, in 1959, an R.J. Reynolds scientist concluded that there was a "distinct possibility" that substances in cigarette smoke could have a carcinogenic effect. By 1962, he was even more sure. He wrote, "The amount of evidence accumulated to indict cigarette smoke as a health hazard is overwhelming, [while] the evidence challenging the indictment is scant."

Such documents were typical of a growing realization among tobacco industry scientists. Had the companies followed their "pledge," they would have disclosed all that they knew about the health risks caused by their products. Instead, they hid what they learned.

Proof of this scheme came once again from the industry's own documents. For example, a 1976 memo, read in part:

> The public position of tobacco companies with respect to causal explanations of the association of cigarette smoking and diseases is dominated by legal considerations...By repudiation of a causal role for cigarette smoking in general, they [the companies] hope to avoid liability in particular cases. This domination by legal consideration thus leads the industry into a public rejection in total of any causal relationship between smoking and disease and puts the industry in a peculiar position with respect to product safety discussions, safety evaluations, collaborative research, etc.

Similarly, a hand-written memorandum dated April 21, 1978, complained that:

> We have again abdicated the scientific research directional management
> of the Industry to the "Lawyers" with virtually no involvement on the
> part of the scientific or business management side of the business.

It took Ciresi and Walburn and their team more than 20 trial court orders and multiple appeals to succeed — but eventually they breached the tobacco wall of falsely claimed lawyer-client privilege, forcing the industry to turn over more than 39,000 key documents on the dangers of smoking to the plaintiffs.

The industry was reeling. But it had another tactic to try: the document dump, to force the plaintiffs' legal team to undertake what amounted to a search for a needle in a haystack in order to find crucial documents. Should document dumps ever be made a stated category in the *Guinness Book of World Records*, the tobacco document disclosure would probably top the list. Big Tobacco lobbed 35 million documents at Walburn and her team. In the end, the team selected only two percent as relevant for use.

With the evidence now in the plaintiffs' hands, the tide had turned. The key now was to devise a way to make the evidence come alive for the jury. That would be the primary responsibility of Ciresi.

As the document wars turned sour for Big Tobacco and trial loomed, one last possible hitch stood between the legal team and the opportunity for victory. Realizing they were on the ropes and having been sued around the country, the tobacco companies attempted to save themselves by reaching what Walburn describes as a "sweetheart deal" that would not only have saved the companies tremendous sums of money and kept many precious documents secret, but as a global settlement, would have immunized them from some lawsuits. Still, the money suddenly put on the table was huge — eventually amounting to billions of dollars for Minnesota alone.

Now, the pressure was on Attorney General Humphrey. Many in the State urged him to accept the deal. After all, Big Tobacco had never lost a case.

"Early-on, I had laid down three goals for this suit," recalls Humphrey. "First, I wanted to make sure that tobacco companies stopped marketing tobacco to kids. Second, I wanted all the documents opened up. No more hiding important public health-related information behind lawyer privilege and other forms of obfuscation. Third, I wanted damages commensurate with the harm caused. The proposed global settlement did not achieve those ends."

As fate would have it, the news of the potential settlement occurred while Humphrey was at a National Association of Attorneys General meeting in Wyoming. "All the media was there, CNN, others," when the news of the potential settlement broke. Some attorneys general wanted to settle. But Humphrey held firm.

"It was a pretty lonely day," he says. "But I was bucked up by [former Surgeon General] C. Everett Koop and John Garrison, the executive director of the American Lung Association. I also wasn't willing to allow other states to force Minnesota into a settlement that did not meet our goals."

Humphrey is glad that the plaintiffs held out. "The tobacco industry wanted to shut down our case," he says. "Because they failed, we were eventually able to obtain a much better result for Minnesotans and obtain millions of documents that would probably have otherwise been disclosed. That is still paying off. We are only just beginning to realize how valuable the information we obtained is to society."

Ciresi and Walburn faced their adversaries in trial court. In his opening statement, Ciresi urged the jury to focus on what the tobacco industry knew about the hazards of smoking, when they knew it, and what they did about it. The answer, out of the mouths of tobacco company executives and the text of industry documents, would end Big Tobacco's reign of legal invincibility.

Ciresi's case was strengthened by the testimony of tobacco company executives, such as Philip Morris CEO Geoffrey C. Bible, whom Ciresi called as part of the plaintiffs' case in chief. Illustrating the devastating nature of the tactic, Ciresi led Bible through a series of duties his company had toward its consumers: to not make false statements, to not make misleading statements, to not knowingly misrepresent the quality of cigarettes. Bible could only acknowledge the duty and agree that the jury should hold the company accountable if it was shown that the many acknowledged duties had been violated.

Day after day, week after week, month after month, Ciresi methodically presented solid proof to the jury of the tobacco industry's egregious wrongdoing. Finally, after four months, 40 witnesses, and 2,500 exhibits, it was over. As Ciresi was prepared to begin his closing argument and ask for substantial punitive damages, the tobacco industry blinked, offering a settlement that could not be refused. The settlement was historic:

■ Damages payable to the State of Minnesota and Blue Cross and Blue Shield totaling $6.6 billion.

- Opening the tobacco document depositories containing tens of millions of documents to the public with the cost of maintaining the records paid by the tobacco industry.

- The industry enjoined from taking any action, directly or indirectly, to target children in Minnesota in the advertising, marketing, or promotion of cigarettes.

- An injunction against making any material misrepresentation of fact regarding the health consequences of tobacco.

- An injunction against any contract, combination, or conspiracy to limit information about the health hazards of tobacco, suppress research into smoking and health, or limit or suppress research into the marketing or development of new products.

- A ban on defendants making any payment, directly or indirectly, for the use of cigarettes in movies.

- Dissolution of the Council for Tobacco Research.

- The establishment of a public health foundation to take action to diminish the human and economic consequences of tobacco use and to fund research relating to the elimination of tobacco use by children and other tobacco control purposes.

This settlement, by any measure a landmark achievement in the history of jurisprudence, changed forever the nature of tobacco litigation, opening the door for other tobacco settlements and verdicts that followed.

In addition to Ciresi, Walburn and Humphrey, other attorneys who deserve recognition for their important work in this case include Richard L. Gill, Corey L. Gordon, Thomas J. Hamlin, John Love, Vincent Moccio, Susan Richard Nelson, Dan O'Fallon, Roman Silberfield, Tara D. Sutton, Gary L. Wilson, and Martha K. Wivell, all of Robins, Kaplan, Miller & Ciresi; Lee E. Sheehy, Eric A. Johnson, Thomas F. Pursell, and D. Douglas Banke, all of the Minnesota Attorney General's Office; and Andrew Czajkowski and Thomas F. Gilde, both of Blue Cross and Blue Shield of Minnesota.

There is no reported decision on the merits in this case.

Michael V. Ciresi   *Roberta B. Walburn*   *Hubert H. "Skip" Humphrey III*

1999: The Case That Targeted the Gun Industry's Marketing Practices

HMO Accountability *Goodrich v. Aetna U.S. Healthcare of California, Inc.*

Product Safety *Philip Morris, Inc. v. Henley*

Product Safety *Williams v. Philip Morris, Inc.*

Civil Rights *Housing Opportunities Made Equal v. Nationwide Mut. Ins. Co.*

Civil Rights *Macedonia Baptist Church v. Christian Knights of the Ku Klux Klan Invisible Empire, Inc.*

Product Safety *Meneely v. S.R. Smith, Inc.*

Government Accountability *Wynn v. Towey*

Toxic Injury Protection *Hall v. Babcock & Wilcox Co.*

Winner

Hamilton v. Beretta U.S.A. Corp.
The Case That Targeted the Gun Industry's Marketing Practices

The finalists for the 1999 Trial Lawyer of the Year Award held nuclear power companies responsible for injuries to radiation victims, battled Big Tobacco, held HMOs accountable for denying medically warranted treatment, exposed and redressed racist violence, improved swimming pool safety, and won proper treatment for brain-injured patients. The winners put the gun industry on notice that manufacturers could be held liable for shoddy sales practices that permit firearms to reach criminals.

HMO Accountability
Goodrich v. Aetna U.S. Healthcare of California, Inc.
Michael J. Bidart

Attorney Michael J. Bidart of Shernoff, Bidart, Darras & Dillon in Claremont, California, obtained the highest verdict ever in a wrongful death case against a Health Maintenance Organization (HMO). The verdict of nearly $120 million sent a powerful message that HMOs would be held responsible if they deprived their members of proper care.

Traditionally, medicine has been practiced on a "fee for service" basis, that is, a patient or insurance company paid the health professional or facility for each medical service rendered. In contrast, managed care health insurance companies — epitomized by HMOs — earn their profits from controlling costs. They actually have an incentive to deny a patient necessary and proper medical care in order to improve their bottom line.

When David Goodrich was dying of cancer, his doctors wanted to pursue critical medical treatment to extend his life. Instead of letting the doctors decide what was necessary for their patient, Goodrich's HMO — Aetna — denied authorization for the care. The denial put tremendous stress on Goodrich because he was forced to pay for the treatment out of his own pocket. After he died, Goodrich's widow sued.

Attorney Michael Bidart tried the case alone against Aetna's team of corporate and outside lawyers, survived the HMO's attempt to force Goodrich's claims into arbitration, produced 2,000 pages of written discovery responses, and attended 76 depositions over three and a half years of litigation. He responded to 56 motions *in limine* before battling Aetna in a 10-week trial. While the jury did not find that the HMO's denial of care directly caused Goodrich's death, the jury did award the widow compensation for her husband's unpaid medical bills and $3.4 million for loss of consortium. Further finding that Aetna acted with fraud, malice, and oppression, the jury awarded an additional $116 million in punitive damages. This case, which is currently on appeal, set an important precedent for the corporate accountability of HMOs that fail to cover appropriate medical treatments.

There is no reported decision on the merits in this case.

Michael J. Bidart

Product Safety
Philip Morris, Inc. v. Henley
Madelyn J. Chaber

In 1996, Madelyn J. Chaber of Wartnick, Chaber, Harowitz, Smith & Tigerman in San Francisco was honored for winning an unusual case against the tobacco industry involving cigarettes that contained asbestos. (See Chapter Fourteen.) In 1999, Chaber took on tobacco giant Philip Morris in the most direct type of personal injury case, a lawsuit on behalf of a 52-year-old woman with inoperable lung cancer caused by the Marlboro cigarettes she smoked for 35 years. The remarkable verdict Chaber won — $51.5 million — included $50 million in punitive damages and was, as of that date, by far the largest jury verdict against a tobacco company. Less than two months later, in a case prosecuted with Chaber's assistance, an Oregon jury would return a verdict in excess of $80 million in another individual suit against Philip Morris. (See *Williams v. Philip Morris, Inc.*, on page 354.)

Chaber overcame massive motions filed on minimal notice; simultaneous, multiple depositions noticed in several different states; and two or three new briefs filed every morning of the four-week trial. At trial, Chaber presented more than 1,000 documents and a multitude of experts to expose the tobacco company's efforts to target underage smokers and cover up the scientific evidence linking smoking with cancer.

The announcement of the punitive damage verdict caused Philip Morris' stock to drop by 10 percent. The trial judge later reduced the punitive damage award $25 million, but he let the remainder of the verdict stand as a scathing indictment of the tobacco company. After Chaber was honored, however, Philip Morris appealed and won the right to a new trial.

The later decision in this case can be found at *Philip Morris, Inc. v. Henley*, 1999 WL 221076 (Cal. Ct. App. Apr. 6, 1999) (not certified for publication) (granting defendant's motion for new trial).

Madelyn J. Chaber

Product Safety
Williams v. Philip Morris, Inc.
Bill Gaylord, Ray Thomas, Jim Coon, and Chuck Tauman

In March 1999, attorneys Bill Gaylord of Gaylord & Eyerman, Ray Thomas and Jim Coon of Swanson, Thomas & Coon, and Chuck Tauman of Bennett, Hartman & Reynolds, all in Portland, Oregon, won a verdict in excess of $80 million against Philip Morris for the estate of deceased smoker Jesse D. Williams. It was the largest verdict to that date against a tobacco company for personal injuries. (Madelyn Chaber, who had won the previous largest verdict less than two months earlier, assisted the team informally in the litigation.)

Attorney Gaylord and his litigation team members — all from small firms — found themselves fighting Big Tobacco's legion of professionals. The team also had to overcome Oregon's eight-year statute of repose for product liability by proving that the lung cancer that killed Williams — a lifetime smoker — was caused by cigarettes purchased in the eight years preceding his diagnosis. The team then had to demonstrate the actual damage caused by the cigarettes because Oregon law did not allow product liability actions based exclusively on tobacco's inherent, carcinogenic qualities.

The jury found Williams and Philip Morris equally at fault and awarded $800,000 in compensatory damages to the estate. The jury additionally found that the corporation had committed common law fraud and awarded $79.5 million in punitive damages. The punitive damage award was later reduced to $32 million, still the largest to that date against a tobacco company.

The result not only validated the civil court system's ability to obtain justice for the individual against a rich and powerful corporation, but also clarified the applicability of fraud principles to mass-marketed products and tested the limits of punitive damage jurisprudence under Oregon and federal constitutional law. After the attorneys were honored, the plaintiff filed an appeal challenging the verdict reduction and the defendant cross-appealed. As of this writing, oral argument is expected to take place in the fall of 2001.

There is no reported decision on the merits in this case.

Bill Gaylord   *Ray Thomas*   *Chuck Tauman*

Civil Rights

Housing Opportunities Made Equal v. Nationwide Mut. Ins. Co.
Timothy M. Kaine, Rhonda M. Harmon,
and Thomas M. Wolf

Attorneys Timothy M. Kaine, Rhonda M. Harmon, and Thomas M. Wolf of Mezzulo & McCandlish in Richmond, Virginia, won a $100.5 million verdict against Nationwide Mutual Insurance Company in a race discrimination case. It was the largest insurance redlining verdict ever.

Testing by Housing Opportunities Made Equal (HOME), a Richmond-based fair housing group, showed that Nationwide had discriminated against African Americans by denying their requests for coverage outright, by offering them coverage at much higher rates than those offered to white testers in comparable homes, and by offering them coverage for the less advantageous market value rather than replacement value coverage.

Litigating against four law firms located in three cities, Kaine, then a Richmond City Council member, worked with Harmon and Wolf to conduct 100 days of depositions and obtain more than 50,000 documents during two years of discovery. Although Richmond voters elected Kaine as Mayor shortly before the trial, he nonetheless served as co-lead counsel at trial.

The litigation team proved the intentional discrimination claim with their grasp of technicalities of actuarial standards, underwriting criteria, and the mechanics of rate-setting, as well as by showing that Nationwide used a variety of means to identify predominantly African-American neighborhoods. The verdict sent a powerful message to corporations that racial discrimination will not be tolerated.

The case settled while on appeal to the Virginia Supreme Court. Attorney Kaine reports that significant payments were made to HOME and the National Fair Housing Alliance and that Nationwide has "embraced a series of reforms to its underwriting practices."

Other attorneys who deserve recognition for their important contributions in the case include William A. DeVan of Mezzullo & McCandlish and Stephen M. Dane of Cooper, Walinski & Cramer in Toledo, Ohio.

There is no reported decision on the merits in this case.

Timothy M. Kaine

Rhonda M. Harmon

Thomas M. Wolf

Civil Rights
Macedonia Baptist Church v. Christian Knights of the Ku Klux Klan Invisible Empire, Inc.

Morris Dees, J. Richard Cohen, and Marcia Bull Stadeker

Attorneys Morris Dees, J. Richard Cohen, and Marcia Bull Stadeker of the Southern Poverty Law Center (SPLC) in Montgomery, Alabama, sent a message to racist groups across the country and effectively crippled the Ku Klux Klan in South Carolina with their verdict of $37.8 million against the Klan for its involvement in burning down a black church. The SPLC team sued four Klan members, the North Carolina parent corporation, the South Carolina affiliate of the Christian Knights of the Ku Klux Klan, and South Carolina Klan leader Horace King, who held the title of "Grand Dragon."

Dees and his investigators uncovered proof against King and his top aides by interviewing dozens of ex-Klan members, sometimes in dangerous locations. Dees sat in jail with Klansmen who had sworn a blood oath to King and the Christian Knights and convinced them to renounce their allegiance to the Klan and testify in court.

King and the Klan organizations raised the First Amendment defense that incendiary racist speech, short of incitement to imminent violent action, is generally protected. Defense attorney Gary White painted King as a feeble old man exercising his right to free speech, claiming King had not authorized the June 21, 1995, attack on the 125-year-old church. But Dees, Cohen, and Stadeker gathered a mass of damning evidence, including videotapes showing that King, garbed in his green Grand Dragon robe, actually authorized racist violence. Witnesses portrayed King as a hatemonger who spoke of burning churches and shielding his men from the law. For example, Thomas Smith, a former reporter for the Richland County weekly *The Star-Reporter,* said he infiltrated the Christian Knights after the fire and testified that King told him that a "race war" was coming by 2000. He said King had also stated, "The only good nigger church is a burned nigger church."

After a five-day trial, the jury, comprised of nine African Americans and three whites, deliberated only 45 minutes before coming up with a unanimous verdict. The jury found all defendants liable and assessed punitive damages of $15 million against the Klan's parent organization based in North Carolina, $15 million against King, and $7 million against the organization's South Carolina chapter. In addition, punitive damages were ordered against four

Klansmen — $100,000 against each of three men and $200,000 against a fourth — who were earlier convicted of criminal charges in the case. The jury assessed $300,000 in compensatory damages.

"That jury's decision was a day of reckoning for the Klan," Dees told reporters. "The verdict shows that there are still some things sacred in the country, still some lines that no one can cross."

"Hate is useless, it is just useless," said Macedonia Baptist pastor, the Rev. Jonathan Mouzon after the trial concluded. He said he offers up his own prayers for the Klansmen.

The verdict marked the end of the Christian Knights as a viable hate group. The plaintiffs' lawyers foreclosed on King's house and the headquarters of the South Carolina chapter of the Christian Knights of the Ku Klux Klan. Proceeds will go to the Macedonia Baptist Church.

Other attorneys who deserve recognition for their important contributions in the case include State Senator John C. Land, III, and his daughter, Frances Ricci Land Welch, both of Land, Parker & Reaves in Manning, South Carolina, and local counsel Tom Turnipseed and Peter J. Tepley, both of Columbia, South Carolina. Tepley is now with the SPLC.

The case marked the third time that Dees had been honored as a finalist for the Trial Lawyer of the Year Award. (See Chapter Six and Chapter Ten.)

There is no reported decision on the merits in this case.

Morris Dees

J. Richard Cohen

Product Safety

Meneely v. S.R. Smith, Inc.

Jan Eric Peterson, Fred Zeder, and Chris Young

A swimming pool accident led to an advance in consumer safety when attorneys Jan Eric Peterson, Fred Zeder, and Chris Young of Seattle's Peterson, Young, Putra, Fletcher & Zeder defeated the National Spa and Pool Institute (NSPI) in a case that punctured the tactic of hiding unsafe products behind the shield of "industry standards." The case began when Shawn Meneely, an athletic 16-year-old, dove from a diving board into a faultily designed swimming pool, breaking his neck on the pool's "hopper bottom" floor. His head struck on the transition slope from the deep to the shallow end of the pool; the impact jammed his vertebrae and rendered him a quadriplegic.

The key defendant was the NSPI, the trade association that sets industry standards for residential pools and spas. In the course of developing standards, NSPI had been provided notice that some people — particularly tall, muscular athletes — could injure themselves diving into swimming pools. Among the 8,000 documents unearthed while litigating the case over six years was a 1982 letter from NSPI's primary expert and consulting engineer, warning that the particular diving board in question was exceedingly dangerous when installed on hopper bottom pools. The expert urged that such boards be removed and decertified by NSPI.

Before trial, Meneely and his family offered to accept a settlement of $160,000 if NSPI would agree to adopt safer industry standards. NSPI refused. The jury heard from 40 witnesses and viewed more than 500 exhibits — leading them to return a verdict of $11 million, including a $6.6 million compensatory judgment against NSPI. The Court of Appeals for the State of Washington affirmed the trial verdict, and the State's Supreme Court denied review.

"The verdict promoted the idea that individuals can hold trade associations responsible for setting and distributing unsafe standards," says attorney Young.

Instead of acting responsibly, NSPI plans to restructure in order to make it more difficult for injured parties to recover damages in the future. According to the May 2001 issue of *AQUA* Magazine, a pool industry trade publication, "...the post-*Meneely* NSPI is likely to look quite different than it does now. ...Currently, NSPI has about 5,900 members who belong to 79 local chapters that are organized within 11 regions." The NSPI Board is reportedly planning to reorganize as a federation in which each industry segment would form its own trade association; these "mini" trade groups would belong to the NSPI federation, which would coordinate the associations.

The magazine report continues: "To make NSPI a less attractive target for future lawsuits, the group needs to find a way to 'hide the money,' as one observer told *AQUA*. One way to do this calls for the federation to own two for-profit subsidiaries. One would be an association management firm, which would assist the trade associations with accounting, administration, etc. The other would be a standards development and public affairs management firm. If the NSPI standards were to come under attack in future lawsuits, the liability would be contained within the standards development firm, which would have fewer assets than the association management firm."

The reported decision in this case can be found at *Meneely v. S.R. Smith, Inc.,* 5 P.3d 49 (Wash. Ct. App. 2000).

Jan Eric Peterson   *Fred Zeder*   *Chris Young*

Government Accountability
Wynn v. Towey
Dianne Jay Weaver and Mike Ryan

Attorneys Dianne Jay Weaver and Mike Ryan of Krupnick Campbell Malone Roselli Buser Slama Hancock McNelis Liberman & McKee in Fort Lauderdale won a landmark $17.99 million judgment against the State of Florida on behalf of Aaron Wynn, a man who suffered from a traumatic brain injury and who had been mistreated and abused in state hospitals. The theory of liability was as important as the amount of the verdict. The case was brought against the State for depriving Wynn of his civil rights.

In 1985, Wynn, then 18 years old, sustained a head wound in a motorcycle accident that left him with symptoms similar to schizophrenia. In April 1988, he was arrested after hitting a policeman and was committed to the South Florida Evaluation and Treatment Center for evaluation. Although the committing diagnosis said he had a possible brain injury, this was ignored.

Wynn spent more than two of his next three and a half years at the treatment center in seclusion and restraints. His caregivers left him for hours or days tied spread-eagled on a bed, covered in his own excrement, and medicated with drugs used for schizophrenia, not brain injury. He nearly lost the ability to walk because he was let up to exercise for only 45 minutes a day before being tied down again.

Wynn returned home in November 1991, extremely withdrawn, paranoid, and disoriented. His mother would sometimes find him cowering in a corner. In July 1993, he became frightened while purchasing bologna in a grocery store and ran out the door. He knocked down 85-year-old Pauline Jackson, who hit her head and died. Wynn was arrested and charged with manslaughter. Jackson's family compassionately urged the court to help Wynn.

He was committed to another state forensic hospital, where he was isolated in a 6-by-10-foot room with no furniture and no windows. More than a year passed before a court ordered his placement in a private facility. The manslaughter charge was eventually dropped. Wynn's attorney, Howard Finkelstein, a Chief Assistant Public Defender and an advocate for brain injury patients accused of crimes, contacted Weaver.

Weaver believed this failure of the Florida Department of Health & Rehabilitation Services to provide proper medical care violated Wynn's civil rights. Pursuing her case, she combed through 27,000 pages of documents on Wynn's treatment to prove that the State's workers had shown deliberate indifference to his medical needs and had substantially departed from medical care standards.

Weaver and Ryan named 21 individual defendants, including those who directed the state facilities, the medical director who developed Wynn's treatment plan, and his physicians, social workers and psychologists.

In her opening statement, Weaver told the jury, "[T]he defendants sought to break Aaron Wynn because he was not compliant. He was put in restraints more than any other individual, ever. As a result of his being tied down, he had lost his mind. He had a brain injury and could have been rehabilitated. He could have had a life. But now he will always be in institutions."

She stressed not just the defendants' liability, but also the jury's responsibility to improve Wynn's life. She told them that the choice they had to make was whether he would be cared for as a human being or "sent back to a state institution to be treated like an animal."

After a seven-week trial, the jury held 17 of the 21 defendants accountable and awarded Wynn $17.99 million dollars — the highest civil rights verdict in Florida's history. The State settled the case for $17.75 million. Finkelstein then used the case to push for a grand-jury investigation of the mental-health system and a number of changes in the justice system. Broward County opened the nation's first court dedicated to trying cases of mentally ill people accused of crimes. Wynn now resides in a facility where he is cared for compassionately and with dignity.

Attorney Gloria Seidule of Stuart, Florida, also deserves recognition for her important work in the case.

There is no reported decision on the merits in this case.

Dianne Jay Weaver

Mike Ryan

Toxic Injury Protection

Hall v. Babcock & Wilcox Co.

Fred Baron, Lisa Blue, Bill Caroselli, Mike Kaeske,
and Kay Reeves

Fred Baron, Lisa Blue, Mike Kaeske, and Kay Reeves of Baron & Budd in Dallas
and Bill Caroselli of Caroselli, Spagnolli & Beachler in Pittsburgh obtained a
$36.7 million verdict for eight residents of Apollo, Pennsylvania, who con-
tracted cancer as a result of their exposure to radiation from a plant that produced enriched, bomb-grade uranium for the nuclear power industry. They
sued Babcock & Wilcox and Atlantic Richfield Company on behalf of 119
Apollo residents who had lived in the shadow of the plant's stacks. For years,
these stacks had spewed smoke laced with radioactive particles. The verdict in
this bellwether trial on behalf of the first eight plaintiffs has been hailed as the
highest ever in a radiation exposure case.

Proving that the defendants generated radiation and exposed the residents
to it was not enough to win the case. Because the case was tried under the federal Price-Anderson Act and concerned the manufacture of enriched uranium,
the plaintiffs had to prove that the exposure was caused by the defendant's violation of specific federal regulations and that those violations caused the cancers. This was no easy task. It took 175 depositions, a review of three million
pages of documents, and the expenditure of more than $2 million in costs over
a four-year period.

The jury finding that the defendants were negligent was a tremendous victory for the plaintiffs, who had sought information about the plant's dangers
for 15 years, but met only resistance and stonewalling. In addition to the compensatory damage verdict, and a separate settlement of punitive damages, the
litigation team achieved a heightened public awareness of the hazards of
nuclear materials. The verdict seemed to indicate that, in our civil justice system, a group of residents from a rural town could prevail in the face of corporate abuses and governmental secrecy. Yet the fight for public justice continues.

Since these attorneys were honored, the case has been bogged down in
appeals and bankruptcy proceedings. Judge Donetta Ambrose of the U.S.
District Court for the Western District of Pennsylvania granted a defense motion
for a new trial and also certified the case for appeal to the U.S. Court of Appeals
for the Third Circuit. Thereafter, Babcock & Wilcox filed for Chapter 11 bankruptcy in Louisiana, gaining an automatic stay of the civil proceedings. Then

the Third Circuit returned the case to the trial court. Co-Defendant ARCO has been ordered to stand trial despite its co-defendant's bankruptcy. ARCO has appealed. If the case proceeds against ARCO, trial is not expected before the summer of 2002.

The reported decision in this case can be found at *Hall v. Babcock & Wilcox Co.*, 69 F. Supp. 2d 716 (W.D. Pa. 1999) (granting new trial on defendant's motion).

Fred Baron

Lisa Blue

Bill Caroselli

Mike Kaeske

Kay Reeves

1999 Trial Lawyer of the Year Award Winners
Elisa Barnes and Denise Dunleavy
The Case That Targeted the Gun Industry's Marketing Practices

New York attorneys Elisa Barnes of The Law Offices of Elisa Barnes and Denise Dunleavy of Weitz & Luxenberg advanced a novel approach to gun safety and responsibility when a jury held gun manufacturers liable on a theory of market share liability for negligently distributing handguns. The landmark verdict they won brought nationwide attention to the gun companies' marketing practices. It also spurred additional litigation across the country, new proposed regulations, and safer practices by some gun manufacturers.

Barnes brought the case in 1995 on behalf of seven victims of gun violence and their families against 25 gun manufacturers. She could not prove which guns were used in the crimes that injured or killed the plaintiffs because the weapons used were never recovered. However, she alleged that the manufacturers were liable for the injuries and deaths because of negligent or even reckless marketing practices that allowed criminals easy access to firearms, resulting in shootings that would not otherwise have occurred.

What is public justice? Gun manufacturers are held accountable if they irresponsibly market their lethal products.

Barnes had just successfully concluded a series of cases involving DES — the drug given to women between 1941 and 1971 to prevent miscarriages that caused reproductive system abnormalities and cancer in female offspring. Most of the women harmed had been unable to identify which of the 300 drug companies that marketed the unpatented drug had manufactured the specific doses they had taken. But New York law permitted the plaintiffs to hold each manufacturer accountable according to its market share of DES sold — an approach known as "market share liability" — which apportions damages based on the amount of overall risk produced. Thus, if a company manufactured eight percent of all DES sold, it would have to pay eight percent of any damage award.

Having worked through the difficult process of obtaining market share liability, Barnes began to reflect on gun violence, which had reached epidemic levels in the period of 1992-1994, especially in poor and/or minority neighborhoods. The carnage made Barnes heartsick.

"I kept reading in the papers about all of this gun violence," Barnes recalls. "I kept thinking that somebody is responsible for the millions of illegal guns in New York. Surely, there must be something the law can do. I came to realize that as far as criminals were concerned, guns were as fungible as DES once was to the daughters of pregnant women."

Barnes contacted New Yorkers for Gun Control, which referred gun violence victims to her. She filed suit in the U.S. District Court in New York on behalf of 25 plaintiffs, naming 49 gun manufacturers as defendants. She analogized handguns and their ammunition to a pathogen leading to injuries and death and sought to hold the gun manufacturers liable for their lax marketing practices that allowed the lethal instrumentalities to get into the wrong hands.

The lead plaintiff was Freddie Hamilton, whose 17-year-old son Njuzi Ray was shot by a 9mm handgun as he walked down a New York City street. The gun was never recovered, and the manufacturer was not known. His alleged assailant was acquitted. Another victim was 18-year-old Damon Slade, who was killed in an elevator when Harry Eberhart kept the doors from closing and opened fire at close range. Eberhart was convicted of the murder, but the handgun he used was never found. Marvin Faretsky, a 49-year-old man, was shot and killed in a robbery at a convenience store in Queens. The bullet that killed him was a .380 caliber, but the gun was never found. Only one plaintiff was a shooting survivor: Stephen Fox was permanently disabled after being shot with a .25 caliber gun, which his assailant admitted purchasing out of a car trunk in Queens. The gun itself was never recovered.

Barnes overcame enormous obstacles, litigating the case by herself for four years and surviving three summary judgment motions and the collective battle tactics of the firearms manufacturers. "The discovery period was horrible beyond imagining," Barnes recalls. "I was a solo practitioner up against 10 large defense firms with hordes of lawyers and unlimited funds. They set about a clear strategy of driving me into the ground. Every day was teeth-clenchingly difficult."

Barnes recalls that defense counsel were cruel to her clients. "They made all of the plaintiffs, most of whom were grieving moms, cry with questions about the kids' school records, or paternity, or drug dealing, or criminal convictions. There were many calls to the Magistrate Judge supervising discovery.

Unfortunately, the defendants' positions were upheld in nearly every case. It was simply brutal." However, due to these interim defense victories, there were no appealable issues available to the defendants based on the discovery phase of the case.

At every phase, the gun manufacturers made Barnes' task more difficult and life more miserable. Defendants repeatedly sought sanctions for minor failures to comply with discovery, forcing her to stay in her office each night until after midnight. She was forced to fly all over the country to take depositions. After Barnes got an order requiring defendants to pay for her airfare, they would put her on obscure airlines with grueling schedules, requiring two or three stops before arriving at her destination. The case consumed all of Barnes' time, so she had to refer potentially profitable cases to other attorneys.

Case costs advanced into seven figures, threatening to exhaust Barnes' ability to continue. Barnes ran up her credit cards well into the six figures, a nonprofit organization put up substantial grant money, and expert witnesses discounted their fees, took delayed payments, or worked without charge. The plaintiffs contributed financially according to their abilities, but also put "sweat equity" into the case by helping photocopy, collate, and do other support work to hold down expenses.

At one point, the pressure almost caused Barnes' knees to buckle. Exhausted and worried about the effect of all her time away from her family, Barnes declared her intention to quit. "My middle child was then eleven," Barnes recalls. "He's a strong kid, but he burst into tears and said, 'You can't do that. You can't do that because I am so scared about guns and you are going to take care of this. Please, don't stop.' I burst into tears and so did my husband and there we all were, sobbing together. And it was so ironic because almost all of the plaintiffs were moms and we joked that this was a 'mom's case' and here was my kid believing that his mom could take care of this awful thing happening in our country."

Before the case could be brought to trial, the court granted summary judgment in the defendants' favor on the plaintiffs' claims for product liability and fraud. It also denied Barnes' request to certify the case as a class action. But in a huge victory for the plaintiffs, the court permitted the case to go forward based on the theory of collective liability for negligence.

The key to success lay in dissecting the marketing plans of the various gun manufacturers and proving both negligence and causation. The plaintiffs would have to prove that a negligent distribution plan proximately caused their injuries. New York law recognizes a duty predicated on the danger of a third person's tortious or criminal misconduct where a relationship between the defendant and either the plaintiff or a third party wrongdoer provides the defendant with the ability to minimize the risk. If such a relationship exists, the defendant is required to take reasonable steps to protect against those risks that are reasonably foreseeable. What might those steps be? This was the heart of the case and required expert testimony.

As the trial approached, Weitz & Luxenberg agreed to donate the services of attorney Denise Dunleavy and other resources. Now, with trial help and staff support, Barnes and Dunleavy sought to prove that in selling to primary distributors, the defendants did not take reasonable steps to reduce the possibility that their guns would fall into the hands of people likely to misuse them.

A key expert witness, Dr. David Stewart, Chairman of the Marketing Department at the University of Southern California, suggested several steps that gun manufacturers could feasibly take to reduce the risks associated with the marketing of their products. For example, the gun makers could franchise retail outlets, restrict distribution to qualified retailers, terminate distribution agreements with distributors who sell handguns irresponsibly, and prohibit sales of handguns at gun shows.

The plaintiffs also scored with the testimony of a former Smith & Wesson executive, who testified that manufacturers could rewrite their distribution contracts to allow them to cut off retailers who make multiple sales to single individuals in short periods of time or who repeatedly have crime guns traced to them. The point was that by implementing more careful marketing strategies, the companies could prevent a significant number of handguns from coming into the wrong hands.

The defendants' argument that the plaintiffs were seeking to hold innocent parties accountable for actions of criminals resonated with the jury. Out of the original 25 plaintiffs, only seven were still parties as the case came to trial, and only 25 defendants remained of the original 49. When the verdict came in after a four-week trial, the defense almost carried the day. The jury found 15 of the defendants negligent. Of these, nine were found to have proximately caused the injuries to one or more defendants. But damages were only awarded to Fox and his mother, in the total amount of $3.95 million for Steven Fox and $50,000 for Gail Fox. These damages were apportioned based on the total national handgun market share for each defendant found liable for damages in Fox's case — American Arms, Inc. (.23% liability, $9,200), Beretta U.S.A. Corp. (6.03% liability, $241,200), and Taurus International Manufacturing (6.8% liability, $272,000). This still represented a stunning victory against long odds.

When asked why she was willing to sacrifice so much for a case with so little chance of prevailing, Barnes replied, "I did it for the plaintiffs, obviously, and for the children of New York. I have three kids of my own. All kids should be able to go to the park and go to baseball games in safety. Urban kids have so much to deal with without worrying about getting shot every 20 minutes. It is outrageous that we can live in a society where kids have easy and immediate access to handguns. We can't have it. It brings social life to a standstill."

The precedent set by the judge's decision on the negligent distribution theory, along with the jury's verdict, helped form the basis for lawsuits filed by municipalities around the country against the firearms industry. After Barnes and Dunleavy were honored, however, the precedent was overturned.

Because a federal court decided the case, and because there were no New York cases directly on point, the district court applied the law it *anticipated* New York would apply under these circumstances. The U.S. Court of Appeals for the Second Circuit certified the case for review by the state's highest court and, in April 2001, the New York Court of Appeals held that the gun makers had no duty based on the facts in the record and, in any event, could not be held liable on a market share basis. The Court of Appeals left open the possibility that gun manufacturers could be found liable if there was a tangible showing that the manufacturers' conduct was a direct link in the causal chain that resulted in plaintiffs' injuries. The Court said it might find a manufacturer liable where there was more of a showing of "substantial sales of guns into the gun trafficking market on a consistent basis." Now that the Court has clarified New York law, the plaintiffs have asked the Second Circuit to remand the case to the district court so they can present the necessary evidence.

The reported decision in this case and the subsequent case history can be found at *Hamilton v. Accu-Tek*, 62 F. Supp. 2d 802 (E.D.N.Y. 1999), *question certified sub nom. Hamilton v. Beretta U.S.A. Corp.*, 222 F.3d 36 (2d Cir. 2000) (certifying question to New York Court of Appeals), *certified question accepted*, 738 N.E.2d 360 (N.Y. 2000), *certified question answered*, 2001 WL 429247 (N.Y. Apr. 26, 2001).

Elisa Barnes

Denise Dunleavy

CHAPTER EIGHTEEN

2000: The Case That Made "Voice of America" an Equal Opportunity Employer

Free Speech *Isuzu Motors Ltd. v. Consumers Union of United States, Inc.* and *Suzuki Motors Corp. v. Consumers Union of United States, Inc.*

Government Accountability *Al-Jundi v. Mancusi*

Government Accountability *Peterson v. Georgia State Dep't of Human Resources*

Auto Safety *Anderson v. General Motors Corp.*

Government Accountability *Willis v. Transamerica Leasing, Inc.*

HMO Accountability *Chipps v. Humana Health Ins. Co. of Florida, Inc.*

Human Rights *In re Holocaust Victim Assets Litigation*

Winner
Hartman v. Albright
The Case That Made "Voice of America" an Equal Opportunity Employer

The finalists for the 2000 Trial Lawyer of the Year Award fought for automobile safety, exposed brutality by prison guards, protected foster children, uncovered public corruption, held an HMO accountable for refusing to provide necessary and reasonable medical care to a child, and won compensation for victims of the Holocaust. The winners battled gender discrimination by the U.S. Information Agency and its "Voice of America" program for 23 years and achieved a record settlement — the largest ever in an employment discrimination case.

Free Speech

Isuzu Motors Ltd. v. Consumers Union of United States, Inc. and *Suzuki Motors Corp. v. Consumers Union of United States, Inc.*
Joseph W. Cotchett, Frank M. Pitre, Steven N. Williams, Barry G. West, and Norma Garcia

Strategic Lawsuits Against Public Participation (SLAPP) abuse the civil justice system by forcing innocent public advocates to defend themselves merely for speaking truthfully about the powerful. (See Chapter Seven and Chapter Ten.) Most often, SLAPPs are filed against individual activists who, lacking insurance to pay the high cost of litigation, are sometimes cowed into silence by these frivolous suits intended to chill free speech and political participation.

But sometimes corporations resort to SLAPPs in an attempt to destroy more powerful adversaries. For example, Isuzu Motors and Suzuki Motors sued Consumers Union (CU), claiming that the consumer advocacy group had defamed them by asserting there was a safety problem with two sports utility vehicles, the Suzuki Samurai and the Isuzu Trooper.

The automakers demanded hundreds of millions of dollars in lost sales plus punitive damages because CU gave the Samurai and Trooper a "non-acceptable" rating. CU based the rating on its independent tests, which demonstrated that the vehicles had a serious propensity to tip up on two wheels during tight turns. The automakers claimed that the CU tests were not scientific, but rigged.

Attorneys Joseph W. Cotchett, Frank M. Pitre, and Steven N. Williams of Cotchett, Pitre & Simon in Burlingame, California; Barry G. West of Gaims, Weil, West & Epstein in Los Angeles; and Norma Garcia of Consumers Union in San Francisco, defended CU's freedom of speech. Using several different law firms to press their claims, Isuzu and Suzuki spent approximately $25 million and $30 million respectively. During Isuzu's discovery effort, the manufacturer took depositions all over the globe — including more than 50 multi-day depositions — of engineers and virtually every editor, test driver, and manager at CU. At the same time, Cotchett and his team were covering more than 70 multi-day depositions from Japan to England in the *Suzuki* case.

During the two-month *Isuzu* trial, the jury heard over 20 days of expert testimony on engineering, journalism, and economics. The trial team presented evidence that Isuzu had attempted to use the lawsuit as a public relations tool and to make Consumers Union "shut up." The jury rejected Isuzu's claims and cleared CU of any liability. And after four years of hard-fought litigation,

Suzuki lost on summary judgment. These victories are of great significance in the battle to defend First Amendment rights against corporations using strong-arm legal tactics to silence critics.

Judgment has been entered in the *Isuzu* case and the company has paid all costs as ordered. The *Suzuki* case is on appeal before the U.S. Court of Appeals for the Ninth Circuit.

Other attorneys who deserve recognition for their important work in these cases include Corey E. Klein and Sylvia Virsik of Gaims, Weil, West & Epstein; Patrick A. Dawson of Dawson & Huddleston in Marrietta, Georgia; Tab Turner of Turner & Associates in North Little Rock, Arkansas; Steven J. Crowley of Crowley, Bunger & Pothitakis in Burlington, Iowa; and Michael N. Pollet of Pollet & Felleman in Yonkers, New York.

Reported decisions on pre-trial motions in *Isuzu* can be found at *Isuzu Motors Ltd. v. Consumers Union of United States, Inc.*, 12 F. Supp. 2d 1035 (C.D. Cal. 1998), and *Isuzu Motors Ltd. v. Consumers Union of United States, Inc.*, 66 F. Supp. 2d 1117 (C.D. Cal. 1999). To date, there is no reported decision on the merits in *Suzuki*.

Joseph W. Cotchett

Frank M. Pitre

Steven N. Williams

Barry G. West

Norma Garcia

Government Accountability
Al-Jundi v. Mancusi
Elizabeth M. Fink, Michael E. Deutsch, Dennis Cunningham, Joseph J. Heath, Daniel Meyers, and Ellen M. Yacknin

Federal district court Judge Michael A. Telesca declared on August 28, 2000, that inmates beaten in the 1971 Attica prison uprising in western New York were treated "like garbage," recounting how the siege left 43 people dead, 80 wounded, and countless more psychologically scarred. He divided up an $8 million settlement to compensate more than 500 inmates and relatives for the abuse that the prisoners suffered at the hands of prison guards following the uprising. The allotment capped one of the longest and most infamous chapters in American criminal justice history, which ended with a landmark agreement between New York State and lawyers representing 1,281 former inmates.

The Attica uprising began in 1971 as a prison revolt over unsafe and unsanitary conditions. It was followed by violent reprisals by prison guards in which inmates were shot, beaten, and otherwise brutalized. The episode ended in 2000 with the largest settlement of a prisoners' rights case in U.S. history. The historic settlement was made possible by a 20-year legal battle by trial lawyers Elizabeth M. Fink of Brooklyn, New York; Michael E. Deutsch of the People's Law Office in Chicago; Dennis Cunningham of San Francisco; Joseph J. Heath of Syracuse, New York; Daniel Meyers of New York; and Ellen M. Yacknin of the Greater Upstate Law Project in Rochester, New York.

The class action was filed in 1974 against New York State and Attica prison officials. It languished for years in federal court in part because it was not energetically pursued. That changed in 1981, when Fink stepped in and saved the case from dismissal for lack of prosecution.

Fink and her team forced the State to disclose once-secret documents that proved harmful to the defendants. They also successfully defended against attempts to decertify the class, and the case went to trial in 1991. The jury found a deputy warden liable. It took six more years of procedural maneuvering to get to the damage phase of the trial. Another victory led to jury verdicts in favor of two former prisoners in the amounts of $4 million and $75,000, respectively. That led to the settlement. The plaintiffs will each receive their proportion of the fund based on the severity of their injuries, bringing a just end to a saga that symbolized the use of excessive force. Several appeals were filed, but none were perfected and all were dismissed.

The reported decision in this case can be found at *Al-Jundi v. Mancusi*, 113 F. Supp. 2d 441 (W.D.N.Y. 2000) (approving class action settlement).

Elizabeth M. Fink

Michael E. Deutsch

Dennis Cunningham

Joseph J. Heath

Daniel Meyers

Ellen M. Yacknin

Government Accountability
Peterson v. Georgia State Dep't of Human Resources
Don C. Keenan

Atlanta attorney Don C. Keenan forced Georgia to enact sweeping reforms to its child protection system by suing the State's child welfare agency on behalf of six year-old Terrell Peterson, whose foster family abused and ultimately murdered him. Keenan's public advocacy both won the lawsuit and prompted the State to pass critically-needed reform legislation.

Despite clear evidence that Peterson's foster mother had repeatedly abused him, social workers failed to protect him. His caseworker failed to appear at a hearing on an assault charge against the foster mother, forcing the judge to dismiss the charge. The caseworker then sent the boy back to live with the foster mother, noting in his file that the judge had found no evidence of abuse. In addition to lying about why the charge was dropped, the caseworker neglected to visit Peterson in the year following the dismissal of the assault charge. The result: the boy died in January 1998. But the coroner could not determine the exact cause of death, because the boy was starving — he weighed only 29 pounds — and had suffered so many bruises, cuts, and burns that the coroner stopped counting them.

Understanding that Peterson was one of hundreds of children who had died of abuse and neglect while in foster care, Keenan set his sights on changing the system. He handled the case *pro bono* and asked not for money damages, but for system-wide reform. To expose the state's wrongdoing, Keenan launched a media campaign around the lawsuit. His strategy worked. The state enacted every reform he requested and the publicity induced state officials to fire those responsible for the inexcusable neglect that infected the child welfare system.

Under the "Terrell Peterson Act," emergency room doctors have the power to take custody of abused children rather than waiting for state action, an independent ombudsman's office was created to work through bugs in the system, salaries for social workers are higher, the governor and state agency heads may now fire poorly performing social workers, and child abuse records are no longer shielded from public scrutiny. Keenan's selfless efforts made Georgia's child welfare system more accountable, undoubtedly saving many lives.

There is no reported decision on the merits in this case.

Don C. Keenan

Auto Safety
Anderson v. General Motors Corp.
Brian J. Panish and Christine Spagnoli

Attorneys Brian J. Panish and Christine Spagnoli of Greene, Broillet, Taylor, Wheeler & Panish in Santa Monica, California, obtained the highest verdict ever in a personal injury case for Patricia Anderson, her four children, and a family friend, who were severely burned when the gas tank of Anderson's 1979 Chevrolet Malibu exploded into flames after a rear-end collision.

The cause of the accident was a known defect in the gas tank. It took Panish and Spagnoli four years of discovery battles, but the pair proved that automaker General Motors (GM) allowed the defective gas tank on the market in order to save $8.59 per car. They also unearthed and presented pivotal evidence never before used in a case against GM, including deposition testimony of former presidential assistant John Ehrlichman, who admitted that GM's chairman had secretly and successfully lobbied President Richard M. Nixon and him to weaken federal fuel tank safety standards.

During the three-month trial, Panish and Spagnoli appeared daily at 7:00 a.m. for evidentiary hearings at which GM objected to the admission of every single document the plaintiffs presented. Arguments on the admissibility of some documents took several days. Nearly every day, the plaintiffs' lawyers also had to combat GM's motions for a mistrial. The jury was convinced that GM should be held responsible for systematically valuing profits over safety, and for knowingly selling a dangerously defective product. It awarded $107 million in compensatory damages and a staggering $4.8 billion in punitive damages, which the judge later reduced to $1.09 billion.

The verdict in this case raised the public understanding of the important role punitive damages pay in curtailing corporate misconduct and uncovered a treasure trove of information now available for use in other cases against GM.

At trial, Carl E. Douglas of the Law Offices of Carl E. Douglas of Beverly Hills, California, represented Anderson, and Mark Robinson, Jr., and Geoff Robinson of Robinson, Calcagnie & Robinson of Newport Beach, California, represented family friend Jo Tigner.

After the verdict, six of the burned plaintiffs offered to give back the punitive damages award if GM would recall the defective fuel systems. GM refused. The plaintiffs, who experienced severe difficulty obtaining burn treatment, have pledged to donate half of all punitive damages collected to the State of California to fund treatment of burn victims.

There is no reported decision on the merits in this case.

Brian J. Panish

Christine Spagnoli

Government Accountability
Willis v. Transamerica Leasing, Inc.
Joseph A. Power, Jr.

Attorney Joseph A. Power, Jr., of Power, Rogers & Smith in Chicago won the largest settlement ever in an accident in Illinois, obtaining $100 million for Janet and Rev. Duane "Scott" Willis, the parents of six children killed in a fiery crash, and drawing nationwide attention to truck safety issues. Even more remarkable than the size of the settlement is that Power's work on the case led to a federal probe of truck license-selling and uncovered a widespread bribery scheme in the state's granting of commercial drivers' licenses.

On November 8, 1994, the Willis family was traveling on Route 94 to Wisconsin to a birthday celebration. The Baptist minister was driving his family's Chrysler minivan, carrying his wife and six of their nine children. The minivan ran over a mudflap/tailgate assembly, which had fallen off a semi-trailer truck. The debris, which weighed 90 pounds, punctured the minivan's floorboards, ruptured the fuel tank, and started a fire. The adults disentangled themselves and managed to escape, but the children were trapped. Five of the six children — Joseph, 11; Samuel, 9; Hank, 6; Elizabeth, 3; and Peter, age 6 weeks — died instantly in the fire. The oldest in the car, 12-year-old Ben, died the next day.

Power sued several defendants, including the driver, the truck leasing company, the manufacturer of the taillight, and the manufacturer of the minivan. He doggedly investigated the responsibility of each defendant in the case, taking more than 100 depositions in 18 months. Eventually, Power's investigation would uncover damning facts that neither he nor the Willis family could have suspected.

During his investigation into the qualifications of truck driver Ricardo Guzman, Power learned from several whistleblowers that hundreds of drivers who were unable to pass their driving and safety tests had bribed state officials to receive their licenses. It eventually emerged that nine people have been killed, and more than 50 injured, in crashes involving truckers illegally licensed in Illinois.

Power then discovered that some of the money obtained from the corrupt sale of these commercial drivers' licenses was funneled into then-Secretary of State George Ryan's gubernatorial campaign fund. Enduring attacks from government officials who vilified him in the media as having a political agenda, Power succeeded in forcing the state to open its records. It then became clear that Power's four-year legal battle was worth it — not only for the case, which settled a few weeks before trial — but for the public good. The work that Power did in this case led to 31 federal indictments relating to the illegal issuance of the licenses, 25 of which resulted in convictions. The investigation is continuing at this time. In addition, thousands of truck drivers in Illinois have had to undergo re-testing or risk losing their licenses.

Attorneys Larry R. Rogers, Jr., Todd A. Smith, and Devon C. Bruce of Power, Rogers & Smith also deserve recognition for their important work in the case.

There is no reported decision on the merits in this case.

Joseph A. Power, Jr.

HMO Accountability
Chipps v. Humana Health Ins. Co. of Florida, Inc.
Edward M. Ricci and Theodore J. Leopold

Edward M. Ricci and Theodore J. Leopold of Ricci, Hubbard, Leopold, Frankel & Farmer in West Palm Beach, Florida, won a $78.5 million punitive damages award on behalf of a child with cerebral palsy whose Health Maintenance Organization (HMO) wrongfully terminated her insurance benefits. This case exposed the deceitful tactics behind the cruel cost-cutting methods of one of the nation's largest HMOs, Humana Health Insurance Company of Louisville, Kentucky.

On December 1, 1995, Mark and Barbara Chipps received an unsigned form letter from Humana Health Insurance of Florida informing them that their five-year-old daughter Caitlyn, born with cerebral palsy, would be terminated from a special medical case management program for catastrophically and chronically ill patients. This denial of coverage was shocking, because Humana had induced the Chipps family to switch insurance companies by assuring them that the girl would be automatically enrolled in Humana's medical case management program and that her level of care would exceed the coverage of the family's previous carrier.

Through four years of painstaking discovery that included bringing Humana to task for violating 100 discovery orders, Ricci and Leopold uncovered widespread fraud within Humana. During the 28-day trial, they proved that the company unlawfully denied special coverage to more than 100 catastrophically ill and injured children in Florida because an accounting company had concluded that coverage of such patients would not be profitable. The attorneys showed that Humana was paying bonuses to physicians and nurses based on the number of medical claims denied each month. And they exposed Hu-mana's deceitful attempts to shield itself from liability by claiming that it had no contractual responsibility for its Florida subsidiary, uncovering a secret indemnification agreement it entered into to save the Florida subsidiary from financial harm.

When the jury learned about the company's deceit and willingness to sacrifice the most vulnerable people to its bottom line, it awarded $78.5 million in punitive damages and $1.029 million in compensatory damages, including $28,763 for medical bills and $1 million for the intentional infliction of emotional distress. Ricci and Leopold's well-earned victory provided rare insight into the operation of a major HMO, spawning national class actions against Humana and other managed care companies.

"Humana tried to cover up the evil of its corporate offspring," said Mark Chipps, "while parents of very sick children struggle through the lies to get the critical care they need. The jury punished Humana in the only place it will understand — in the pocketbook."

After these attorneys were honored, AIM Insurance Company, one of the insurance carriers of Humana, removed the judgment to federal district court, asserting that the claim had to be arbitrated pursuant to an international arbitration agreement because Humana's liability insurance company was a foreign corporation headquartered in Bermuda. The district court dismissed this contention and remanded the matter to state court, where it is now on appeal.

The later decision in this case can be found at *Humana Health Ins. Co. of Florida, Inc. v. Chipps*, 748 So. 2d 280 (Fla. Dist. Ct. App. 1999) (affirming trial court judgment without opinion).

Edward M. Ricci

Theodore J. Leopold

Human Rights

In re Holocaust Victim Assets Litigation

Melvyn I. Weiss, Robert A. Swift, Morris A. Ratner, Michael Hausfeld, and Professor Burt Neuborne

During World War II, virtually every German company used slave and forced labor. "Slave laborers," about half of whom were Jewish, were held in concentration camps and subjected to the Nazi "annihilation through labor" program. "Forced laborers," most of whom were not Jewish, were civilians from German-occupied territories who were taken from their homes and forced to work for German businesses in support of the war effort.

More than 50 years after the war ended, a team of trial lawyers obtained an unprecedented settlement, convincing German industry and government officials to establish a $5.1 billion fund to compensate a worldwide class of approximately one and a half million Holocaust survivors who were slaves or forced laborers during the Nazi regime. This was truly a remarkable achievement.

The Holocaust-era litigation team filed about three dozen class actions in numerous U.S. courts to obtain compensation for the exploited laborers, in addition to many other lawsuits designed to compensate others with claims against banks and insurance companies. Litigating these class actions required extensive historical and legal research, enormous out-of-pocket expenses, and the development of novel legal theories that would permit U.S. courts to adjudicate cases on behalf of a worldwide class against private companies that engaged in misconduct in foreign countries. The settlement negotiations alone lasted 15 months. Each session required the logistics of an international conference, typically attended by more than 80 people from eight countries, with simultaneous translation into five languages.

The settlement offers public recognition of the suffering of these laborers and broadens the concept of "human rights" by focusing on economic abuses during wartime, opening the door to other cases against private entities that try to profit from human rights atrocities.

Members of the Holocaust-era litigation team who were honored as finalists for the 2000 Trial Lawyer of the Year Award were Melvyn I. Weiss of Milberg Weiss Bershad Hynes & Lerach in New York; Robert A. Swift of Kohn, Swift & Graf in Philadelphia; Morris A. Ratner of Lieff, Cabraser, Heimann & Bernstein in San Francisco; Michael Hausfeld of Cohen, Milstein, Hausfeld & Toll in Washington, D.C.; and Professor Burt Neuborne of the Brennan Center for Justice at New York University School of Law.

Other attorneys who deserve recognition for their important work in these cases are Deborah Sturman of Milberg Weiss Bershad Hynes & Lerach; Robert L. Leiff and Elizabeth J. Cabraser of Lieff, Cabraser, Heimann & Bernstein; Irwin Levin and Richard Shevitz of Cohen & Malad in Indianapolis, Indiana; Professor Arthur Miller of Harvard Law School; Israel Singer of the World Jewish Congress in New York; Dr. Hans Reis of Hanover, Germany; Allyn Z. Lite of Lite, De Palma, Greenberg & Rivas of Newark, New Jersey; Martin Mendelsohn of Washington, D.C.; Stephen A. Whinston and Edgar Millstein of Berger & Montague in Philadelphia; and Lawrence Kill and Linda Gerstel of Anderson, Kill & Olick in New York.

The reported decision in this case can be found at *In re Holocaust Victim Assets Litigation*, 105 F. Supp. 2d 139 (E.D.N.Y. 2000) (approving class action settlement).

Melvyn I. Weiss   *Robert A. Swift*   *Morris A. Ratner*   *Professor Burt Neuborne*

2000 Trial Lawyer of the Year Award Winners

Bruce A. Fredrickson, Susan L. Brackshaw, Linda M. Correia, Jonathan C. Puth, and Jeffrey E. Fallon

The Case That Made "Voice of America" an Equal Opportunity Employer

Attorney Bruce A. Fredrickson of Webster, Fredrickson & Brackshaw in Washington, D.C., shared the 2000 Trial Lawyer of the Year Award with Susan L. Brackshaw, Linda M. Correia, Jonathan C. Puth, and Jeffrey E. Fallon, all of Webster, Fredrickson & Brackshaw in Washington, D.C., for the work he performed in his very first case — an unprecedented feat in the award's history. More remarkable, Fredrickson filed the case as a new associate in his first legal job and ultimately settled it after he was a principal in his own firm, 23 years later.

The case began when women applying for various jobs at the U.S. Information Agency (USIA) during the 1970s were denied employment and advancement due to their sex. It would end with the federal government agreeing to a settlement of $508 million plus attorneys' fees, the largest settlement ever in an employment discrimination class action.

What is public justice? The government both enforces and respects the laws barring gender discrimination.

Fredrickson was assigned the case as a new associate in a Washington, D.C., law firm. Perhaps it was a matter of youthful idealism and zeal, but he *knew* from the very beginning that this case would eventually be a winner. Little did he know the personal sacrifice he would have to make to keep the case alive.

Early on, Fredrickson successfully obtained a ruling certifying the case as a class action. It would eventually involve nearly 1,100 women who alleged that they were denied employment or promotions because of gender discrimination between 1974 and 1984. The next step, in May and June of 1979, was to try the issue of liability in federal district court, where he hoped to get a ruling that the plaintiffs had established a *prima facie* case.

If Fredrickson succeeded in establishing liability against USIA for the entire class, then the burden of proof would shift. Rather than the plaintiffs having to prove that each member of the class did not receive a job or promotion due to sexual discrimination, the government would have to prove that each refusal was founded upon non-discriminatory bases. Fredrickson presented testimony and expert statistical analysis. For example, he demonstrated that, over a five-year period, the USIA had hired 103 radio technicians and none of them was a woman. He also demonstrated that in the radio industry, at a similar time, the ratio of female to male hires for similar positions was demonstrably higher.

"I thought it was a compelling case," Fredrickson recalls. "The statistical disparity just couldn't be denied."

But the judge did not accept the statistical comparisons, so the plaintiffs could not meet their burden of proof. Fredrickson's superiors considered the adverse ruling a deathblow to the case; they were ready to give up. Yet he still believed in the cause. He wrote a memo for his firm supervisors briefing the legal approach he proposed to take on appeal. But the partners were not enthusiastic. They worried that even if a reversal were obtained — a prospect they considered highly unlikely — the judge would simply find another way to defeat the class claim. They decided to drop the case. At this point, Fredrickson made an extraordinary offer.

"I think I can win this case and, if you will let me do it, I'll work on it during my spare time," Fredrickson offered. "I'll do it at nights and on weekends. I'll take vacation time if need be to do my research, drafts, and to attend oral argument."

The firm agreed — on the condition that it not adversely impact his other firm responsibilities. Fredrickson was now a full time lawyer in a busy firm — hardly a nine-to-five job — who was also responsible for researching, writing, and arguing a difficult appeal in his "off" hours. Soon he left his employment and opened his own firm, then Webster & Fredrickson, taking the sex discrimination case with him. The fledgling firm was soon bolstered by the addition of Susan Brackshaw, who climbed into the trenches beside Fredrickson and remained throughout the campaign.

The Court of Appeals validated Fredrickson's faith in his case in 1982, reversing and remanding for further hearings on the issue of whether the plaintiffs could prove a *prima facie* case on the issue of sex discrimination. Confirming that Fredrickson's optimism was warranted, the trial court decision issued on November 16, 1984, was good news for the plaintiffs and the class. While the trial court still found no *prima facie* case with respect to retaliation, it concluded both that the plaintiffs had established a *prima facie* case of gender discrimination in hiring and then the government had failed to rebut it.

The court summarized the discrimination that had occurred against one of the plaintiffs, Rose Kobylinski. The court found that Kobylinski had not applied for a position because she knew it had "been preselected" for a male USIA employee. More important, the court accepted the statistical evidence presented by Fredrickson as proof that sexual discrimination was rife at the Agency. The court found "gross statistical disparities" in USIA's hiring practices. The court also accepted expert testimony that a "significant underutilization of women" existed at the USIA in six out of 10 job categories studied: Electronic Technician, Foreign Language Broadcaster, Production Specialist, Writer/Editor, Foreign Information Specialist, and Radio Broadcast Technician. These were plum positions and represented 50 percent of the jobs available.

The next milestone came in 1988, when the district court directed the USIA to cure its discriminatory practices and to notify women worldwide of their rights to file claims in the suit. The court ruled that, except for Foreign Service applicants, class members who wished to participate in class relief would be entitled to individualized determinations of their claims. Most significant, the court laid out the remedies to which successful claimants would be entitled. Demonstrating the totality of the victory that had been hard won by Fredrickson and his team, the court ruled that damages would include:

- Back Pay: The government wanted back pay to be determined based on "established salary schedules," but the court agreed with the plaintiffs' legal position that equity favors the use of a "proxy salary" formula, i.e., that the earnings of the man actually hired for the job the class member was denied would be used to calculate her lost back pay.

- Value of Fringe Benefits: "In addition to back salary," the court ruled, "victims of discrimination are entitled to the monetary value of fringe benefits in their back pay awards." These included "vacation leave, sick leave, and medical coverage," as well as "the value of overtime and shift differentials."

- Front Pay: Plaintiffs "who request employment with the Agency but cannot be hired immediately" were ordered to receive "front pay," that is, compensation equivalent to what they would have received if a proper position were available. Front pay would be calculated in the same manner as back pay and would last until an appropriate position was found or until a date certain, based on an estimate of the period it was expected to take to find employment.

- Hiring Priorities: Members of the class were ordered to receive hiring priorities and once hired, each class member's appointment date "will be retroactive to the date which she would have been hired absent the discrimination."

The court also ordered that the claimants would have to mitigate the government's damages. This meant that the amount of the awards would be reduced "by amounts that claimants earned or could have earned with reasonable diligence." However, the plaintiffs were explicitly not required to accept "employment beneath their skills."

In addition, the government was ordered to begin reevaluating previously rejected female applicants for positions in the Foreign Service and to hire officers from the ranks of the plaintiff class. Notification of the reevaluation process was sent to nearly 30,000 women, more than 9,000 of whom sought to participate. By court order, the Agency hired 39 officers from the class to serve in positions around the world.

On a separate track, more than 1,100 women filed forms asserting more than 2,500 claims of rejection for civil service employment with the Agency. The USIA was ordered to file sworn affidavits addressing each and every claim, as well as provide documentary evidence in support of those defenses. During 1991 and 1992, the Agency filed hundreds of declarations and served more than one million pages of supporting documentation responding to the claims.

The team members analyzed the reams of documents in anticipation of spending years trying each individual case. Their analysis suggested which cases to bring forward in the earliest hearings because of their potential to undermine or eradicate defenses common to a number of claims. This decision-making process was critical to the overall success of the case, since the Agency had destroyed thousands of documents necessary for some trials as part of its "routine" document destruction practice. Nevertheless, to prepare for each individual hearing, the team had to master thousands of pages of documents.

In 1996, the hearings opened and continued for nearly four years. Fredrickson and his legal crew tried 48 cases. At these trials, the team demonstrated that the testing process had not been anonymous, that test evaluators in some cases knew the precise identities of the test takers, and that scores were raised or lowered to assure hiring of male and rejection of female applicants. In one case, they proved the existence of a "buddy system" whereby male test evaluators assured the success of other male friends in the supposedly anonymous process. The depth of detail adduced at these hearings led the Special Master to write opinions in some cases exceeding one hundred pages per claim. In some cases, the Special Master found the evidence so compelling that he said the plaintiffs had proved sex discrimination "beyond a reasonable doubt."

By the end, the plaintiffs had won 46 of the first 48 trials. The average prevailing class member was awarded nearly $500,000 in back pay with additional relief, including front pay, retirement benefits, and instatement orders for many. The total awards for these claimants exceeded $23 million.

In the meantime, the Agency had sought refuge in the appellate courts. It appealed the class certification order in 1994 and the liability determination in 1996. When those appeals failed, it sought U.S. Supreme Court review, which was denied in 1997.

Finally, the government realized that further fighting made no sense. In a record-setting settlement, it agreed to pay $508 million (plus accrued interest and minus amounts needed for unreimbursed administrative expenses) to be divided equally among the class members. Each woman in the class would receive approximately $450,000. Women whose hearing victories amounted to less than this amount received the difference between their individual award and the average share under the consent decree. Non-monetary forms of relief, such as job placement and the establishment of retirement accounts, were also agreed upon.

"There is no doubt that that the government could have settled the case for a far more modest price earlier in the litigation," Fredrickson says. "One of the reasons that the settlement is so enormous is that it covers in some cases 25 years of back pay."

Altogether, the legal team had invested more than 100,000 hours in the case and advanced hundreds of thousands of dollars in costs. David had, once again, defeated Goliath. Looking back at the effort, Fredrickson expressed the certainty he had felt all along: "I knew we were right. We always had been right about it. Sex discrimination denied hundreds of women fruitful and productive careers with the USIA. We are all looking forward to distributing to these patient and courageous women the product of nearly a quarter century of effort."

Other attorneys who deserve recognition for their important work in the case include Douglas Huron and Stephen Chertkof of Heller, Huron, Chertkof, Lerner, Simon & Salzman of Washington, D.C., who assisted with damage calculations; and Tom Gies, Laurel P. Malson, Terence Flynn, Lisa Greenlees, Glenn Grant, and Cary Flanery of Crowell & Moring of Washington, D.C, who assisted in the remedial phase of the case.

There is no reported decision on the merits in this case.

Bruce A. Fredrickson

Susan L. Brackshaw

Linda M. Correia

Jonathan C. Puth

Jeffrey E. Fallon

Epilogue

THE FINALISTS FOR THE 2001 TRIAL LAWYER OF THE YEAR AWARD were being selected as this book went to print. While we do not know their names yet, we do know what they have done. Like the finalists and winners before them, they have spent enormous portions of their lives, time, and money fighting for public justice. They have taken on powerful interests for people who would have no chance without them. They have battled for access to justice, human rights, product safety, government accountability, civil rights, medical safety, HMO accountability, consumer rights, auto safety, insurer accountability, workers' rights, drug safety, religious freedom, environmental protection, gun safety, toxic injury prevention, free speech, or the innocent on death row. They have made a real difference.

And the finalists are…

Table of Cases

L

Lockheed Toxic Torts Litigation, 283
Lousiana Energy Services, Inc., In re, 316-317

M

MacDonald v. Ortho Pharmaceutical Corp., 43, 54-59
Macedonia Baptist Church v. Christian Knights of the Ku Klux Klan Invisible Empire, Inc., 358-359
Mahoney v. Carus Chem. Co., 93-94
Malley v. Briggs, 73-74
Marbled Murrelet v. Babbitt, 290-291
Marbled Murrelet v. Pacific Lumber Co., 290-291
Martinez-Baca v. Suarez-Mason, 133-135
McKay v. Ashland Oil, Inc., 138-139
McLendon v. The Continental Group, Inc., 173, 187-192
McMillian v. State, 223-225
Meech v. Hillhaven West, Inc., 68
Meneely v. S.R. Smith, Inc., 360-361
Meyers v. Philadelphia Housing Auth., 22-23
Millison v. E.I. du Pont de Nemours and Co., 120-121
Minnesota v. Philip Morris, Inc., 327
Miranda v. Arizona, 253

N

National Ass'n of Radiation Survivors (NARS) v. Derwinski, 193, 203-210
National Ass'n of Radiation Survivors (NARS) v. Walters, 193, 203-210
National League of Cities v. Usery, 167, 168, 169

O

O'Gilvie v. International Playtex, Inc., 61, 75-82
Okeelanta Corp. v. Bygrave, 220
Orr v. Sonnenburg, 155, 167-172
Ortiz v. Gramajo, 261, 275-281
Oxendine v. Merrell Dow Pharmaceuticals, Inc., 20-21, 65-66, 112, 266-267

P

Patterson v. E.I. du Pont de Nemours & Co., Inc., 298
Paul v. Avril, 261, 280-281
Pedroza v. Bryant, 32-33
Peterson v. Georgia State Dep't of Human Resources, 378-379
Pfost v. State, 67-68
Philip Morris, Inc. v. Henley, 352-353

R

Rappaport v. Suarez-Mason, 133-135
Rastello v. City of Torrance, 162-164
Reilly v. Schneider, 140-141
Roberts v. Texaco, Inc., 308-309
Rosario v. Diamond Shamrock Corp., 312-313
Roxas v. Marcos, 302-303

S

Sabine Pilot Service, Inc. v. Hauck, 52-53
Sarchett v. Blue Shield of California, 9-10
Sierra Club v. Tri-State Generation & Transmission Ass'n, 318
State v. See name of opposing party
Sterling v. Velsicol Chem. Corp., 84-85
Strom v. Boeing, 177-178
Suzuki Motors Corp. v. Consumers Union of United States, Inc., 374-375
Synder v. American Ass'n of Blood Banks, 262-263

T

Tabler v. Wallace, 71-72
Tanner v. Decom Medical Waste Sys., Inc., 193, 212-215
Taylor v. State Farm Ins. & Cas. Co., 331
Taylor ex rel. Walker v. Ledbetter, 158-159
Technical Equities, In re, 131-132, 146-149-
Texas Dep't of Mental Health and Retardation v. Petty, 131-132, 152-154
Todd v. Panjaitan, 261, 279-280
Toyota Motor Co. v. McCathern, 334-335
Turner v. Dist. of Columbia, 122

U

Ueland v. Reynolds Metals Co., 46-47
United States v. See name of opposing party
United Steelworkers of Am. v. Milstead, 166
United Steelworkers of Am. v. Phelps Dodge Corp., 165-166

V

Von Stetina v. Florida Medical Center, 11-12

W

Wallace v. City of Los Angeles, 241, 256-260
White v. City of Newark, 292-293
Williams v. Philip Morris, Inc., 352, 354-355
Willis v. Transamerica Leasing, Inc., 382-383
Wixted v. Pepper, 69-70
Wollersheim v. Church of Scientology, 90-91
Wynn v. Towey, 362-363

X

Xuncax v. Gramajo, 261, 275-281

Index

A

Access to justice
architects no-action statutes found
unconstitutional as violation of
equal protection, 71–72
attorneys' fees. See Attorneys' fees
banks and brokerage houses held
liable for lending their name to
support fraudulent real invest
ment firm which could not pay
judgment due to bankruptcy,
131–132, 146–149
child's right to sue for loss of
parental companionship, 46–47
damage caps. See Damages
Fireman's Rule unreasonably
shielded reckless and wanton
defendants from liability to
injured firefighters, 93–94
malpractice damage cap violated
constitutional right to jury trial,
86–87
mandatory arbitration clauses in
medical treatment agreements
not enforceable against
consumers, 69–70
Oregon statute of repose barring
suit for auto manufactured
more than eight years earlier,
x, 301, 319–325
SLAPP suits to prevent. See Libel
speedy trial under California Code
of Civil Procedure to provide
redress for defrauded clients,
146–149
statute of limitations. See Statute of
limitations
Veterans Administration, attorneys'
fees cap as bar to filing suits
against, 193, 203–211
Agriculture
fern workers in Florida who
worked year round not fairly
paid due to exemption from
AWPA, 221–222
migrant farm workers' class action
against apple advertising
commission for fraud in
recruiting ads, 174–176
migrant sugar cane cutters cheated
of promised pay in Florida, 220
"SLAPP-back suit" filed by
California farmers group
silenced by contrived libel suit
by agricultural corporate giant,
142–143
Air pollution. See Toxic injury
prevention
Aisenberg, Bennett, 239
Alien Tort Claims Act, 133, 134, 248,
275
Allison, Robert, 191
Altman, Michael, 95–97
Amato, Theresa, 338
Anderson, Leland, 234–239

Anesthesiology
ventilator malfunctioned during
surgery, 2–3
Annunziata, Rosemarie, 86–87
Arbitration
mandatory arbitration clauses in
medical treatment agreements
not enforceable against
consumers, 69–70
Architects no-action statutes
statute of limitations found
unconstitutional as violation of
equal protection, 71–72
Argentina
human rights cases against Suarez-
Mason, 133–135
Armstrong, Sarah, 274
Arnold, Phillip, 46–47
Arrests
acquited Samoan-Americans' suit
against L.A. police for beating
and arresting them without
justification as they attended
bridal shower, 288–289
rape suspect arrested and questioned by Tucson police who
denied his constitutional rights
in hope of confession, 241,
250–255
state trooper liable to arrested
couple when his action lacked
probable cause, 73–74
Asbestos
cigarette manufacturer's use of
asbestos fibers in filters causing
smoker's lung tumor, 284–285
manufacturer's liability found
despite defense of "state-of-the-
art" shield, 1, 13–17
workers' compensation, employer's
knowledge with substantial
certainty that injury will result
allowed exemption from statute,
120–121
Assumption of risk defense
Fireman's Rule unreasonably
shielded reckless and wanton
defendants from liability to
injured firefighters, 93–94
Atomic bomb testing
navy serviceman exposed,
government's duty to warn
when health risk discovered
after discharge, 63–64, 203–211
radiation damage to people living
downwind of bomb test sites,
19, 34–41
Attorney-client privilege
tobacco industry cases,
manufacturers' research
documents in, 342–344
Attorney's fees
medical malpractice claimant
prevails under Florida's "loser
pays rule," 11–12
Veterans Administration, fee cap in

cases against, 193, 203–211
Automobile insurance
California Proposition 103 to lower
auto insurance rates,
constitutionality of, 132,
150–151
soft tissue injuries denied medical
coverage by using independent
medical examinations by
insurer-chosen doctors, 264–265
Automobile safety
computer chip sensor's failure
causing accident known to
manufacturer GM which was
engaging in "silent recall,"
185–186
crash test damage to Honda
passengers, faulty design and
manufacturer's failure to act
despite knowledge, 6–7
gas tanks on passenger cars
crashworthiness testing, faulty
design and manufacturer's
failure to act despite
knowledge, 28–29
known defect causing fire in
collisions, GM allowed to
save trivial sum, 380–381
minivan fire caused by road
debris from truck, resulting
investigation found bribery
scheme in Illinois licensing
of truck drivers, 382–383
gas tanks' side saddle design on
GM pickup trucks
company knew of faulty,
dangerous design,
218–219
statute of repose barring
suit, x, 301, 319–325
passenger-side airbag not provided,
faulty design and manufacturer's
failure to act despite knowledge,
24–25
rear shoulder harnesses not
installed based on manufacturer's
cost-benefit analysis, 114–115
rolling over of Toyota 4-Runner,
defective design as cause of
personal injuries, 334–335
"SLAPP-back suit" filed by
consumer advocacy group
which auto manufacturers
sought to keep from criticizing
Isuzu and Suzuki sports utility
vehicle safety, 374–375
Avril, Paul, 261
AWPA (Migrant and Seasonal
Agricultural Worker Protection Act),
221

B

Banke, D. Douglas, 347
Barnes, Elisa, 366–371
Baron, Fred, 364–365
Baron, Lawrence, 319–325
Barrera, Ricardo, 239
Baxter, George T., 262–263
Beasley, James, 22–23
Beasley, Jere Locke, 185–186
Beck, Thomas, 288–289
Bell, Griffin, 270
Bendectin
  morning sickness drug, pregnant
    woman not warned of risk to
    fetus from, 20–21, 65–66,
    88–89, 112–113, 266–267
Benlate
  fungicide sprayed on pregnant
    woman resulting in birth of
    child without eyes, 306–307
Berger, Daniel L., 308–309
Berger, Max W., 308–309
Berman, Robert, 339
Bernheim, Bernie, 331
Bertsche, Robert, 281
Betz, Thomas, 191
Bianchi, David, 140–141
Bidart, Michael J., 350–351
Bikini Atoll
  atomic bomb testing, navy
    serviceman's exposure and
    governmental liability, 63–64,
    203–211
Birth control pills
  manufacturer's duty to warn
    patient of risks, 54–58
Birth defects. See Pregnancy
Bleakley, Thomas H., 267
Blood transfusions
  HIV screening not established by
    blood industry trade association,
    causing HIV from transfusions,
    262–263
Bloom, Michael J., 250–255
Blue, Lisa, 199, 364–365
Blue Shield
  refusal to cover hospitalization for
    diagnosis, 9–10
Boats and ships
  motor without propeller guard as
    cause of swimmer's injuries,
    136–137
  oil spill by tanker Exxon Valdez in
    Alaska, 261, 268–274
Bollack, Patricia, 166
Boucher, Raymond P., 256–260
Bowman, William S., 49
Brackshaw, Susan L., 388–393
Bradtke, James, 338
Brake, Timothy, 144
Breidenbach, Francis, 30–31
Bribery
  Illinois licensing of truck drivers,
    investigation of minivan fire
    caused by road debris from

truck led to discovery of bribery
  scheme, 382–383
  oil company executives' complaints
    about bribery of foreign officials
    led to their wrongful
    termination, 138–139
Bricker, Ross B., 221–222
Bright, Stephen, 194–195
Brockovich, Erin, ix–x, 310–311
Broder, Sherry P., 248–249, 294–295,
  314–315
Brosnahan, James, 95–97
Bruce, Devon C., 328–330, 383
Bryant, Arthur H., vi, xiii, 178
Bryant, Neil, 320
Butler, A. Bates, 95–97
Butler, James E., Jr., 218–219

C

Cabraser, Elizabeth J., 387
Cachere, Matthew, 281
California Consumer Legal Remedies
  Act, 332
Campbell, Glenn J., 245
Canan, Penelope, 212
Cancer
  HMO, to save costs, denied
    appropriate medical treatment
    to patient, 244–245, 350–351
Cap on damages. See Damages
Capital punishment. See Death penalty
Carlson, Eric J., 328–330
Carlson, Jon G., 328–330
Caroselli, Bill, 364–365
Castle, Roger, 239
Cathcart, Daniel C., 302–303
Cathcart, Peter T., 303
Center for Constitutional Rights
  (CCR), 183, 275–276
Chaber, Madelyn J., 284–285, 352–353,
  354
Chapnick, Ellen, 274
Cheeley, Robert D., 218–219
Chemicals. See Toxic injury prevention
Chertkof, Stephen, 393
Cheseboro, Kenneth, 328–330
Chevrolet Chevette, 28–29
Child Abuse Protection Act, 122
Children
  birth defects. See Pregnancy
  child abuse
    foster care system in Georgia
     failed to properly screen and
     place child, 158–159, 378–379
    government agency has special
     duty to enforce law, 122
  child-proof containers and
    warning labels on household
    drain cleaners, 50–51
  lead-based paint poisoning,
    Newark city agency to provide
    protection to children at risk,
    292–293

parental companionship, right to
  sue for loss of, 46–47
  vaccinations, drug company using
    cheaper version of DPT despite
    availability of safer formula,
    50–51
Chiosso, James, 286–287
Chromium 6
  PG&E poisoned groundwater with,
    in case investigated by Erin
    Brockovich, ix–x, 310–311
Cigarettes. See Tobacco industry
Ciresi, Michael J., 340–347
Civil rights. See also Hate crimes
  burning of African American
    church, Klan speech inciting
    outside of First Amendment
    protection, 358–359
  capital punishment, disparate
    sentencing of black defendants,
    194–195
  damage cap set by Colorado
    Government Immunity Act
    challenged under §1983, 217,
    234–239
  glass ceiling prevented women
    from advancing at company,
    246–247
  home insurance company engaged
    in redlining to discriminate
    against African Americans,
    356–357
  housing discrimination in Illinois
    village's redevelopment plan,
    338–339
  insurance company discriminated
    against women in hiring of sales
    trainees, 200–202
  mental commitment in state facility,
    improperly diagnosed brain
    injury and subsequent
    mistreatment denied
    plaintiff of his civil rights,
    362–363
  nuclear plant to be placed in
    Louisiana African-American
    community, NRC convinced of
    racial discrimination in choice
    of site, 316–317
  police beating of political
    demonstrator, §1983 violation
    by San Francisco, 181–182
  prima facie case of sex
    discrimination by government
    agency shown by hiring
    statistics, 373, 388–393
  restaurant engaged in pattern of
    employment race discrimination,
    226–227
  tapes of company executives
    revealed employment race
    discrimination by Texaco,
    308–309
Clancy, Kenneth P., 44–45
Clarno, Bev, 320, 321
Clean Air Act, 318

F

rights in hope of confession, 241, 250–255

shooting in police confrontation of suicidal culprit, cover-up and lack of police training for crisis intervention revealed, 286–287

Lawrence, Scott, 239

Lead-based paint poisoning children at risk to be protected by Newark city agency, 292–293

Lebedoff, David, 270, 271

Leiff, Robert L., 387

Leonrad, James L., 44–45

Leopold, Theodore J., 384–385

Lerner, Bruce, 166

Levin, Irwin, 387

Lewis, Forrest, 239

Libel
"SLAPP-back suit" filed by California farmers group silenced by contrived libel suit by agricultural corporate giant, 142–143
"SLAPP-back suit" filed by consumer advocacy group which auto manufacturers sought to keep from criticizing sports utility vehicle safety, 374–375
"SLAPP-back suit" filed by environmental activist whom medical waste incinerator company sought to silence by libel action, 193, 212–215

Linfield, Deborah, 108–109

Liquid Plum'r, 50–51

Lite, Allyn Z., 387

Litman, Roslyn, 189

Long, Thomas J., 133–135

"Loser pays rule"
medical malpractice claimant prevails under, 11–12

Love, John, 347

Lowery, Joseph, 195

Luce, L. Ames, 118–119

Lutz, Ellen L., 133–135

Lyons, Dianna, 182

M

Malman, Jerome, 239

Malpractice, medical.
See Medical safety

Malson, Laurel P., 393

Manes, Hugh, 288–289

Manheim, Karl, 151

Mardirossian, Garo, 288–289

Margolis, Sol, 114–115

Marlin, Donald I., 116–117

Martens, Mark, 239

Mason, Wally, 281

Masry, Edward L., 310–311

Massey, Jonathan, 328–330

Massey-Ferguson, 196–197

Maxine Waters Act, 332

McAllister, Gary D., 328–330

McCall, John, 138–139

McCrory, Michael, 165–166

McDonnell, Jill P., 310–311

McGarvey, Allan M., 336–337

McGarvey, Dale L., 337

McIntyre, Daniel, 187–192

McKenna, James, 26

Medical safety
anesthesiology ventilator malfunctioned during surgery, 2–3
attorney's fees, claimant prevails under Florida's "loser pays rule," 11–12
blood screening for HIV not established by blood industry trade association, causing HIV from blood transfusions, 262–263
damage cap in malpractice cases violated constitutional right to jury trial, 86–87
emergency room staffed by independent contractors, hospital still liable for negligence of, 118–119
hospital pediatric unit insufficiently staffed to monitor newborns, 92
hospitals held accountable for quality of their doctors' care, 32–33
orthopedic surgeon unqualified to perform Posterior Lumbar Innerbody Fusion (PLIF) surgeries harmed patients, 140–141
preeclampsia's causal connection to death from Adult Respiratory Distress Syndrome (ARDS), 48
pregnancy risks not told to patient, 8
statute of limitations, time should run from discovery of negligence, 44–45

Mehri, Cyrus, 308–309

Mendelsohn, Martin, 387

Mendez, Juan, 133–135

Mental anguish
accident victim compensated when difficulty of choosing medical treatment caused distress, 49

Mental commitment
failure to review justifiability of confinement on regular schedule, 132, 152–154
forced labor without compensation during violated Fair Labor Standards Act, 155, 167–171
state facility failed to properly diagnose brain injury and then mistreated plaintiff, denying him of his civil rights, 362–363

Mescaline
medical experiments with, conducted under Army contract

without subject's knowledge or consent, 108–109

Meyers, Daniel, 376–377

Michaud, Gerald L., 75–82

Migrant and Seasonal Agricultural Worker Protection Act (AWPA), 221

Migrant workers
class action against apple advertising commission for fraud in recruiting ads, 174–176
fern workers in Florida who worked year round not fairly paid due to exemption from AWPA, 221–222
sugar cane cutters cheated of promised pay in Florida, 220

Military, U.S.
atomic bomb testing by.
See Atomic bomb testing
attorneys' fees capped in cases against Veterans Administration, 193, 203–211
Court of Veterans' Appeals, creation of, 210
medical experiments with mescaline conducted under Army contract without subject's knowledge or consent, 108–109

Miller, Arthur, 387

Millstein, Edgar, 387

Miltenberg, Ned, 328–330

Mining
strike, mining company's use of law enforcement to break, 165–166

Minority rights. *See* Civil rights

Moccio, Vincent, 347

Montana's State Torts Claims Act, 67–68

Morin, Jose Luis, 281

Morrison-Knox, William C., 210

Mouzon, Jonathan, 359

Muckle, Melanie, 274

Murray, Leslie M., 49

Myers, Richard, 69–70

N

NAACP Legal Defense and Education Fund, 226–227

Nace, Barry J., 20–21, 65–66, 112–113, 266–267

National Spa and Pool Institute swimming pool standards found unsafe, 360–361

National Traffic and Motor Vehicle Safety Act, 114

Neal, James, 270

Nelson, Susan Richard, 347

Neuborne, Burt, 386–387

New Jersey Tort Claims Act, 116

New Yorkers for Gun Control, 367

Newberg, Herbert, 178

Nolting, Laddie Montague, 274

COLOPHON

This book was set in Minion®, a typeface inspired by the classical, old style typefaces of the late Renaissance. A 1990 Adobe Original typeface by Robert Slimbach, Minion has an elegant, beautiful style typical of the Renaissance period. Created primarily for text setting, Minion combines the aesthetic and functional qualities that make text type highly readable with the versatility of digital technology. Berthold Imago, the typeface used in headings, was designed in 1982 by Germany's Günther Gerhard Lange of the Berthold foundry, renowned for crafting high quality typefaces. Berthold continues this tradition today, offering one of the world's leading type collections.